THROUGH TRAVEL AND ERROR

To Don

I hope that you have a few laughs.
Maybe when the kids are older you will hit the road.

Marty Hamilton

THROUGH TRAVEL AND ERROR

CONFESSIONS OF AN ASYLUM-SEEKING CANADIAN

Matt Hamilton

iUniverse, Inc.
New York Bloomington Shanghai

THROUGH TRAVEL AND ERROR
CONFESSIONS OF AN ASYLUM-SEEKING CANADIAN

Copyright © 2008 by Matthew Hamilton

All rights reserved. No part of this book may be used or reproduced by any means, graphic, electronic, or mechanical, including photocopying, recording, taping or by any information storage retrieval system without the written permission of the publisher except in the case of brief quotations embodied in critical articles and reviews.

iUniverse books may be ordered through booksellers or by contacting:

iUniverse
1663 Liberty Drive
Bloomington, IN 47403
www.iuniverse.com
1-800-Authors (1-800-288-4677)

Because of the dynamic nature of the Internet, any Web addresses or links contained in this book may have changed since publication and may no longer be valid.

The views expressed in this work are solely those of the author and do not necessarily reflect the views of the publisher, and the publisher hereby disclaims any responsibility for them.

ISBN: 978-0-595-45677-2 (pbk)
ISBN: 978-0-595-71360-8 (cloth)
ISBN: 978-0-595-89979-1 (ebk)

Printed in the United States of America

For Anne Price, who is an amazing woman with a dynamic spirit and an everlasting energy. She is an inspiration to me and to countless others around the world.

Contents

FOREWARNING ix

** *DOWN THE ROAD* ...

CHAPTER 1	THE FIRST HURDLE. 3
CHAPTER 2	THANK YOU, ANDY ROONEY 8
CHAPTER 3	RUNNER. 14
CHAPTER 4	WHY NOT?. 20
CHAPTER 5	GET LOST. 30
CHAPTER 6	THE PRAGUE EXPERIMENT. 44
CHAPTER 7	A YANKEE MOMENT 53
CHAPTER 8	GET A JOB 60
CHAPTER 9	ACTUALLY, THE FLOOR WASN'T THAT BAD 66
CHAPTER 10	GANGSTER'S PARADISE 78
CHAPTER 11	A NAME FROM THE PAST. 89
CHAPTER 12	EXPECTATIONS 101
CHAPTER 13	WHO KNEW?. 109
CHAPTER 14	MONDAY 119
CHAPTER 15	A TRANSKEI BUY. 128
CHAPTER 16	WERNER. 150

Chapter 17	THE CHASE	156
Chapter 18	SHIT HAPPENS	162
Chapter 19	BLAME CANADA	170
Chapter 20	TRUST	182
Chapter 21	A TO B	192
Chapter 22	FINDING MALAWI	206
Chapter 23	B TO C	217
Chapter 24	HOLD THAT THOUGHT BABY … HOW BIG?!	234
Chapter 25	LIVING IN REALITY	239
Chapter 26	THE EMAIL	255
Chapter 27	CULTURE SHOCK	266

REFERENCE	275
ABOUT THE AUTHOR	277

FOREWARNING

Many authors like to include an introduction or a foreword to offer insight on their books. It can be an account of their rigorous research, funny anecdotes, publication difficulties or other various projects.

However, because I have my readers' interests at heart, I consider it my duty not to call the following an introduction or foreword but to call it, more accurately, a fore*warning*.

I'm writing this forewarning well before the end of the book is anywhere in sight, because it is important to warn you that I don't really know what I'm doing. But that is okay.

I have done many things in my past where this was the case, so why break the pattern now. The way I see things, if my attempt at bohemianism fails, the worst-case scenario is that this text ends up as some sort of twisted journal that I can laugh and cry over in my old age. Thankfully, I'm still a long way from there.

Currently, I've been working on *Through Travel and Error* for about a year and a half. When people ask me about its progress, my standard answer is, "I'm working on half of the book," which is more or less correct. One of my problems is that I don't know how or where to start writing. My method so far has been to write a few middle chapters, then, when I feel so inclined, I might write a touch more at the end. Then, maybe, I'll skip back to the beginning. The whole time, I'm hoping that all the writing and stories will magically fit together like some sort of literary puzzle. I think the principles of chaos theory might be necessary for a reader to detect any writing pattern that I may have used.

Nonetheless, I am working on half the book. My big concern about saying this, however, is that I've been saying it for the past six months.

Granted, there have been obstacles that hindered the progress of the manuscript. Although beautiful settings, a bus, a noisy dorm and the beach aren't the most productive writing environments. However, the most significant obstruction is that I spent the first year writing the book with a pen and paper. Can you believe that? I'm living in the 21st-century, and I'm using the same tools Shakespeare used hundreds of years ago! Ink and paper for Christ's sake! How that guy ever completed a play is well beyond my understanding or patience. The confusions and frustrations of using pen and paper are many. You have to scratch out spelling mistakes and reorganize thoughts and sentences. Pages are tossed about and lost by a sudden gust of wind on the beach. And then there was my terrible handwriting and my cramped hand. The quandaries almost made me pack in the whole idea before it really got rolling.

Thankfully, a fellow backpacker provided a second-hand laptop, and even though the settings and programs were in Italian, my daunting task of writing a book took a quantum leap forward. My new toy motivated and re-energized me to get back up on the horse of lore and give writing another whirl, which is exactly what I did. I discerned the mishmash of notes, stories and ideas from the tattered scraps of paper that I'd been protecting for a year among the litter of my backpack. Encouraged, I began working on new material. But that old fear crept back up my spine.

Despite having the luxury of a laptop, there was still one major hindrance impeding the book's completion. It's an obstacle I face when I look at myself in the mirror every morning. It's one I've worked long and hard to grasp and come to terms with. It's one that is proving quite the Everest to conquer. This hindrance is that my ignorance proves a nasty snag when it comes to writing a book.

During university, I studied history and political science. Although some of the history essays I submitted could easily have been considered creative writing, I never formally enrolled in any English or writing courses. As a result, I haven't read enough of "the classics," I don't understand style, my vocabulary is limited, and my grammar is pretty shitty. Basically, I was lacking all the ingredients essential to becoming a good author and writing a quality book.

My formal education attempted to teach me that effective writing concisely and clearly expresses ideas. My professors said that a solid piece of work consisted of a to the point introduction followed by a strong, supportive body and ended with a well-constructed conclusion. I didn't do very well at university, and thankfully, I never fully understood or adapted to this boring, structured and monotonous approach to writing. Of all the history essays I plagiarized over the years, and there were many, I never once read one that was, if technically correct, mildly interesting.

If I had used this style writing a book, I would have died of boredom ages ago.

Luckily, being from the heart of Western civilization, I had another valuable educational tool at my disposal. This tool was a mentor that I idolized and listened to daily without fail. Without its influence, I wouldn't have attempted to write this book. While it's nice to know that my lack of grammatical knowledge and all around ineptitude could be concealed with the aid of skilful editors and spell-check, I knew that a manuscript, no matter how grammatically correct, would never see the inside of a publishing house if it didn't have style. Style baby. It's what got your foot in the front door. Style is where I would have been in trouble had it not been for my 36 inch mentor, the good old TV.

The style I adopted is the "'Seinfeld' technique."

The genius of "Seinfeld" was that it was a television program about nothing … well, almost nothing. Millions stopped what they were doing every Thursday night to watch four people do the same nothingness they had the week before. Why were we addicted to this sitcom? Brilliant writing? Talented acting? Mass advertising and promotional campaigns? We had nothing better to do at nine on a Thursday? Subliminal messages? While these are all possible explanations, I believe that maybe, just maybe, it was because these irrelevant, silly scenarios offered something we could relate to.

Maybe we knew that through the characters, situations and predicaments, even in the most irrelevant circumstances, we could find a common point of interest.

I believe it is the same with *Through Travel and Error*. My stories are really quite irrelevant to everyone's day-to-day existence. At initial glance, they may appear like no more than ridiculous yarns by some unknown, unimportant, everyday type of guy. And honestly, that is more or less what they are.

However, if you allow yourself to open your mind, you might discover that within my blatant idiocies there is something everybody can relate to, whether you've put a pack on your back or not. Within my random predicaments and experiences, there exists a point we can all learn from.

If this haphazard approach worked for "Seinfeld," it might just work for me.

Through Travel and Error may be a book for travellers timelessly floating across the globe without a return flight home and questioning what "it" is all about. Perhaps it's for those who are unhappy being comfortable. Or perhaps it's for those people stuck in their well-paying, nine-to-five routines who seek some motivation or excuse to change the monotony of their existence. Or, when all is said and done, the book could be strictly for my parents, whom I constantly reassured that my seemingly endless travel would have a point.

I really don't know.

However, what I do know is that the stories are my actual experiences and observations about this funny little chunk of rock we live and move about on.

I do know that the opinions expressed are solely my own, which is reassuring in a way.

I do know that I made Canadian political history in the most improbable of ways in the most unusual of places.

I do know that some of the names were changed to protect the innocent or, in some cases, the extremely guilty.

I do know that some of what I have written will be left on the cutting room floor (or whatever the editing room is called in the publishing racket), and for those omissions, I apologize. But the creative editing was probably done to keep your dodgy author from being sued, extradited, or severely beaten up. And all in all, that's not a bad thing.

And I do know that if you are anybody other than my immediate family and you are reading this, I have overcome the literary and personal hurdles of my writing marathon and made it to print.

Whoever you are, I hope you enjoy the read.

Good luck.
Matty Hamilton

** DOWN THE ROAD ...

My predicament was grim.

My predicament was beyond grim. It was gruesome. It was tragic. It was so mind-bogglingly inconceivable that I still wasn't totally convinced it was actually happening.

I hesitantly looked back over my shoulder. There was nothing but the pitch-black night staring back at me. The darkness confirmed my implausible reality.

How did I let myself get so completely abandoned in the middle of some rinky-dink, Third World, piss-poor African country? All I knew with a bleak certainty was that I was standing somewhere on a road in the middle of the night. I was all the more demoralized because I had absolutely nothing to my name. No wallet, no money, no passport, no backpack. Nothing.

There was nothing *except* the massive crisis waiting for my return.

Waiting for what? I didn't want any part of that catastrophe. Even if I did want to play the role of a hero, I wouldn't know where to begin. Maybe in a perfect world, I would know what course of action to take. In this utopian world, I would be cool, calm and collected. I would handle this gigantic problem with the skill and confidence of a natural-born leader.

But this wasn't a perfect world.

I wasn't composed. I was tiptoeing on the edge of sheer panic.

I hadn't bargained for this type of turmoil. This wasn't part of my master scheme. I was in way over my head, and I didn't have the slightest idea how to get my ass out of it. A conservative assessment of my dilemma would be that I was up shit creek without a paddle, there was a hole in the boat and a nasty hurricane was looming on the horizon.

As much as I racked my brain or scoured for a quick fix, I knew deep down that I didn't have any alternatives. There wasn't going to be any easy way out of this one. My ability to drop and run at the first sign of trouble, a weapon I had used countless times over the past two years, wasn't available. There was nowhere to run.

As much as I wished otherwise, there was only one place I could go.

I went back to deal with the carnage and the bodies.

My only consolation was that I looked stylish.

1
THE FIRST HURDLE

SEPTEMBER

"Glasgow?! Why would you want to start your travels in a dump like that?"

"Stab City?! Why would you want to go there?"

"Glasgow? Never heard of it?"

These were the first comments I heard when I told friends I was planning on beginning my trip around the world in Glasgow, Scotland. Had they heard of Glasgow, they thought I was crazy for choosing such a dreary and dangerous destination. If they hadn't heard of Glasgow, they thought I was crazy because there were so many other beautiful and obvious destinations. Either way, they thought I was nuts.

When I choose Glasgow as my starting point, I was unaware the town had the dubious nickname of "Stab City." This ignorance came as no surprise to me. Sure, I knew my basic global layout and some of the countries' capitals. But generally, when it came to knowledge about cultures, beliefs and practices, I knew jack shit. Honestly, I wasn't even positive where Glasgow was located in Scotland. I certainly wouldn't have bet anything substantial on it. I had a roommate in university who would say what I didn't know could fill an ocean. He was being kind. I was smart enough to know I was pretty dumb.

You are probably asking too, "Why Glasgow?"

It wasn't based on any knowledge or insight into the city. It was more process of elimination.

Having never travelled anywhere on my own, let alone outside of North America, I figured it would be prudent to start somewhere that I knew somebody. Not only would I have local insight into the city and culture, but I would also have an emergency contact if and when I got my ignorant ass in trouble.

And Glasgow was the only city outside of North America where I knew somebody.

I had a university friend from Glasgow whose address and phone number I kept from an old student directory. He only spent one year in Canada, and we hadn't been in contact since, but he was as good as it was going to get in terms of international connections.

A few days before I left home, I called Colin's number to let him know I would be in his neck of the woods. The number was to the home of his parents, who kindly informed me that Colin had moved to smoggier pastures, London. In hindsight, it would have been wise to call him before I booked my flight.

I hadn't even left Canada, and I already made the first of what I was sure would be many mistakes.

Not surprisingly, it didn't take long to expose my next oversight.

The second reason I chose Glasgow was because of my roots. I'm half Scottish and half Irish. I carried the ridiculous belief that something in my genetic structure would recognize and help me adapt to Scotland or Ireland better than, say, Kenya or China. Since I didn't have a contact in Ireland, it had to be Scotland.

Already I felt I was grasping at straws. This was a weak reason for choosing Scotland, and I knew it. I was never strong in the sciences, but even the most challenged student would agree that the genetics of a third generation Canadian know sweet nothing about Scotland. I could have had Robert the Bruce's genes, and it wouldn't have helped a lick. And I was right. I'm sure my genes, just like the rest of me, were shitting their pants when I arrived in Glasgow. If there were any Scottish instincts in me, they didn't make it through customs.

This was blunder number two.

Regardless of my first two mistakes, the third reason I chose Glasgow was the fail-safe backup plan that would ensure my survival. Having never travelled outside North America and not having the slightest idea what I was doing, I thought it would be wise to begin my travels in a country whose native language was English. It would be easier to take those first critical steps of finding somewhere to sleep and something to eat if I could communicate.

The plan would have been fine and dandy except for one small but critical hitch I was completely unprepared for: the Glaswegian accent.

I knew my travels would be filled with learning experiences. I knew I would be in many situations where I wouldn't have a clue what was going on. This was okay with me because I hoped that I would adapt and learn from my mistakes. I hoped diving headfirst into my travels would be the best way to educate myself about how and why this baffling, mysterious planet works the way it does.

I was prepared to be unaware and ignorant. I was prepared to be confused. I wasn't prepared for the Glaswegian accent.

As I mentioned, there is a shitload about the planet that I don't know. The harshness of the Glaswegian brogue was one of those little pieces of information that had avoided my knowledge. When I mention the Glaswegian accent, I'm not just referring to the thick, guttural intonation but also the vocabulary and slang, which no one but Glaswegians and the most talented linguists can decipher. Discovering the new language was my first life-on-the-road lesson.

After I had cleared customs, I was trying to figure out my next move.[1] That move was getting my ass out of the airport and finding somewhere to crash. I was tired, and I needed a bed.

I asked a guy standing next to me if he knew how one might find a hostel.

And the smiling Glaswegian said, "Alright big man, where yea fae? You heading into toon then? Nae worries. You git yoursel' oot those doors and stick your hand up at that big bus, and he'll take ya up the city. Tell the mucker tae take yea tae Argyll Street and flag a black oot west, and you'll git yoursel' sorted. Watch yoursel' big man and enjoy a dram in Glesgow."

It had been a long day of travelling. Perhaps my ears hadn't popped from the change in pressure, and that was why his words were muffled and not registering.

I asked the man to repeat himself. He did.

I briefly considered that I had boarded the wrong flight and landed in Iceland instead of Scotland. (I had heard Björk attempt to speak English, and it wasn't pretty.) However, I quickly dismissed this notion when I saw the massive sign hung above the arrival terminal saying, "Welcome to Glasgow." I was in the right place.

So I asked the man to repeat himself again.

And the very kind Glaswegian did repeat himself again. And therein lay the problem. If I didn't understand him the first two times, then there wasn't much chance I'd decipher it the third time around.

I didn't.

I don't care how many times you listen to the dialogue in *Braveheart* or *Trainspotting*, it won't prepare you in the slightest for the thick, Glaswegian brogue.

---

1. My ignorance almost prevented me from getting into Scotland. Apparently, immigration officers don't like the answer "I don't know" for the questions "How long are you staying" and "Where are you going next." Mind you, my ears were still dripping wet and I had loads of money. The officer must have thought that someone this unacquainted and naïve isn't here to screw the system. If anything, the system is going to screw him. So she let me in.

I knew the man was speaking English. He had to be. I mean, I was in Scotland. I knew they spoke English in Scotland; it was one of the few things I did know.

He may as well have been speaking Dutch or Zulu for all I could understand.

I couldn't ask this guy a fourth time, so I politely nodded as if I understood. I smiled, said thank you and sat on a bench to think things through. It didn't take long to reach a conclusion. I was fucked.

How could I not be? Reason one for coming to Glasgow had moved to London. Reason two was flat out stupid. And reason number three, the benefit of understanding the language, my fail-safe reason, failed miserably.

Maybe I should have done more research before I left Canada. And by that, I mean done any research. Perhaps I should have organized something simple and essential like where I might sleep my first night on the other side of the planet in a place where I didn't know a soul. This was one of many critical details that I completely ignored.

I literally left Canada with a one-way ticket to Glasgow, the pack on my back and a totally unprepared notion to travel around the world. That's it. That's all.

This was shaping up to be the biggest mistake I ever made.

How could I get it so wrong? Could I be this brainless? Was I this over my head? If I couldn't get out of an English-speaking airport, then what was I going to do in Spain or Vietnam or anywhere? These were my forefathers, and I couldn't comprehend what they were saying.

I wasn't sure what to do or even where to begin thinking.

Then it dawned on me. I could go home.

Why not? I was sitting in the airport. My bag was packed and ready to be tossed onto a plane. I had the money. I could catch a flight and be back in Canada in a flash. In fact, with the time change, it would almost be as if I had never left at all. I could tell my friends and family I was only kidding about going around the world. Did they seriously think I would or could leave the comfort and safety of my home, family and friends for a timeless trip around the planet by myself? I could tell them I had spent the weekend boozing in Toronto. This story would also explain any signs of jet lag.

I'm sure I could get my job back.

But ...

But what about my anger? What about my rage? If I returned to Ottawa now, in this frame of mind, I'm sure, even though I'd never thrown a punch in my life, I'd end up killing someone. No doubt about it.

I didn't really have a choice. I couldn't go back. Not a chance.

I had only one option other than homicide and a life in a Canadian prison. I could deal with the situation at hand and figure out what the hell people were saying.

I took a deep breath, closed my eyes and began to think.

I thought of a friend who had travelled extensively by herself. I thought of what she would do in this situation. I thought of how she would be laughing her ass off at my predicament. I also thought of the going-away card she had given me, which for some reason, I decided to bring on my travels. I dug it out of the top of my pack and read the passage on the front, "A journey of a thousand miles begins with a single step."

I gave those simple words some thought. They made a lot of sense.

A wonderful calmness replaced my anxiety.

It was as though a completely different and enlightened mentality took over. It was a dose of positive reality that made my bleak future look much brighter.

I realized that I may be ignorant, but I wasn't inept. I didn't understand a word these people were saying, but I'd still find a way to communicate. I wasn't going to starve. I would find a bed for the night. I would figure out how to find wherever the hell that bed may be.

I did have the ability to walk out of the airport and figure out … well, just figure out.

I took a couple of deep breaths, swallowed back the fear that was trying to escape from my body in the unpleasant appearance of vomit, put my pack on my back and made my way to the exit doors, which seemed the logical first step to getting out of the terminal and starting this travelling thing.

It was.

I glanced to my right. Nothing. I glanced to my left. There was a bus.

Public transportation. This seemed to be another rational step to getting away from the airport and finding somewhere to sleep. I asked the driver if he was heading to the city centre, a logical part of the city to look for accommodation. Much like the first guy I had asked for help, the driver spoke an incomprehensible Glaswegian dialect. However, unlike the first guy, my question required a simply yes or no answer. Thankfully, he used the international sign of approval, or at least so I hoped, which was a simple nod. This was as much help as this naive and terrified traveller was going to get.

I got on the bus and sat down.

I had taken my first thirty steps of what would hopefully prove to be thousands of miles.

It wasn't much, but it was a start.

2
THANK YOU, ANDY ROONEY

SEPTEMBER

As I was sitting on the bus, watching the unfamiliar city of Glasgow roll past the window, I was still not 100 per cent convinced it was taking me to where I needed to go. I began to question what could possibly have made me leave everything and everyone I knew and loved for what seemed a difficult and lonely journey.

Ultimately, what I came up with was that I couldn't hit a damn curveball.

As a little guy, I always knew I wanted to be a professional baseball player. Some kids wanted to be firemen. Some kids wanted to be policemen. I wanted to be a ball player. It wasn't about the money, although that would have been a nice perk; it was simply that I loved the sport, and the thought of playing a game for a living was ideal. I often said I would have played for rent money and a case of beer. Baseball was my passion.

When I was 19, I got a chance to play in an American collegiate summer league in New York state. It was where American college kids played to improve their skills for the upcoming school season. It was also a league that professional teams frequently scouted. For a 19-year-old Canadian still in high school, it was a fantastic opportunity.

I was on my way to becoming a professional baseball player. At least I thought so.

As it would happen, in one short season, my dreams and ego were simultaneously crushed.

The talent that surrounded me was too good, or more accurately, I wasn't anywhere as good as I thought I was. I was painstakingly aware that no matter how much training I did, I would never develop the natural, raw, God-given skill that the other players seemed to ooze.

Plus, I couldn't hit a decent curveball if my life depended on it.

I knew at age 19 that I was never going to be what I truly wanted to be.

So instead of pursuing an unattainable career in baseball, I decided to use another part of my body that still had potential, my brain, and I enrolled in university. Based on its reputation and the admission standards, I was accepted at a top school. During my first semester as a student of history and political science, I was keen and enthusiastic. I attended every lecture and read every page of the required reading.

However, I quickly became disenchanted.

Lectures sucked. They were a waste of my time. The dispassionate and uninspiring professors were regurgitating the same material I had reviewed and read the previous night. I can read. I understand English. History is basically a story with a setting, plot, characters, beginning, middle and end. Unless one of the professors had access to a time machine, then they couldn't offer any further insight beyond what had already been written. What they knew they got from books others wrote—books I was reading.

Studying history at university turned out to be an expensive library card.

I also came to the dispiriting conclusion that university professors didn't give a rat's ass about their students. These people weren't teachers like I found in other educational institutions; they were researchers and authors. They weren't there to teach; they were there to lecture. And I could tell by their lack of enthusiasm during lectures that they didn't even want to do that. The three hours a week spent addressing undergrads was three hours not spent working on their own more important projects. They didn't do any of the grading either. That important task was left to an unqualified teaching assistant. It was apparent that if you were an undergrad at Queen's University, then you weren't worth two shits in the eyes of the faculty.

By my second semester, I was pissed off. I began to develop a "fuck them" attitude.

This was around the time I discovered marijuana.

A few of my buddies and I would get together every Wednesday and buy a quarter ounce of weed to smoke. The evening was called "Wacky Weed Wednesday," and it was the highlight of my week. We'd get stoned, play some music and shoot the shit. We'd talk about anything and everything. Topics ranged from current events and politics to video games and comic books. We'd also delve into asinine subjects such as which superhero had the best strengths or which mythical beasts would win if forced to fight.

We'd also discuss philosophy—lots of philosophy.

Sometimes these discussions were deep; sometimes they weren't. Regardless, my brain began to think, expand, wonder, challenge and question.

Although these were not the topics I thought I would be discussing while studying history at university, they did produce the advancement and thought development I had hoped to find when I enrolled.

Marijuana broadened my creativity, and it helped subdue my frustrations. Barely.

"Wacky Weed Wednesdays" were soon accompanied by "Totally Token Tuesdays."

Not long after, marijuana became a daily fixture.

I smoked my way through the next three years with some creative essays and minimal enthusiasm. Two months after my release from academic prison, with barely a moment to question, "What now," I found myself chasing cheese in the rat race.

I got a job working for an insurance brokerage. I got to wear good-looking suits and received a good paycheque. I had good steady work, Monday through Friday, nine to five. There was even a good corporate ladder to climb.

On paper, things were looking good.

The next year and a half flew by.

However, something wasn't good. I was angry all the time.

It appeared that the seed of rage planted during my years at university was nurtured by the pace and mentality of the rat race. Even the soothing powers of marijuana couldn't suppress my frustrations.

I couldn't get through a day at work without getting pissed off and having it turn sour. The workplace and its activities seemed so trivial and pointless. They seemed fake and scripted. It was almost like a little performance, except we weren't onstage and nobody was watching. The plot to this 'Canadian drama' was straightforward as well ... Go to work, pay your taxes and retire.

Everything was a race to see who could get the most the fastest. And the brutal irony was that regardless of how hard we worked and our position on the economic ladder, we were essentially doing the exact same thing. It didn't matter if you were the CEO of Coca-Cola or working the counter at McDonald's. Both were waking up, hitting the snooze button, going to work, coming home, paying some bills and going to sleep. Then they'd repeat five to six times a week for 40 years. The only disparity would be the size of the home and the expenses.

Same difference.

If I could somehow get through a day at the office remaining calm, then all would be lost when I turned on the six o'clock news.

Every single day, the news was filled with negativity, hatred and violence. The message I took from these horrifying images was, "Hey buddy, don't worry about your little issues and discontentment. Your life in Canada is much better than these poor bastards."

Most of us would agree. We'd say it was a tragedy then get back to our lives. We'd feel better about ourselves, thankful our city hadn't been bombed or swallowed by an earthquake, and not give the actual disaster and its actual victims a second thought. I regarded the media as an attempt to subdue and blind us from our own unhappiness. They were there to keep us afraid, productive and consuming. We were being brainwashed into complacency.

We were exploring Mars and cloning sheep, but the most interesting and anticipated story was where the President of the United States stuck a cigar and what was going to be done about it.

Kosovo was a massacre, the Russian market collapsed and everybody was in a panic over the "millennium bug." This high-tech dilemma was going to cost an estimated $600 billion to fix.

The world was going insane right in front of me, and there was nothing I could do about it.

My fire of discontentment and frustration was burning out of control.

I was pissed off with the government.[1]

I was pissed off with the media.

I was pissed off with my co-workers.

I was pissed off with bad drivers.

I was pissed off with the 'system'.

I was pissed off. Period.

I urgently needed a change, or I was going to crack.

The urge to travel had been tickling way back in my head the way it does with most Canadians. We tell ourselves we would love to see the world, but we have a job, girl, house, bills, safety, routine or commitments and, therefore, really can't go anywhere. We appease our wanderlust and sense of adventure by simply talking about leaving it all, and we satisfy our cultural enlightenment by taking our two-week, all-inclusive holidays in Cancun or Hawaii.

We are afraid of giving up what was safe and secure. I was no different.

---

1. Don't even get me going on the follies of the Canadian government. That is an entire book in itself. Between the mismanagement of taxpayers' money (think about how many times an item is actually taxed *before* you pay tax on it) and the ridiculous waste of time openly displayed by the politicians, it came as no surprise to anyone that I was a "Canadian anarchist."

I had conceded to a life in the velvet rut, that smooth **slide** through existence with minimal variety and limited exposure outside the **North** American reality bubble.

I could easily visualize myself as a grey, balding, retired 65-year-old.

However, I couldn't visualize anything that had happened in between. The velvet rut had held me to the point of retirement, and I had done nothing. I had simply existed ... Life had passed me by.

Thankfully, the final push I needed to jump the Canadian ship and go explore came from the crustiest, grumpiest old dinosaur of a journalist living today—Andy Rooney.

Andy Rooney has been a journalist since before there was paper. He is particularly well known for his surly social comments at the conclusion of the respected investigative news program "60 Minutes." This particular observation, which I happened to catch one Sunday evening, really opened my eyes and made me re-evaluate my priorities in life.

This is what he said:

"The most unfair thing about life is the way it ends. I mean, life is tough. It takes up a lot of your time. What do you get at the end of it? A death. What is that, a bonus? I think the life cycle is backwards. You should die first; get it out of the way. Then you live in an old age home. You get kicked out when you are too young, you get a gold watch and you go to work. You work forty years, until you are young enough to enjoy your retirement. You do drugs, alcohol, you party and you get ready for high school. You go to grade school, you become a kid, you play, you have no responsibilities, you become a little baby, you go back into the womb, you spend your last nine months floating ... and you finish off as an orgasm."

Damn ... that made sense.

That was all I needed to truly realize and believe that life is short, and that we only get one crack at it.

I needed to make the most of my one run. Mentally, I was already gone.

I made my decision to leave Canada and explore the planet. And honestly, making the *conscious* decision to leave home was the hardest part.

Not maybe. Not someday. Now.

I would say goodbye to everything I knew and travel around the world without an itinerary or deadline in search of everything that I didn't know. I was going to take my time.[2] If I liked a spot, I'd stay. If I didn't, I'd leave. As simple as that.

The logistics of leaving home fell into place with relative ease. I bought a backpack and a ticket to Glasgow. Quitting my job was a no-brainer and a relief. I explained to my family and friends that I needed to go and that my decision had nothing to do with them. I got overwhelming support—everyone understood that this was mandatory for my sanity.[3]

After a few going-away parties and dinners, I was ready to go. I left with all the stuff I didn't need, such as a poncho and massive pair of hiking boots, and none of the stuff I did, like knowing what I was doing.

Before I could get my head around what was happening and the dramatic life change I was throwing myself into, I was sitting on board a Boeing 747. I was somewhere over the Atlantic, heading towards Scotland and crying my eyes out.

I was hoping one of two things would happen to me during my travels. With option one, I would find a country that was more conducive to my mentality and lifestyle. I would find somewhere to make and call my home. The alternative would be my acknowledgment that Canada was an okay place to live after all. I'd somehow learn to accept and deal with all the "western shit" that was driving me out of my mind.

At least that was the plan.

Mind you, I was off to a shaky start. The "Glaswegian fiasco" aside, I still didn't have any idea what I was doing or where I was going. I left home with a one-way ticket to Glasgow, a bit of money and a lot of time. That was it. I didn't have any guidebooks or even a basic knowledge about a destination or, for that matter, the world of budget travelling. Frankly, I wasn't prepared.

The driver pulled into what looked like a central terminal in the heart of the city, and everybody got off the bus. I assumed that was the end of the line. I stepped off the bus not sure what my next move was going to be.

Staring me straight in the face was a large billboard that read, "Information." It was an encouraging sign, no pun intended.

I was going to do it. I had to.

As Yoda, the great Jedi Master once said, "Do or do not. There is no try."

---

2. Even though my trip was "timeless," I was guessing it would take me two years to go around the planet.
3. My nickname prior to leaving was "Rage-a-holic Prick." A couple of mates even wrote a song about my anger using the same name.

3
RUNNER

SEPTEMBER

This could go down as the mother of all hangovers.

I was stretched out on my dorm bed not wanting to move. My head was pounding. My eyes were swollen. My tongue felt thick and furry. My throat was raw. My stomach muscles felt as though they had endured ten rounds with Mike Tyson.

I was a mess.

As I said, this *could* go down as the mother of all hangovers, but it didn't. There was one factor preventing my suffering from ranking among the most sadistic of all time. It was an anomaly to the traditional, physical characteristics of a massive hangover. Despite my agony, I was smiling. I was feeling ecstatic.

My friends know I'm good at holding my booze; they know I'm even better at losing my booze.

When I lose it, I do so in a loud, painful and violent manner. The blood capillaries in my cheeks and eyes burst, leaving my face puffy, bloodshot and downright ugly. When I puke, it is always a ghastly and excruciating experience.

My friends also know this is the only time I contemplate taking religion into my life, for I continuously plea with the heavens to deliver a quick end to my horrible suffering.[1]

Therefore, they know there was no way I could feel human, let alone ecstatic.

Thankfully, there was a difference between this and all my previous hangovers.

---

1. To be honest, my screams of "Christ," "God" and "Jesus, Mary and Joseph" were purely blasphemous. I was cursing the powers that be for giving me free will and allowing me to consume copious amounts of alcohol. There is no way I could accept Christ into my soul during toilet-hugging times like these. I wouldn't be able to keep him down.

This difference was the reason I was smiling.

I was hungover *in Scotland*.

Was it possible that this minute and irrelevant component was helping me to avoid the misery of a hangover? There was no doubt. Had I been feeling this rough in Ottawa, I would have been a miserable prick.

If I were at home, I would have been irritable because I was hurting. If I were at home, I would have been frustrated because the rest of my weekend was wasted due to my incapacity to move. Luckily, I wasn't in Ottawa, and that was the wonderful point of it all. I wasn't in Canada. It was starting to sink in. I had escaped the velvet rut. I was on the road. I was beginning a timeless journey of discovery.

I was in Scotland. This was a Scottish hangover. It was the result of a heavy night of drinking in Scotland—drinking Scottish drinks in Scottish pubs with Scottish people.

Let me rephrase that. Scottish *women*.

The night began innocently enough, or should I say, I began the night innocently enough. I found a club called *The Garage* on Sauchiehall Street, the main party drag in downtown Glasgow. The club had a long line of waiting people. I assumed a lengthy line meant a popular club.

This was the first time I had ever gone into a bar without knowing a soul inside. I had to admit, I was in a bit of shock and wasn't sure how to behave or approach anybody. Ultimately, I ended up doing what any terrified rookie traveller would do. I bought a beer, found a spot near the bar, planted my feet and watched, completely petrified to move. This is how I spent the entire evening.

When the music stopped and the lights came up, I began to unglue my feet and head for home when a girl approached me. She said, "Awright gorgeous? Where ye fae? You've been standing there wi tha bevy fa ages."

I explained that I had just arrived in Glasgow, didn't know anybody and was still trying to soak it all in.[2]

The girl was obviously smashed. She had a full pint in her hand and was staggering back and forth. This resulted in the beer spilling over the edge of the glass and onto her. She giggled, wiped away the spilt drink and continued. "Me and

---

2. Although I wasn't totally sure what this girl was saying, I was able to pick up the general gist of it. Throughout the day and night, my ear had been adjusting to the Glaswegian brogue. I don't think I'll ever understand it, word for word, but if I can pick up a few phrases and fill in the blanks, then I'll consider it a small victory in communications.

ma pals are aff tae *Nice n' Sleazy* at eight bells tomorrow. If you wanna see a good night in oor city, get yoursel' in there, and we'll tak ya for a ride down Sauchie."

Her friends, also ripped, came by, grabbed the girl's arm and dragged her toward the door. Between gulps of the remaining pint, she pointed out the club's front doors and continued to shout, "*Nice n' Sleazy.*"

I left a few minutes later and saw, to my pleasant surprise, a pub called *Nice n' Sleazy* half a block away.

Of course I hooked up with them the next night. What else did I have to do?

Canadians can drink. Don't let anyone tell you otherwise. However, all the boozing I had done in my short yet prolific drinking career did not prepare me for the alcoholic bender that Fiona and her five girlfriends put me through.

I should have known these lasses could drink. I'm not sure if it was their obscene language, their trampy and way-too revealing clothing or the amount of booze they were guzzling, but Fiona and her five friends personified words such as rough, nasty and hard-drinkers. They struck me as the type of girls who would burp and fart loudly and proudly.

I knew I was in trouble.

I'm not sure at what point I lost count of my drinks. But I do know we were still in *Nice n' Sleazy*, and we were still drinking Pernod and lemonade. Seemingly endless rounds made their way to the table and down the throats of the Glaswegian women. These girls could drink longshoremen under the table.

I was in big trouble.

If I had been in Canada, I would have passed out right then and there after having consumed so much alcohol in so short a time. However, I had a double dose of pride, Canadian and male, that was keeping my head elevated. I couldn't let these Glaswegian gals destroy the cocky Canadian lad on his second night on the road.

Despite all signs indicating that I would be, I couldn't be the first to go down to the drink.

Please, one of them, just one of them, bail me out by saying quits.

Not a chance. It was time to pub hop.

Where we went is still a mystery to me.

What wasn't a mystery was that wherever we were, we were surrounded by loads of alcohol, and the girls weren't slowing down. Worse yet, they weren't showing any signs of doing so. I was nearing my last breath, and these mad women still had their second wind in the waiting.

I was in colossal trouble.

There were signs that I was about to pass out. I had the spins. My tongue felt heavy and pasty. I was seeing double, therefore doubling the amount of alcohol around me. Fuck Canada and fuck machismo. I knew if I got another whiff of booze, I was going to chuck my guts right then and there.

I was about to bow out as gracefully as a stumbling, drooling, slurring drunk could, when one of the girls,[3] bless her heart, said, "I'm pure steaming hen. I need ta get ma arse inta a hacknie."

The other girls aye'd and proceeded to get up. I didn't have a clue what was just said, but it appeared, to my joy, we were leaving. I was saved. I was going to escape this depraved adventure with my pride, a handful of brain cells and, most importantly, my dinner.

But when we got to the door one of the girls, may she rot in hell, said, "Na way ya mad bird, get yar arse back in there fae another bevvy."

The other girls aye'd and turned around. I didn't have a clue what was just said, but it appeared, to my horror, we were going back in for more alcohol.

The mere thought of having to put another drink to my lips sparked a massive revolt and exodus in my guts.

I puked everywhere.

With my pride and Canadian manhood splattered on the walls and in various puddles on the floor, there was no need for me to stay. I'm not sure if Fiona had been flirting with me during the evening. Christ, I'm not sure how my legs worked during the evening. But if she had been coming on to me, any chance of a romance was like my dinner—gone. I think I thanked Fiona and her friends for a memorable evening while silently cursing them. Miraculously, I stumbled back to the hostel and passed out fully dressed.

This hangover had teeth.

The novelty of a Scottish hangover and my smile were quickly disappearing. The reality of pain and suffering, regardless of the continent, was entrenching itself into every cell in my body.

To make matters worse, Brian came into the dorm.

Brian was the first person I met in Glasgow. He spotted the Canadian flag on my pack as I was wandering up Sauchihall Street looking for a place to sleep.

"So, you're from Canada, eh?"

I told him I was from Ottawa.

---

3. I truly don't remember any of the girls' names. I'm lucky I remembered Fiona's name. I'm lucky I remembered *my own* name.

"Hey great. I'm from Edmonton," he said with enthusiasm. "Are you looking for the hostel? I can show you where it is if you want?"

I had been following the map from the information booth, but I was concerned my fatigue would prevent me from finding where I needed to go. I quickly and happily accepted his offer.

After about 30 seconds, I could tell that Brian and I had absolutely nothing in common or ever would. It wasn't that he was rude or offensive. He was actually quite friendly and helpful. He was just quite strange. He oozed oddity. It was hard to discern exactly what it was about Brian that was weird. Regardless, my instincts were screaming, "Hey man, heads up! This guy enjoys dissecting small animals and plays *Dungeons & Dragons* a little too intently."

He did, however, lead me to the hostel.

The flight and emotions of the day had drained me. I was dead tired, and all I wanted to do was sleep. I checked in, turned around and bumped right into Brian, who had been lurking in my shadow.

"So, what do you want to do now?"

He clearly meant "we."

I explained that I was tired from the long flight, and I was going to take a shower and crash.

"So, how long are you going to nap?"

I wanted to say, "When I'm done sleeping you tit," but all I could spit out was an, "I don't know."

"If you want, I could hang around and wait for you, and we could go out somewhere together."

Was this guy serious? I tried to clarify that I was tired, and with jet lag, there was a chance I'd sleep through till morning. I didn't want to waste his evening.

"That's alright. I don't mind waiting. I don't have any plans anyhow."

Now there was a surprise.

When I did wake up, I did my best cloak and dagger routine in an attempt to avoid Brian. Thankfully, I was able to escape detection and sneak off to my evening at *The Garage*.

This went on for two days. I would peak around corners and then scamper off when there wasn't a sign of him. I was becoming an expert at evading Brian.

Unfortunately, in my state of extreme weakness, he tracked me down.

He was oblivious to my misery, and his voice was like a jackhammer on my brain. He asked me what my plans were. Without thinking (thinking wasn't something I was good at in the state), I managed to convey that I planned to stay in Glasgow for a few more days then make my way to Edinburgh.

He must have smelled my weakness. "Hmmm. That sounds like a great idea. I think I'll join you."

Brian had left the room before my brain fully registered what he said. When my grey matter eventually deciphered his words, I went into a panic.

I didn't know how to tell Brian that I didn't want to travel with him, and I didn't have the heart or personality to tell him to fuck off. So, I did the only thing that I could do.

I did a runner from Glasgow.

This was one of the benefits of travelling alone—complete and total selfishness. I needed to be selfish for awhile. Without being aware of it, family and friends can be very demanding of your time and energy. Of course there is a give and take, and being there for those you love is part of any successful relationship.

Unfortunately, for the past couple of years, I found I had been giving too much energy to others and not expending enough on my necessities.

I needed to be selfish in a way that would help me find what I needed to find. I needed to look after myself and myself only.

I was hoping that travelling alone would open a door of freedom, allowing me to do what I wanted, when I wanted and with whom I wanted.

I wouldn't compromise my plans for anyone, especially someone like Brian.

I suppressed the pain of my hangover, packed my backpack, did a quick hall check for Brian, paid my bill and made a direct line for the train station.

I had an hour to kill before my train departed for Edinburgh. Miraculously, my hangover was more or less gone. The thought of travelling with Brian had washed away any lingering symptoms. I was petrified that Brian would show up at the station, bags packed and ready for our trip, completely ignorant of my attempts to ditch him.

Thankfully, my fears were unwarranted. Brian didn't show, and I was safely on the train en route to Edinburgh.

I was smiling again. I could get into this freedom thing.

4
WHY NOT?

OCTOBER

"I can give you a ride to Dublin."

I was listening to every word Sabrina was saying. It was irrelevant that the pub was jam-packed or that I was, once again, blind drunk. I heard every syllable that came from her lips. I was listening to her because she was the first South African I'd met during my short time on the road. I was listening because she was the first person to tell me anything positive about her country. I was accustomed to the Western media's bleak portrayals of South Africa as a troubled and dangerous nation. I was listening because she was telling me about Cape Town's brilliant landscape, its exceptional nightlife, amazing beaches, friendly people and cheap weed.

I was listening because she was drop-dead gorgeous.

I decided to take the ride.

Besides Sabrina's beauty, it was the only feasible way to visit Dublin during my weeklong trip to Ireland.

After a fantastic time in London hanging out with my friend from university, I had decided to fly across to Ireland. I was going to catch up with a girl I met the day I flew from Canada to Glasgow. Sinead was from Cork and visiting Canada for the summer. She was dating my friend's roommate but returned to Ireland a couple of days after I started my travels. She had given me her phone number and said I could visit anytime.

I decided to take Sinead up on her invitation.

Why not?

Unfortunately, I had underestimated how long I would need to see a decent portion of the emerald countryside. A week wasn't going to scratch the surface.

Unfortunately, I had also underestimated how drunk I was going to be in the land of Guinness.

Okay, I had been fairly loaded since the moment I began my travels. I had been in full-on party mode. I kept having these out-of-body sensations that reminded me I wasn't in Canada anymore. Instead of being aware of places, I was experiencing places with my own eyes and my own perceptions. Whether strolling at the foot of Edinburgh castle or swimming in Loch Ness or wandering around Piccadilly Circus, I was bombarded with the constant realization that I had escaped the velvet rut.

And much like any escapee, I was celebrating my new-found freedom.

Ireland was a continuation of this celebration.

From the moment I arrived at the Cork airport, Sinead and her brother Willie John had been keeping the pints continuously flowing down my throat. Everywhere we went, we got drunk. When Sinead took three days off work and travelled with me around the Dingle Peninsula, we drank. When Willie John took me on a rugby road trip to Galway, we drank. When we hung out with their friends, we drank. So did the friends; so did everybody in sight. In my short time in this festive and friendly country, I concluded that Ireland was a land overpopulated with the likes of Fiona and friends.

My time in this boozy haze, not surprisingly, had disappeared.

Therefore, Sabrina's offer appeared to be an ideal situation. I would catch a free ride to Dublin, work some charm on the South African beauty, go drinking for the evening then hop on a bus back to Cork to next day. It *appeared* to be an ideal situation.

The first problem was that we left at 5:00 AM.

That ridiculous time is bad enough under normal circumstances. However, 5:00 AM is diabolical when you wake up somewhere between drunk and what promises to be one nasty, draft beer hangover.

Fortunately, I was still closer to drunk than hungover.

Unfortunately, I was even closer to passing out, which is exactly what I did the moment my pitiful ass hit the car seat. I was at that stage of intoxication where I couldn't properly fall asleep, yet I still didn't have the mental or physical capacities to formulate complete sentences, keep my eyes open or keep my mouth from hanging agape. My plan of charming the pants off Sabrina drooled, literally, down my face.

I was awoken a few hours later by an unnecessarily loud and aggravating voice. The voice had been angelic and enthralling the previous evening.

"We're here, China."

I was no longer drunk. Now I was fighting a nasty headache. Through red and swollen eyes, I took in the Irish capital. All I could see was a dingy port and a couple of warehouse-like buildings. With a hairy tongue, I grumbled that Dublin looked awfully hick.

"We're not in Dublin bru. We're in Wexford."

I was sure Sabrina had said, "We are here." I was also sure that here was supposed to be Dublin. I was also sure that she said she could give me a ride to Dublin.

"Ag shame. I said I could give you a ride *on the way* to Dublin. I'm heading back to Wales from here on the ferry. You are two hours closer to Dublin though."

This was my second problem. It appeared my ride to Dublin wasn't going to Dublin.

In my drunken state the previous evening I must have misheard Sabrina's offer. Or maybe I had heard what I hoped to hear. Either way, I was stuck in Wexford.

It would have been bad enough being dumped in Wexford, but it was countless times shoddier being stranded in the town's barren and cold port, which is exactly where Sabrina dropped me. My hangover was now pounding. All I wanted was to sit down on the bus and pass out. It was becoming a question of needing to sleep as opposed to wanting to sleep. Mercifully, one of the few buildings in the immediate vicinity was a bus station.

"The next bus to Dublin leaves in three hours."

My first, bleary thought was that the ticket guy knew he had a hammered tourist on his hands and was having some fun at my expense. However, as I waited for him to laugh, I gazed around the empty departure lounge and realized it wasn't a joke. I also realized that uncomfortable bus seats are about a million times more restful than the curved, blue plastic seats I had to wedge my hurting body into for the next three hours.

I hit my third problem. Sleep was not an option.

Sometimes three hours can fly by. This, painfully, wasn't one of those times.

The eventual ride to Dublin didn't improve my mood or comfort.

I got stuck sitting next to a guy who had forgotten the benefits of hot water and a bar of soap. The only thing reeking more than the guy next to me was the stench escaping the guy behind me. For unknown reasons, the guy sat so far forward in his seat that his putrid breath was continuously wafting over my shoulder. To keep himself propped forward, he wrapped his hands, which smelled of bad cheese, around my headrest.

Sleep was not an option.

After what seemed like the longest journey of my life, I arrived in Dublin and found a small hostel several blocks from the bus station.

Sleep was the only option.

I awoke a few hours later to an empty dorm. I got dressed and strolled into the common lounge and found it empty except for one person sitting on the couch smoking a joint.

"Hey mate. I'm Gavin, but everybody calls me Gav. Fancy a toke?"

And this is how I met Gav. We smoked a spliff and shot the shit. Gav was a fashion photographer from London who was visiting Dublin for much the same reason as I—to go on a bender. It looked as though I had a partner in crime.

I'm quite comfortable with my sexuality, so I don't mind saying that Gav was the most stunning man I'd ever seen. He was about 6'4, solid as a rock, mulatto, dreadlocks pulled into a ponytail, big sensitive eyes and a great smile. He was all around stunning. Basically, Gav was the type of guy that everybody looks at when he walks into a room. Every single woman, regardless of her relationship status, will do a double take. When Gav made his entrance, conversations were put on hold; trains of thought were lost and burning matches charred fingertips.

Most of the evening was spent pub hopping around Dublin. I drank with Gav and chatted with the women who were anxiously waiting to chat with him. I was having a blast. My night was unfolding exactly as I had hoped. However, around 11:00 PM, the fatigue of the day's marathon journey and the previous week's debauchery began to take control. Gav caught me in a yawn.

"You fading on me, mate?"

I explained, to which he replied, "Up for doing some speed?"

Why not?

A compelling "why not" might be that I had never tried speed, and doing so for the first time in a strange city might not be the wisest of ideas. This, however, wouldn't be the first time I experimented with a new drug. I was very open-minded and curious when it came to most drugs. I was intrigued. I wanted to expand my understanding. I wanted to delve into old thoughts using new and alternative perceptions and realities. It is hard to describe exactly the feeling of tripping on acid, but some of my deepest and most enlightened introspections came during such times.

Regardless, my experimentations with drugs were simply that—experiments. I was never concerned about becoming addicted nor was addiction ever a problem.

I did have two rules I always obeyed. The first was that I knew something about the drug, such as its physical effects in the short-and long-term. I also wanted to know what sensations the high would bring. I knew that amphetamines were a stimulant and probably the ideal drug for my current energy level and setting. I knew that speed was as harmful to the system as any Class A drug, such as ecstasy or cocaine, and that nothing positive could come from long term use. However, the same can be said about alcohol, nicotine or sitting in traffic twice a day for 40 years breathing noxious fumes.

The second and more important rule involved being in the right frame of mind. I would never try anything because of peer pressure nor would I consume something if I was troubled. Most angry, aggressive drunks are reacting to shitty days. Alcohol is not a wise remedy for depression. The same is true for any drug from marijuana to LSD. I almost guarantee a nasty acid trip if your girlfriend has just dumped you. On the other hand, if your mindset and environment are positive and upbeat, then your experience will be the same.

Gav and I hit it off the moment we met, and we continued to connect throughout the evening. Although he had hordes of gorgeous women throwing themselves at him, he spent the night talking with me. Notwithstanding the length of our friendship, I liked and, more importantly, trusted him. I've always been an excellent judge of character, and I was detecting a positive energy from Gav.

As far as being in the right frame of mind and environment, it is hard to beat celebrating the rediscovery of my freedom in the Dublin pubs.

Was I up for doing some speed? The answer was a definite yes.

We slipped into a stall in the men's room. Gav pulled out a small plastic bag containing a whitish powder, which we dabbed on our tongues. The taste was bitter, similar to chewing on aspirin. However, it did the trick. Within no time, I was bouncing around the dance floor and talking a mile a minute. It is a good thing that the women were interested in talking to Gav as opposed to me because I don't think I was making any sense. Besides which, at the rate I was talking, nobody would be able to get a word in edgewise.

We dabbed some more speed, then the unthinkable happened. The pubs closed. It seemed implausible and irrational that bars would kick people out at midnight on a Saturday, arguably a pub's most lucrative time of the week.

Nevertheless, that is exactly what happened. Everything shut down.

How could this be? I don't know why the lawmakers thought it would be prudent to close the pubs at this time. But whatever their argument, a guy flying on speed and looking for a party is going to vigorously disagree.

Bur regrettably, there is nothing he can do about it.

With nowhere to go, out on the streets we went. Gav, despite several direct and personal invitations from women I would have chewed my left arm off for, decided to stick it out with me. Maybe he knew he had a rookie speeder on his hands, and he felt it was best to see me home. Maybe he felt responsible for my well-being, or maybe he was too messed up himself to actually go home with the stunning women. I didn't care. It was great to have somebody listen to me chatter.

The two of us made our way back to the hostel only to find nobody awake.

"Don't worry, mate. I've got a chunk of hash that'll help us come down."

I grinded a thanks through my teeth.

We settled in the common lounge and smoked joint after joint to help ourselves mellow from the speed rush. Despite Gav's generosity with his gear, I found that the hash wasn't helping me come down off the nasty chemical.

Then, to make matters considerably worse, Mick stormed into the lounge.

Mick, who was born and bred in Belfast, looked like your stereotypical Ultimate Fighting Champion. He had tattoos up and down his massive arms, an even larger frame, missing teeth and a menacing glare on his ugly, oversized lump of a shaved head. All his knuckles were freshly cut. This made me wonder what the other guy looked like and what gutter he was laying in, unconscious and bleeding.

I know you shouldn't judge a book by its cover, but in this case, the book was wide open.

Mick was as drunk as a sailor and a self-confessed racist who thought the world would be a better place if every Chinaman was dead and rotting. In the best circumstances, Mick was a bastard to tolerate. I was still speeding off my nut, however, and that made the difficult situation that much more strenuous. Mick sat and spewed racism for a solid 15 minutes and chugged a couple of beers. He smashed the last on his forehead, belched and left.

Thank Christ.

The hash must have been working on Gav because he remained cool during Mick's racist tirade. I, on the other hand, was having a hard time. Listening to this stupidity and racism was nearly impossible. Still, Mick's size and the likelihood of him kicking my ass made it relatively easy to bite my tongue. Gav, in contrast, was massive and had about six inches on the drunken, Irish fool. I was sure he could have pounded the Belfast prick into next week. I asked how he kept so calm with that moron ranting and raving.

Gav answered between deep drags of the mammoth joint. "There are some people in the world who just don't get it and never will. They have their own fucked up ideas. People like that slob are ignorant. Nothing I say will get through his thick melon. No sense in even trying, mate. That Muppet is a waste of my breath and time."

Gav was right. There was no point dwelling on Mick's narrow-minded perception of the world. I had more pressing and personal issues to handle, namely coming down off speed.

We smoked another joint. Gav looked as though he was ready to crash, so when he asked me if I would be able to fall asleep, I told him I could. It was a lie. The poor guy had turned down woman I would consider paying for and gave me enough hash to tame a tiger. He'd done enough to make sure I'd recover. The rest was up to me.

I made my way to the dorm, and as my jittery hands fumbled with the doorknob, I heard the smash of a beer can and a loud burp behind me.

"Hey, Canadia. It looks like we're in the same fucking room."

Shit. It was Mick.

There is an unwritten law among backpackers. When you sleep in a dorm room and come in late, you try to be as quiet as possible so you don't disturb your fellow, sleeping travellers.

Most travellers abide by this considerate and simple guideline.

Not Mick.

The Belfast racist kicked the door open, flicked on the lights, burped and stomped through the room, which was filled with sleeping backpackers. In one of the bunk beds, there was a guy cuddled up with a girl. Mick walked up to him and began yelling. "I fucking told ya not to bring yar fucking sluts back here ya fucking cunt!"

Then, WHAM! Mick drilled the poor sleeping bastard in the mouth. WHAM! Mick clocked him again.

Mick yanked the dazed kid from the bed and began slamming him around the room. Everybody woke up. When they realized the maniac known as Mick was involved, everybody decided it was in their best interest to roll over and go back to sleep. The girl was screaming hysterically. She grabbed what clothes she could find and ran naked from the room.

The fight continued. Mick landed the majority of punches. When I say the majority, what I really mean is all of the punches. It was a beating. The kid, bleeding like a stuck pig, managed to free himself from Mick's grip and ran out of the room.

I was left with the raging psycho.

"I was going to fucking kill him," the maniac screamed.

And with that death threat, Mick reached into his ass-stomping boot and pulled out a knife.

Lovely. Now the violent lunatic has a weapon.

He waved the blade in my face in an inquisitive manner and asked, "Do ya think that I was right?"

I wasn't sure what to say.

He asked for my opinion on the assault and battery a second time. "Do ya think I was fucking right?"

Everything was unfolding way too fast for my liking.

I had a hammered, homicidal maniac who, for no apparent reason, pounded some sleeping kid. Now he was asking me, a guy who was seriously confused and stressed about his situation, if I thought his blatantly unjustifiable actions were justified.

I needed to choose my words very carefully.

Despite the speed in my system, I was able to put together a lucid thought. I said it very quickly, but at least it was coherent.

I conveyed that I had no idea what their history was and that maybe things would seem better in the morning. I babbled some crap about tomorrow being another day and that my best advice would be to sleep on it.

I didn't know if my suggestion had gotten through his thick, hammered melon, or if the lunatic was about to launch into another violent outburst. He just stared at me. He stared with his chest heaving, his nasty, liquored breath wafting on my face and always with the knife gripped in his hand.

The silence was broken only by my grinding teeth.

Then an amazing thing happened. Mick broke from his pig ugly gaze and said, "Ya know ..."

He still had the knife in my face. However, he wasn't shaking it aggressively anymore. He was waving the blade in a way that indicated deep thought,

"Ya know," he continued, "I think you're fucking right."

Miraculously, my bullshit worked, and I was able to subdue the monster. Mick belched one last time. He lay down on his bed fully dressed, closed his eyes and passed out with the knife still in his hand. Before I could exhale, Mick began to snore. In fact, the noises roaring out of his face well surpassed the boundaries of snoring.

What just happened?

Within a minute of walking into a peacefully sleeping dorm, I witnessed a seemingly unprovoked and certainly unfair fight, had a screaming naked girl run past me, watched a guy get his head bloodied, heard a murder threat, had the potential weapon shoved in my face, got asked my opinion about the assault, pacified a maniac, watched him pass out and discovered a new noise that humans are capable of producing.

Combined with the speed racing through my system, sleep was not an option.

Gav found me the next morning fidgeting in the common room.

"Jesus man. You look knackered. You holding up?"

I recounted the previous night's adventure.

"Fuck mate. That is one speed trip I wouldn't wanna be on."

Cheers for the advice.

"Hey brother, this will help calm you down. Take it for the road. I've got tons." Gav handed me a massive joint.

I thanked Gav for the smoke, said goodbye and made my way to the bus station. I had an hour to kill before my departure back to Cork. Although I was close to coming off this nasty drug, I felt that a joint would unquestionably assist me on the road to recovery. I looked around and discovered that the only place to smoke the spliff was in a park behind the terminal.

I sat down, sparked up and reflected on the previous evening's exploits. Despite the Mick incident, the Dublin bender had been amazing. On top of a great night out with a cool guy and breathtaking women, I came away with valuable lessons. The first lesson: speed wasn't a drug for me. For the amount of damage it would do to my body, the high didn't seem worthwhile, and I despised the immediate aftermath. Even if you took Mick's tirade out of the equation, last night's come down was indisputably the worst come down from any drug I had explored.

It was safe to say that my experimentation with speed was finished.

Second and more important, I reaffirmed my ability to read a person's character. Anyone with a fragment of a brain could see Mick was a complete and total idiot. However, the same couldn't be said for Gav. I was happy to discover that my initial analysis of his personality was accurate. Gav was a friendly, generous and considerate soul with a positive outlook on life. He did his absolute best to make sure I had a great party and that I was well looked after. He could have easily ditched me anytime during the evening for carnal pleasure of the utmost quality, but he didn't. Instead, he made sure I got home safely and had the easiest time possible coming off the speed.

I knew there would be many moments on this trip when I would have to put my trust into complete strangers, and my ability to assess their true intentions would not only be a valuable skill but a necessary tool if I was going to succeed in travelling across the planet by myself.

You never know whom you will meet. All walks of life are out there.

There are the good, the bad and, in Mick's case, the ugly.

It was indispensable to know who was who.

Luckily, I sat next to one of the good on my ride to Cork. What made this individual good in my opinion had nothing to do with his character or personal hygiene but everything to do with his willingness to shut up and let me get some long overdue sleep.

I took full advantage of the silence and finally fell into a deep and long slumber.

I called Sinead when I got to Cork.

"How was Dublin?"

I began telling her about the evening's mayhem, but she cut me off. "We're going to *Shakespeare's* for a good ol' piss-up tonight. You can tell me every detail of your story there. See you there at nine?"

Why not?

5
GET LOST

NOVEMBER

"It breaks down like this. It's legal to buy it. It's legal to own it, and if you are the proprietor of a hash bar, it's legal to sell it. It's legal to carry it, but that doesn't really matter 'cause—get a load of this—if you get stopped by the cops in Amsterdam, it's illegal for them to search you. I mean, that is a right the cops in Amsterdam don't have."

—Vincent Vega—*Pulp Fiction*

When John Travolta's character explained the liberal ways of Amsterdam to his nefarious partner in the opening scene of Quentin Tarantino's classic film, *Pulp Fiction*, he was also disclosing this innovation to North American potheads. Many of these potheads, because they were potheads, were not aware that such a smoking Mecca existed.

I was one of them.

Although most North American potheads could not point out Amsterdam on a map or even say what country the city was in, some were determined to visit.

Again, I was one of them.

Even though I discovered the benefits of marijuana relatively late in my youth, I had taken to the green bud with a devoted passion.

To begin, I have an issue calling marijuana a "drug." That is, I have an issue putting marijuana under the same umbrella as cocaine, speed, acid and ecstasy. Those are chemically engineered narcotics produced in a lab. Marijuana is a plant. It comes from the earth.

In over 2000 years of its reported use, not a single person has died from a marijuana overdose. The difference is obvious and undeniable.

I'm a big proponent of legalizing marijuana or at least decriminalizing it. The shocking waste in manpower and resources to arrest, prosecute and incarcerate weed smokers is beyond my comprehension. People are still assaulted, raped and murdered; yet police continue wasting their valuable efforts by arresting non-violent marijuana users.[1]

As far as I can tell, the only victim of a chronic smoker is the refrigerator.

Howard Marks, the infamous British marijuana smuggler, best summarized the madness and confusion of legal priorities when he remarked that the date of his release from Terre Haut Penitentiary in Indiana was the same day as Mike Tyson's release from jail.

"I had been continuously in prison for the last six and a half years for transporting beneficial herbs from one place to another, while he (Tyson) had done three years for rape."

Does this make any sense?

I've always been very open about my attitude towards marijuana as well as my consumption of the plant. Luckily, my friends and family were extremely tolerant and accommodating when it came to my smoking.

Regardless, the one place that wasn't tolerant or accommodating was the one environment I would have most enjoyed smoking a joint. That location was in a bar with my buddies. It was bad enough sneaking off like some junkie to smoke a doobie in the middle of summer. But to have to leave the warmth of the bar to brave the negative 30 degree Canadian cold in order to blaze up was downright painful. Through chattering teeth we would always mutter, "F-f-f-fuck. If we were in Amsterdam we c-c-ould be smoking this b-b-baby indoors."

So, it should come as zero surprise that Amsterdam was topping my must-see list.

I wasn't going to Amsterdam for the museums, architecture, windmills, clogs or cheese. I was going to Amsterdam for the dope. I was going to Amsterdam to get stoned.

Chilling out and smoking weed for a few days would be exactly what my polluted body needed to detoxify. Ireland was, to use a local expression, a "crack,"

---

1. There was a man in Oklahoma who had multiple sclerosis. He grew and smoked marijuana, because it eased his pain enough that he could play with his small children. He was arrested, tried and sentenced to 48 years in prison for intent to distribute. The sentence was automatically doubled because he possessed the plant in front of minors. The prosecutors forced his wife to testify against him, or they would have convicted her as well, leaving their kids parentless. 96 years in prison because a suffering father smoked weed in order to play with his kids without feeling pain. Have we really lost our grip on reality that badly?

but ultimately it was like every other destination on my trip. It turned into one long, vicious hangover. I'd been drinking way too much.

I needed to slow down.

I needed to mellow out.

Amsterdam's red-light district was an idyllic location to do so.

I said goodbye to Sinead, thanked her for helping destroy billions of my brain cells and got my drunken ass out of Ireland and on a plane to the Netherlands. After a quick and easy train ride from Schipol Airport, I was standing in front of Amsterdam's Central Station. I stared at the beautiful skyline, and the red-light district enticed me to sample its offerings.

I couldn't wait to smoke a joint.

I found the nearest hostel and I was shown into an eight-man dorm room that was full except for my bed. Everybody introduced themselves. They were all from Canada or the United States.

"We are about to go to the District. If you want, you can come with us. We can show you around."

Despite spotting Brian-like qualities from a few of them, I accepted their invitation. I was being cautious. I didn't know what to expect in the District that promised prostitution and drug dealers. After learning the language lesson in Glasgow, and being in a new country with another tongue, I figured it might be wise to have company who knew the area and customs.

This was a bad call.

We easily made it from the hostel to the edge of the infamous red-light district, but then the headache began.

The group stopped. They pulled out a map. They argued about which café to see, and they debated which route they should take. The group expressed their concerns about getting lost. They consulted their maps and deliberated some more.

Were they serious?

Were we not in the red-light district? Were there not coffee shops and, therefore, weed to smoke everywhere? I smelled the sweet odour of burning buds; the aroma seemed to emerge from every direction. It didn't matter to me where we went or how we got there. All I wanted to do was smoke a joint in a public venue.

It was dumb enough arguing where we should smoke, since the answer was anywhere. But to stand there with a map? We weren't Hansel and Gretel in the Black Forest. There were people everywhere. How could we possibly get lost? When I was at my snapping point, the group decided on a destination and marched out.

Thank Christ.

We crisscrossed through the cobblestone alleys past countless cafés more than suitable for my quest. It was torture.

I desperately wanted to smoke.

I could have burned several joints by the time we arrived at a café, a venue that was frustratingly identical to every one we had skipped. Regardless, we were there, and I could get some weed and chill out. I was told during the lengthy journey that if I wanted to buy some dope, I had to go to the bar and ask to see a "menu."

It was the first thing I did when we walked in the door.

I didn't know where to start. White Widow? K2? Super Skunk? Northern Lights? Purple Haze? Transkei Red? The incredible selection of marijuana and hashish all seemed tantalizing. I eventually settled on a gram of K2 and a gram of Purple Haze knowing I would work my way through the entire assortment.

I was close. I had my weed

All that was left was roll a joint, light it, smoke it and chill out.

It was not to be.

I made the critical mistake of going back to the table of Americans from the North.

Sure, I rolled my joint. I even lit it and smoked a bit. Nevertheless, the loud, obnoxious dribble accepted as conversation made it impossible to chill out.

The idiot next to me was from Florida. I knew this because that was all he could jabber about. Florida is better than this. Florida is better than that. Florida has bigger this. Florida has bigger that. Florida … Florida … fucking Florida.

I wanted to ask the guy why he left if he had such an obvious hard-on for the place. I honestly didn't give a shit if Florida had better weed or better drive-through banking. In case he hadn't noticed, we were in Amsterdam. There wasn't an orange grove in sight. I wanted to tell the guy to mellow out, so I could focus on the task at hand—getting stoned.

I didn't though. I kept my mouth shut. He kept blabbing.

I did the only thing I could other than tell him to shut up.

I palmed my spliff and said I was going to the toilet. I locked myself into a stall, sat down and relit the joint. I took a deep, long drag, leaned back on the porcelain and smiled. I thought of Russ, Chris, Danny and my other toking buddies. I wished they could share this smoke with me.

It was only then that I properly chilled out.

It wasn't the most glorious venue for my first joint in Amsterdam, but at least it was in a public place.

The K2 knocked me on my ass. Going back to the table with the loudmouths was not an option. Thankfully, the toilet was in a place that allowed me a quick and undetected escape. For the second time on my travels, I successfully pulled a runner from a group of North Americans.

I don't dislike Americans and Canadians. It's just that I left home to get away from home. I knew North America, and to be brutally frank, I wasn't a huge fan. I didn't fancy our philosophies, attitudes and goals, which I felt represented a small minority of humanity. Many North Americans, like buddy from Florida, are so in love with their home that they are biased and close minded about anywhere else.

It didn't take a fortune-teller to see that a discussion about the Western world with Mr. Florida would end in confrontation.

So I bailed.

This escape gave me the freedom to explore and sample different coffee shops in the District. My initial anxieties about wandering by myself proved unjustified. The language difference was a non-issue for everybody spoke English. There were a lot of Nigerian and Moroccan drug dealers who popped out of dark alleys when I walked by. They came right up into my face and asked with wild, dashing eyes, "Want some coke? Want some E?"

Although this invasion of personal space was mildly intimidating at first, I found the problem was resolved by firmly stating no and continuing my stride. The dealers accepted the stern rejection and would slouch back into the shadows.

The prostitutes, on the other hand, caught me off guard.

Much like marijuana, prostitution in the Netherlands is legalized and controlled. In the red-light district, there are alleys lined with windows, in which nearly naked women try to seduce you into their booths for paid passion. Red lights above the windows indicate where love can be bought. There are many red lights in the District.

The real oddity, however, is the variety of women in the windows.

There are your leggy, gorgeous blonds that are very difficult to ignore. These beauties I expected to find. However, I wasn't expecting the multitude of ugly prostitutes. Nor did I anticipate alleys devoted to fat women. Every age, nationality and body type was represented. One moment I was staring at an Asian supermodel, and then I was looking at a 300-pound African mama. And around the next corner, I'd discover a hooker who looks a lot like somebody's grandmother.

Something for everyone I guess.

This was one strange and fascinating city.

I'm not sure what time I got in to the dorm that evening, but I do know that I was very, very stoned. I also know that I was woken up well before I was supposed to be awake.

I opened my eyes to Mr. Florida shaking me and telling me to hurry up. Still unsure if I was conscious or stuck in some cruel dream, I asked why.

"Well, we've got a busy day planned. First, we're going to the Anne Frank museum. From there it's off to see the Rembrandt. After that, we should be close to lunchtime. There is a great little café near the museum. After lunch we're heading to …"

It was way too early for this dribble. I had to put an end to it.

I explained that I was still tired from last night, and I needed to sleep. In fact, I was certain I would be sleeping for quite some time, and that they should go off on their own. I would be fine by myself.

I thought the same excuse that I used with Brian in Glasgow might work with this bunch.

Regrettably, they were just as persistent as my first friend.

"Well," Mr. Florida asked, "do you even know where you are going?"

He asked in a tone that suggested I was a fucking idiot who didn't know how to tie his shoes.

I explained that I didn't mind walking around aimlessly. I said it was next to impossible to actually get lost in a city.

Mr. Florida looked at me as if I had just farted on a baby's head. He spat out, "Fine then," and he stormed out of the room. The rest of the group grabbed their packs, maps, water bottles, compasses, bread crumbs and whatever other piece of survival equipment they needed for the wild streets of Amsterdam. They followed the alpha male out of the dorm.

The room was left with an icy chill.

I knew when I was outnumbered and when a situation was uncomfortable. This was another opportunity to apply my "avoid conflict if at all possible" philosophy. Therefore, my first priority of the day would be finding a new place to sleep. This mission proved easy, for I had passed a vibrant hostel the night before called *The Smoking Hobbit*. As it turned out, it was much closer to the heart of the action. After checking into a room, I did what I had promised.

I began to wander; I began to get lost.

How lost could I really get, though? I was in a city. I was in the tourist section of that city. If it was the worst-case scenario, and I was really desperate and starving, I could hop into a taxi.

As I zigzagged through the maze of alleys and canals, I took in the sights and sampled various local herbs. During my search for anything, I came across the Museum of Hemp and Marijuana. It was a definite find.

The small museum was filled with documentation about the history and uses of the plant. The information confirmed a lot of what I already knew.

One section of the museum was a hydroponics growing centre. As I was staring at the beautiful, green buds, a deep, raspy voice spoke from behind me. "Would you like to try some of this?"

I turned around. Sitting at a table was a guy with a long, grey ponytail who looked about 50-something. On the table was a massive contraption that resembled an oversized laboratory beaker.

I asked what he was offering.

"Vaporized weed. Puuure THC, man."

The man introduced himself as Buffalo Jim, a Cherokee Indian from Arizona and self-proclaimed fugitive. Buffalo Jim explained that THC is the chemical in marijuana that gets you high. He added that when you smoke weed, you are also, unfortunately, inhaling a large amount of tar. The vaporizer extracts the THC from the plant and allows a clean, pure and unpolluted high.

I was fascinated.

Buffalo Jim took about five grams of weed and put it into a small dish. He slid the dish into the neck of the massive bong. Then he fired up the paint remover gun, which he aimed directly through the top of the funnel. The bowl began to fill with mist. After about a minute, he put down the paint remover gun, took out the plate of weed and threw the ganja into the garbage.

The professional pothead must have detected my disbelief that he had thrown away buds that appeared freshly harvested because he said, "Not potent anymore." Tapping the bowl filled with mist, he continued, "All the THC is in here. Go ahead. Have a hit."

I gripped the mouthpiece and inhaled the mist deep into my lungs. I'm not sure what I noticed first. Maybe it was the taste … or lack of taste. It was amazing. It was like standing over a humidifier and breathing clean, damp, tasteless air. The nasty taste of smoke was non-existent. This revelation barely had a chance to register before the THC hit my blood stream.

I was immediately high.

It was as clean a high as I've ever experienced. There wasn't any sensation of being "stoned." I didn't have that smoky feeling behind my eyes or in the chest. I didn't feel lethargic. I felt energized.

Buffalo Jim had a toke and glanced around the room. "It's pretty dead in here today. Go ahead and have another hit."

So I did. So did he.

We each hit the bong of vaporized weed four more times.

When I stumbled out of the museum, I was as high as I had ever been.

It was time to get lost again.

Along with its attitude towards drugs and prostitution, Amsterdam is also quite liberal about its live sex shows. Viewing a live sex show is something most tourists put on their Amsterdam must-see list. The live sex clubs in the District were as common as McDonald's at home. Each club had a guy standing at the front door, promoting the show and trying to entice you in for the next performance.

I guess I wandered by the same club a few times during my goofed walk to nowhere because I started to recognize one particular guy. He obviously recognized me. Each time I passed, he smiled and nodded. And unlike most of the promotion guys, this dude wasn't going for the hard sell. He acted as though he didn't care if I came in. He was simply saying hello.

As I wavered by for the third time, the guy smiled and said, "So man, you going to come in and check out the show?"

Like most travellers in Amsterdam, seeing a live sex show was on my agenda. I was planning on seeing one at some point. I figured, as high as I was, now was probably the best time to see what all the fuss was about.

I paid my twenty guilders and went downstairs into a small theatre that held about 50 people. The seats faced an elevated stage that was draped in purple velvet curtains. The walls were adorned with paintings of ancient Roman orgy scenes.

There were only about 30 of us seated when the show began. The tacky curtains were pulled back to reveal a stunning brunette standing onstage. She began to dance. Then she began to strip.

Once she was fully undressed, she stopped dancing. She looked at the audience and asked for a volunteer.

Nobody flinched.

With a seductive tone, she asked again. "Please. Isn't there anybody who would help me?"

Maybe the gentleman in me felt bad for this poor, desperate girl onstage. Without question, being high as a mountain goat gave me added courage. Regardless of the reason, I raised my hand and volunteered, having no idea what I was setting myself up for.[2]

I hopped up onto the stage. Following a quick introduction, she lay down on her back and spread her legs as wide as possible. She gave me an extremely sensual look, and in the most seductive voice she asked, "Do you see anything interesting?"

Was that a trick question?

"Anything pink?"

Now I knew she was messing with me. However, upon further inspection, I did notice something interesting and pink. There appeared to be a pink ribbon protruding from her vagina.

I cautiously answered that I did see something.

"Go on and give it a little tug."

So I did. I tugged, and I tugged, and I tugged some more. Before I knew it, I was going arm over arm with the seemingly endless supply of pink trimming. After a good 50 feet, I finally pulled out the end of the magical ribbon.

I was impressed.

She stood up and thanked me for my help with a kiss on the cheek. I sat down thinking if that was the opening act, then what in the world could be next?

I didn't have long to wait.

Another girl, even more beautiful than the first, took the stage and began her striptease. And once again, after she was completely naked, she stopped and asked for a volunteer from the crowd.

Since I already had my experience onstage, I didn't bother putting up my hand. I figured I shouldn't be greedy and should share the interaction with my fellow patrons.

To my utter disbelief, no one raised his hand.

I was baffled. Had these people not witnessed what just transpired with the pink ribbon? Why weren't they crawling over each other to volunteer?

I gave it another couple of seconds then dutifully raised my hand. This decision had nothing to do with being high or a gentleman. This decision was based on curiosity and the desire to have a bird's-eye view of whatever bodily accomplishment the girl might perform.

I made my way front and centre, did the introduction formality and again, the girl lay naked on her back. I thought I knew what I was supposed to do, and I was close to diving in and exploring.

I think the girl could sense my anxiousness because she quickly said, "No, there isn't anything in there ... yet."

---

2. Okay...she was hot.

Yet?

With that, she pulled out a foot-long vibrator from the bag she had brought onstage. She asked, "Do you know what to do with this?"

Was she kidding? An elephant would be hard pressed to know what to do with something that huge.

I think the girl noticed my eyes popping out of my head and guessed that the machinery overwhelmed me. She said, "Here, let me show you."

She took the monstrosity and inserted it between her legs as if it was a toothpick. I thought the miracle of childbirth was something to see, but this spectacle was out of this world.

The girl took a break from her masturbating and looked up at me. "Do you think you can help me now?"

I didn't know if my wrists were strong enough, but I was willing to give it an attempt.

With two hands, for I was afraid of tearing a muscle or dropping the thing on my foot if I used only one, I grabbed the vibrating beast. The contraption gave out as much power as a jackhammer and allowed me the same amount of control. Its use may have registered on the Richter scale.

Again, I was impressed.

I was also laughing my ass off.

I was, once again, having one of those little out-of-body moments that confirmed I was a very long way from home. I was high as a kite. I was inserting a foot-long vibrator into a Dutch beauty in front of complete strangers on a Thursday afternoon.

Was this city for real?

After what was a rather convincing orgasm, the girl thanked me and I, once again, returned to my seat.

My personal involvement in the first two acts made me a tad biased, but the couple that performed the choreographed sex routine didn't captivate me anywhere as much. Sticking with the "Conan the Barbarian" theme, the man and the woman would screw in a variety of positions. He'd be nailing her in the missionary position, and with a quick, fluid, almost acrobatic flip, he'd have her doggy style.

The climax of the feature event was, surprisingly, the climax.

At the very least, the main event answered one of my burning questions—where they got the mould to make act two's foot-long vibrator. I was amazed the girl was able to walk off stage.

I wasn't sure if clapping was the appropriate response in that situation, but nonetheless, that is what I did.

I wondered if the Americans had found the Anne Frank Museum.

I began laughing again. Considering I left the hostel without a plan, my day turned out quite action-packed. I know the Yanks had an itinerary to take in all the sights, but I strongly doubt that a Rembrandt provided as much entertainment as my walk to nowhere. It dawned on me that when you get lost, you discover things that you never knew existed.

I had a feeling I was going to encounter a lot of unknowns on my voyage.

After my day of discovery, I began coffee house hopping. I eventually stumbled upon a small, funky little café located just outside the District that particularly caught my attention. *Morrison's Café* hooked me because the first time I walked in, they were playing Canada's best rock music from a band called The Tragically Hip. The café had immediate potential to become my regular smoking venue. The dope was potent. The barmen were friendly. The coffee was delicious. What more could I ask for?

Morrison's Café became a fixture of my daily routine in Amsterdam. I'd wake up and head to *Morrison's* for my morning cup of coffee and morning spliff. At some point in the afternoon, I'd go back to *The Smoking Hobbit* for a nap. At some point in the evening, I'd wake up, get a bite to eat and return to the vibrant café for the rest of the night.

On first appearance, it doesn't look as if I did much in Amsterdam other than get stoned. That is only partially true. I didn't do anything physical, but my brain received a notable workout.

While I took the lazy approach to backpacking and plunked my ass down in one spot all day, the rest of the energetic world would come and go. They would move for me. I'd roll a joint in my cozy corner underneath a trippy painting of Jim Morrison, and somebody would inevitably sit down on the cushions next to me. Joints would be passed and conversations started. After they would leave, a new person would take their seat. The faces and nationalities would change, but the spliffs and chatter remained consistent.

How sweet was this? I was meeting a variety of people from the four corners of the planet while smoking weed and listening to great music. And I didn't even have to move.

The routine entrenched itself rather quickly and easily.[3]

I was having a hard time prying myself away from the city. Two weeks flew by. I had certainly accomplished my desire to stay off the booze and chill out. I knew I had to start travelling again, but I also knew it wasn't going to be easy to get motivated. Amsterdam had a lot going for it. I loved the city. I loved the mentality and openness of the Dutch. I loved the weed. I loved the coffee. I even loved mayonnaise on french fries.

How long was Vincent Vega stuck in Amsterdam? Three years?

There was the strong possibility that I too could get trapped.

Thankfully, it was Mother Nature who provided the push I needed.

The weather had turned shitty. It was now the beginning of November, and the cold Dutch rain made its presence known. Walking to *Morrison's Café* had become a chilly and damp endeavour. The bitter and drizzly winter was getting ready to kick off with a vengeance.

Before I began this trip, one of the requirements I had made was to travel with the sun. I'd spent 24 years living with cold winters, and I had yet to find a truly appealing aspect to it. Skiing? Snowboarding? Skating? Sure, they can be fun. However, all enjoyment is frozen with negative 30 degree temperatures. That is negative 30 not including the wind chill factor. And I can only play so much. Most of my time is spent doing the living in the rut shit, such as going to work, taking out the garbage and shopping. Furthermore, just to get anywhere I had to shovel snow from my driveway and scrape ice off the windshield of my car. How could I not loathe winter?

Therefore, having left Canada's barren, frozen, winter wasteland, I vowed to experience an endless summer.

It was time to get my cold, wet ass to somewhere hot.

I contemplated exactly where somewhere was going to be as I smoked a joint and chilled on the massive cushions in the communal smoking area of *The Smoking Hobbit*.

Being stoned, I was having a hard time staying focused on the task at hand. My eyes began wandering aimlessly around the groovy hostel. Much like my walk to nowhere, my eyes began to get lost. Because I was baked and stretched out on

---

3. I did leave once. I had met a girl in Dublin from Bonn, Germany who said I could visit anytime. Bonn was about a three-hour train ride from Amsterdam. I saw this as the perfect opportunity to escape from my routine. However, this decision created a new dilemma. She lived with her brother who sold weed. We smoked in the morning, afternoon and evening. We smoked all day at no cost. It was like a Cheech and Chong movie. I was actually smoking more weed in Bonn than I was in Amsterdam! At least in Amsterdam my smoking was placed under some form of economic restraint. I could only afford to smoke so much. Not so in Bonn. I could feel my cognitive skills disappearing. Consequently, I went back to Amsterdam.

the comfy cushions, I could see a poster nestled behind the hostel's bar. Underneath a shelf of glasses, I had yet to observe it in any vertical position.

The poster was an advertisement promoting *Hades' Hideaway*. It was an intriguingly named backpackers' getaway located in Corfu, Greece. There were pictures of invitingly warm and sunny beaches.

Having a few Greek friends at home, I did know a little bit about the country. I knew Greece was on the Mediterranean. I was somewhat confident that the Med was warm this time of year. Unquestionably, Corfu would be warmer than Amsterdam.

That was all the knowledge I required to make my decision. My next destination was going to be *Hades' Hideaway*.

That is, after I finish smoking this joint.

Buffalo Jim and his potent vaporizer.

Your slightly goofed author seated and blazing beneath a painting of Jim Morrison. It was this comfy corner in *Morrison's Café* that consumed the majority of my time in Amsterdam.

6

THE PRAGUE EXPERIMENT

NOVEMBER

"Aren't you a little short to be a Stormtrooper?"

The question stopped me dead in my sandals. I slowly turned around and discovered a girl sitting on the bar counter in *Hades' Hideaway*'s groovy, in-house pub.

She repeated her question, pointing to the Stormtrooper logo on my T-shirt. "I said, aren't you a little short to be a Stormtrooper?"

The Galactic Empire's foot soldier is easily recognizable to any fan of the *Star Wars* films, but there are many who don't have a clue what a Stormtrooper could possibly be. Unfortunately for my libido, the majority of those who don't know or care are women.

I'm fully aware that *Star Wars* represents the childish and nerdish side of my personality, but nonetheless, it is a part of who I am.

I'm a devoted *Star War*ian. *Star Wars* was a part of my childhood foundation. It was the first movie I ever saw in the theatres. I played with *Star Wars* toys. I was there for the original release. I was there for the re-release. I knew I would be there when George Lucas eventually releases the prequels. In truth, *Star Wars* was such an integral part of my upbringing that I would subtly quiz first dates to gauge their *Star Wars* knowledge and thus determine compatibility. Answers such as "that little green thingy" or "the scary guy in the mask" pretty much guaranteed there wouldn't be a second date. Although, perhaps my asking the questions was the reason there was never a second date.

So when this mystery girl not only correctly identified the Stormtrooper on my shirt but also used a quote from the movie to do so, she had me hooked. She was even more captivating because the quote she applied was appropriate. I *am* too short to be a Stormtrooper.[1]

I had to know this girl.

We began talking. Just to make sure her comment regarding my shortcomings as a Stormtrooper wasn't a lucky guess I asked her if she was a fan of *Star Wars*. She looked at me as if I was daft.

"I'm the Jedi Master," she brashly replied.

I was taken aback. Proclaiming to be a Jedi Master is an extremely bold statement. There can be many Jedis but very few Jedi Masters.

I couldn't let her off with my standard first date interrogation. Questions such as "who is Luke's father" and "what is the name of Han Solo's ship" would not be appropriate following the presumptuous declaration that she was a Jedi Master.

I increased the level of difficulty. I decided to ask her a question that the casual viewer of the film would most certainly not know. The answer to this particular question would require not only an extensive knowledge of the films and characters but planetary geography and hardware as well.

My question was this: "What did Luke want to buy at Toshi Station?"

She gave me that "man, are you ever daft" look again. She said matter-of-factly, "Not only can I tell you how much Luke would have paid for his power converters, but I can also tell you where he would have gotten a better deal."

I was awestruck. She *was* a Jedi Master.

That was the moment I fell for Stacey.

It had been a very long time since I met anybody who knew more than I did about *Star Wars*. And I guarantee that whoever that science fiction nerd may have been, he wouldn't have been as beautiful as Stacey. *He* wouldn't have been a *she*.

We immediately had an amazing connection. It was almost as if the "force" was flowing between us. As our conversation delved deeper into the philosophies and ideologies of *Star Wars*, our attraction to one another grew.

We decided to go for a walk on the beach.

I asked if I could hold her hand, and I made some cheesy comment about the moonlight dancing off the waves.

And there, on the sand underneath the stars, with the Ionian Sea lapping at our feet, I had my first kiss during my travels.

However, after one night of romance, she was gone.

This wasn't the first time a woman disappeared from my life after one night with me. Surprisingly though, it wasn't anything I said or did that made Stacey

---

1. I don't actually know how tall one has to be to be a Stormtrooper. I do know that the chances of me being too short are pretty good. My friends would say I was lucky to get onto rides at the fair.

leave *Hades' Hideaway* the following morning. There was another factor involved. Stacey had a flight to Amsterdam.

This, so it would seem, would be an unfortunate aspect of the travel romance. Plane tickets, dates and departure times would dictate the life of love on the road, not the strength of the connection or passion between two people.

This was one of those times.

As we kissed goodbye and waited for her taxi to take her to the airport, Stacey proposed an idea. She said she was only going to be in Amsterdam for a couple of days, and then she was going to make her way to Prague. She suggested that I meet her there. She had been told Prague was a romantic city, and she thought it would be amazing to spend her week there with me.

The taxi arrived, and after one more kiss, Stacey was gone.

I began to miss her immediately.

I thought about her invitation. It was tempting.

However, as much as I would have loved to meet Stacey in Prague, it wasn't possible. I'd been in Greece for two and a half weeks, and all of that time was spent in Corfu. Rather, all of that time was spent at *Hades' Hideaway*.

The place was a lazy trap. Set right on the beach, this warm weather hostel was the perfect setting to do nothing but relax and work on your tan. During my moments of baking on the beach, I had planned my next few months of travel. I planned to trek through the rest of the Greek Isles then make my way into Turkey. From Turkey, I'd continue onto Israel and most likely find work on a kibbutz. After a couple of months working, the plan would be …

Hold on a second. What had really been planned? I hadn't bought any tickets. I wasn't meeting anybody. Turkey wasn't going anywhere. Israel should still be there. In fact, I had only made this "plan" to travel the Middle East a couple days ago.

Just because I had haphazardly planned to go to Turkey and Israel didn't mean I actually had to go. I certainly didn't have to go now.

It dawned on me that nothing was set in stone. Until it actually happened, everything was just a possibility.

Wasn't this the selfishness and freedom I was searching for?

I had the power to do what I wanted, when I wanted, where I wanted, with whom I wanted, for however long I wanted.

I had spent a great night with Stacey. I had also been told that Prague was a beautiful and romantic city. It was a fantastic place to be with a girl.

Did I need any more reason?

Nope. I was going to Prague.

This plan wasn't going to be easy to implement. However, my true dilemma wasn't travelling to the other side of the continent, although that was a daunting mission. It wasn't even finding Stacey, assuming I got to Prague, even though I didn't know where she would be staying.

The difficulty was leaving *Hades' Hideaway*.

Well … the difficulty was not being too hungover to leave *Hades' Hideaway*.

I mentioned that *Hades' Hideaway* was a lazy trap, although I wasn't completely forthright why. The lethargic mentality of the travellers staying here was in part due to the relaxing climate, but ultimately, it had more to do with most being too ruined to physically leave the hostel. It was very easy to convince yourself to recuperate another day in paradise instead of travelling while feeling miserable. However, with alcohol as my staple diet, waking up without a hangover was a rarity.

I should have been wary when I checked in and they gave me a shot of ouzo. This could have been viewed as a welcoming gesture to a new guest if it hadn't been eight-thirty in the morning. There was steady consumption of booze throughout the day at *Hades' Hideaway*. However, it was at night that the alcohol pounding began, and the madness truly made its presence known. The place turned into a sex-crazed, drunken zoo.

I had attempted to leave *Hades' Hideaway* on several occasions but failed miserably every time. I hadn't even been able to attempt the first segment of the 48-hour journey to Prague—a ferry from Corfu to Brindisi, Italy. The problem had to do with the departure time of said ferry. The boat left the docks at eight in the morning. This schedule is very tough to keep when you pass out in bed at five. Making dinnertime is tough when you pass out at five in the morning.

Numerous people missed their rides because their going-away parties never ended.

I was determined not to be one of these people … anymore.

It was not to be.

I drank. I danced. I partied. I might have even smashed a plate or two, and I got to bed at five.

When my alarm went off two hours later, I almost cried. My eyeballs felt like bowling balls. My tongue took up most of the space in my mouth. I began debating whether or not I should get up and go or simply sleep it off and try it all again tomorrow. To my amazement, I convinced myself to get up. The decisive factors were that I had packed the day before, and I was still too drunk to fully comprehend the length of the journey ahead of me.

Getting onto the bus for the ferry wasn't a problem. It was a problem when the bus started to rock and bump. It was at this exact moment that all the alcohol in my system decided to gang up and teach me a lesson.

Incredibly, I was able to retain the contents of my guts during the treacherous and bumpy ride to the harbour. Predictably, the moment I got off of the bus, souflaki and ouzo were everywhere.

Astonishingly, I somehow steadied my composure and was able to purchase a ferry ticket to Brindisi. I found a bench in the waiting lounge, stretched my shivering body across the seats and passed out. Well … I wasn't completely out. In my state of semi-consciousness, I was able to hear comments regarding my current state.

"Boy is that guy ever messed up."

"Do you think he will be all right?"

"Is that puke on his foot?"

I wanted to answer, "Brilliant observation Sherlock," "Yes, I'll be fine" and "So what? It washes off." But all I could muster was an "Arghoooouaaahhh," which probably answered their questions in a more appropriate manner. It seemed that my basic functions of communication were taking a breather.

I have no idea how I got on the ferry or what any of the eight-hour journey to Brindisi was like. I'm assuming that other travellers from *Hades' Hideaway* helped me on board and found a corner to dump me. I spent the next eight hours sleeping it off. Although I don't know if you can call being sprawled out on a metal deck and sweating the aftermath from the previous night's bender "sleeping it off."

When I awoke, the ferry was docking in Brindisi, Italy.

I should have felt fantastic. Sleeping through eight hours of slow travelling should put any backpacker in a magnificent and refreshed mood.

Regrettably, I didn't feel magnificent. I didn't feel refreshed.

I felt rough as sandpaper. My head hurt. My back was sore. My mouth was dry and tasted like an ashtray. My coordination was askew, and I had four hours before my train left for Venice, which was the next leg of my two-day marathon.

I roamed around the town like a zombie trying to kill time, but my brain and body were having none of it. They needed rest and recuperation. I found a café close to the train station, sat down and ordered a coffee. I have zero recollection of Brindisi, other than watching the clock slowly tick around and around.

Four, painful hours later, I was sitting on a train destined for Venice. The hangover had begun to wear off, but the next leg of my journey, a 40-hour train ride across the continent, was going to require all my energy and patience.

And to make matters more trying, I had somehow picked up two travel companions.

Mark and Will were from Boston. They had been staying at *Hades' Hideaway* and were heading to Prague too. The problem with Mark and Will was that they didn't shut up. They talked endlessly about nothing. It was almost as if they were performing for each other and anyone else in earshot. Their ramblings were filled with giggles and inside jokes that didn't make sense to anyone but themselves. Even the beautiful Italian scenery couldn't distract me from their endless babble.

From Brindisi to Venice they talked shit. From Venice to Vienna they talked shit. From Vienna to Breclev they talked shit. Miraculously, from Breclev to Prague they slept.

It was miraculous because the train was the bumpiest ride I'd ever taken in my life. I guessed we were riding some old, World War II Russian cargo train that had been salvaged for passenger use. The three of us were bouncing around the sleeping compartment like Mexican jumping beans. How the two yapping Yanks were able to sleep was beyond me. I certainly wasn't able to crash.

Was I really putting myself through this torment for a girl I'd just met?

The metal death trap eventually pulled into Prague's central train station around eight in the morning, which was a tortuous 48 hours after I had departed *Hades' Hideaway*.

I stepped off the train not feeling much better than when I left Corfu two days earlier. I hadn't really slept. I hadn't really eaten. I was a tad delirious, and I still didn't have a clue about the country and city I was in, how to find Stacey or where to stay.

Fortunately, the last issue was resolved for me. Ten steps from the train, I was bombarded by a mass of Czechs who were frantically trying to get me to rent their apartments. Under the best of circumstances, this situation would have been a battle, but in my current state of delirium, I had zero control.

I think Mark and Will were dazed as well. They had stopped talking shit about an hour before we pulled into the station, which was a strong indicator that the lengthy journey had zapped their brains. Despite their ramblings over the past two days, Mark and Will were all right guys. My friends from home and I aren't much different when we are together. We also talk non-stop shit, and our conversations are always littered with inside jokes. So when the mass of Czechs pounced on us, we decided to stick it out together. Between the three of us, we had the total functioning capacity of one brain.

Everybody was screaming for our undivided attention.

Men and women were pushing each other out of the way to get into a better position to shove photos of their apartments in our faces.

It was bedlam.

I've never been a big fan of the hard sell. I can't stand it when pushy salespeople try to convince me I need something that I actually don't need. Granted, I desperately needed a place to sleep. But after my two-day journey, I wasn't in the mood and I didn't have the mental stability for the in-your-face approach by the potential landlords.

Through the blur of grabbing hands, pleading faces and photos, one guy stood out. He did so for a couple of reasons. The first was that he was standing still at the back of the insane crowd and, therefore, was easy to focus my red and blurry eyes on. He carried the same demeanour as the guy in Amsterdam who had enticed me into his sex show. He behaved as though he didn't give a rat's ass if you rented his apartment or not. I concluded that this passive guy would be easier to negotiate with than the rest of the frenzied Czechs.

The other reason I noticed this guy was because he looked as though he could be a dad—anyone's dad. He had greying hair, glasses, a warm friendly face and dressed like your typical dad on a Saturday: jeans, fleece jacket and white running shoes that were at least 20 years old.

He looked like my best option.

I pushed my way through the mass of insistent and aggressive people towards the "Czech Dad." Mark and Will were right on my ass. I asked if he had an apartment to rent.

He said he did. The place had two bedrooms, was fully furnished and would cost us 20 American dollars a day.

He said it was close to the city centre, and he showed us some pictures.

I saw a bed in one of the photos. That was all that I needed. I was sold.

The four of us made our way out of the madhouse train station and into his car. The city was a blur as he took us across town. He could have been driving in circles for all I knew. We eventually arrived at an apartment, and true to his word, there were two bedrooms and, more importantly, beds.

I was unconscious before he closed the door.

I slept for the dead.

I woke up around three in the afternoon. I felt a million times better than before I crashed. I had slept off most of the wear and tear of the 48-hour journey. I was recharged. I was refreshed. I overcame the epic cross-continent excursion in one piece.

Now that I was in Prague, I had my next problem to tackle. I had to find Stacey.

I got dressed and went for a walk to get my bearings. To my pleasant surprise, I discovered that our apartment was indeed very close to the city centre and the famous, statue-adorned Charles Bridge. I found an Internet café nearby and sent Stacey an email.

> Hey there Stacey,
> You convinced me … I'm in Prague! Where are you staying? I've got an apartment, 295 Yugoslavska. Come by anytime! Otherwise, I'll try and hook up with you at a bar called *Joe's*, which is on the north side of the Charles Bridge. I'll be there between eight and eleven tonight waiting for you. I can't wait to see you!
> Your Stormtrooper …

All I could do now was wait. And wait I did.

I sat at *Joe's* from eight until eleven, drinking Budvar and watching each face as it entered the door. Unfortunately, there was no sign of Stacey. When she didn't show by eleven, I decided to stick around a few more minutes just in case she couldn't find the bar or was running late. No luck. She still hadn't shown by half eleven.

I decided to call it a night and go back to the apartment.

As I walked home, I questioned my decision to drastically alter my plans for a girl I had just met. After all, I had only spent one night with her. Yes, she had said, "Come meet me in Prague," but was she actually expecting me to come?

Maybe she wasn't that into me.

Maybe she was just whispering sweet nothings in my ear. Maybe she knew that nobody in his right mind would leave the warmth of the Greek Isles to travel for 48 hours to the opposite end of the continent to see a person they had just met.

Maybe my being in Prague would actually freak her out.

And if my uncertainties about coming to the Czech Republic weren't troublesome enough, Prague was fucking freezing.

I got back to the apartment a little after midnight. The brisk and lonely walk had given me time to clear my head. I had eliminated all negative thoughts and scenarios. I had accepted that what was done was done. They say that things happen for a reason. Therefore, for whatever reason, my travels had brought me to the Czech Republic. I'm here, I thought. I might as well make the best of it … with or without Stacey.

If anything, coming to Prague proved that nothing on this trip was finalized. I had a complete freedom and liberty that I had never experienced before. Despite coming from a "free" country, I didn't have this type of absolute independence at home. I had commitments and responsibilities. I had bills and debts. I was, in essence, a slave to the system.

I decided that as far as worst-case scenarios are concerned, redefining and truly understanding what freedom could be wasn't that bad.

I was about to shut off the lights and go to bed when I heard a faint knocking at the door.

Could it be?

I opened the door to find a smiling Stacey, who threw her arms around me and gave me a huge hug and kiss. "I'm sorry that I missed you at *Joe's*," she apologized. "I only read your email an hour ago."

She looked at me with her big, brown eyes and asked in a very seductive tone, "May I come in?"

I had a feeling that Prague was going to be a very romantic city.

7

A YANKEE MOMENT

DECEMBER

One feature that all Canadian backpackers have in common is that every one of us travels with at least one of our nation's flag sewn onto our packs. More often than not, a Canadian traveller will have the maple leaf plastered not only on their packs but also on every conceivable piece of clothing they own. There are loads of Canucks who have gone so far as having the red flag tattooed on their bodies.

I was surprised to discover we were the only nation that had this identification ritual. When I bought my travel gear, there was a massive barrel full of Canadian flags of all sizes located next to the cash register. I thought a flag was part of the travelling package; I thought it was as essential as the pack itself.

I bought two.

However, it didn't take long to figure out why we unfailingly display the flag. It's not that we are more patriotic than any other nation. We wear the flag because we don't want to be mistaken for Americans. And our desire to clarify our nationality is not because of *our* dislike of the United States. Rather, it is a result of the rest of the world's obvious aversion and prejudice towards the Yanks.

In Canada, we have a long stemmed rivalry with the States. We dominate at hockey. And ridiculous questions such as "Y'all ride dogsleds up there?" or "Do you know Bob in Vancouver?" keep us laughing and shaking our heads at the backwards perceptions of Canada. Americans are, more often than not, the butt of our jokes.

However, world opinion regarding the United States differs dramatically from that of Canada's. In Canada, although we heckle the shit out of the Yanks, we do maintain a level of respect based on the understanding that our southern neighbours are our best economic partners and the primary reason that we don't have a multi-billion dollar defence budget. We employ a "don't bite the hand that guards you" ideology.

The rest of the world, however, seems to possess an animosity toward the global superpower. It seems that the world's aggravations can and are blamed on the United States. I imagine it is very similar to the way the rest of the world regarded the English during their rule as global superpower a couple of centuries ago when "the sun never set on the British Empire." Didn't *everybody* hate the English back then? I've never seen a period film in which the English weren't portrayed as nasty, evil bastards.

The mentality isn't very different today.

The superpower may have changed, but the loathing hasn't.

So it's not hard to understand why we wear the Canadian flag as conspicuously as possible. We wear them as a safety precaution, as do a lot of Americans for the same reason.

Due to my accent, when I met travellers for the first time, they often assumed I was American and asked where in the States I came from. This question was typically asked in a tone that suggested they really didn't give a shit.

I'd tell them I was from Canada.

They would then respond in one of two ways.

Mostly, their reaction was one of relief and relaxation. They would express an enthusiastic interest in where I was from and who I was. The same people who, thinking I was a Yank, wouldn't piss on me if I was on fire, were now willing to open up and have a genuine conversation.

The other reaction was to be apologetic. Knowing how much Canadians hate to be mistaken for Americans, they profusely apologized for making such a horrible blunder.

However, this mix-up does not bother me. In fact, it is highly understandable. Our accents are, more or less, the same. Our cultures, interests and economies are virtually identical. Even I have to listen long and hard to determine from which side of the border a North American accent originates.

Unfortunately, there are Canadians who become enraged and defensive if you mistakenly call them American. They are actually insulted. They are offended by the assumption.[1]

Inevitably, this same high and mighty Canadian will go off on the "we're so much smarter than Americans" tirade. When they finish their rant, ask them who the president of Mexico is. I bet they don't know the answer. Why not? They should. There are only three countries in North America. Mexico is one of our

---

1. I bet the same Canadian would be hard pressed to tell the difference between an English and Scottish accent.

major trading partners. Intelligent Canadians would like to think they know the name of the Mexican president, but most do not. I guarantee these same Canadians would tear into Americans for not knowing that the capital of Canada is Ottawa or that we have a prime minister instead of a president.

Despite the few sketchy encounters I've had with Americans on my trip, I quite like and get on with the Yanks. I think Americans are far from stupid. Their brains are more than capable of retaining information. The problem is the information that they retain.

For a very long time, those in a position to feed knowledge have fed the population crap.

It is not the individual American's fault that he/she is generally uneducated about the rest of the world. I don't hold their ignorance against them.

I blame that one entirely on "Uncle Sam."

About 40 years ago, during the peak of the Cold War and the communism scare, the U.S. government needed to have its population 100 per cent behind the American way of life. The education curriculum, controlled and designed by the government, was intended to teach students about the merits of the United States and the United States only. The media helped pound the message home that the U.S. of A. was the greatest place on earth. There was no need to report what was going on with the rest of the world if it didn't include the U.S.

It worked.

The end result was a population of zealously patriotic Americans with a biased perspective on their country's place in the world.

Today, despite the Cold War ending long ago, the media's "America Only" agenda not only continues but has expanded with the inception of the 24 hour news channel. Further, consider the schools where metal detectors, armed security guards, gangsters and drug dealers are as common as pimples, and it should come as no surprise that most American kids have never heard of Ottawa, their neighbour's capital. Schools are more like warzones than learning environments.

Yes, the Yanks can be quite ignorant to the ways of the world and quite obnoxious with their observations.

Nevertheless, you should be aware that the Yanks aren't the only ones living under the secluded North American bubble.

Canadians can also be quite uninformed about the rest of the world.

Well … at least this Canadian.

I'm not a smart man. I didn't fully grasp this knowledge until my first day on the road, and then it hit me like a ton of maple leaves. Don't get me wrong; I don't think I'm stupid. A more accurate way of describing my intellectual situation is that I'm not as smart as I thought I was. Or better still, I'm not as smart as Canadian society led me to believe. Despite what the "system" wants me to accept as true, just because I went to school, read some Shakespeare, did some math and went to a top university doesn't mean that I'm intelligent.

There is more to intelligence than listening to what you are told and reading a few books.

I believe that true intelligence comes through experience.

I undoubtedly gained some intelligence and enlightenment through my Prague experiment. As sweet as Stacey was, the more time I spent with her, the more I recognized that I had travelled to Prague just because I could. Subconsciously, I needed to test a few theories regarding what real freedom meant. I learned that freedom didn't just mean being able to get smashed and not having to worry about work, bills and the rat race.

Freedom meant that I could follow my intuitions and take advantage of opportunities as they presented themselves. Freedom meant that I could deviate from a plan if it suited me.

After the romantic and educational week in Prague, Stacey flew back home. I spent another few days on my own, taking advantage of the beautiful city, unbelievable nightlife and drop-dead gorgeous women.[2]

However, with the cold weather, I decided it was time to head south towards warmer climates. Still, there wasn't a chance in hell I was going to do another marathon journey like the one from Greece to the Czech Republic. Therefore, my next destination had to be relatively close to Prague.

I pulled out my map.

Austria was just to the south.

Although, I knew very little about the country, my first impression of Austria had been a reasonably good one.

During the mission to Prague, I had spent a couple of hours in Vienna waiting for the connecting train to Breclev, which was on the Czech border. Despite the fatigue of the journey, Mark, Will and I decided to walk around. We aimlessly wandered for a few blocks and eventually found a pub. We had a couple of drinks, went back to the station and caught our next train. It was not much of a first impression, but it was certainly not a bad one.

---

2. Czech women are still the best looking women that I've seen anywhere in the world. It was like an endless gauntlet of beauty.

It wasn't my first impression of Austria, however, that made me think about visiting the country. It was my first impression of *Austrians* that made me work on my yodelling.

I met Mariella and Sabine in Amsterdam while sitting underneath the painting of Jim at *Morrison's Café*. Other than their striking beauty, they caught my eye because the blond had a cast on her arm and therefore couldn't roll a joint. Her brunette friend was failing miserably in an attempt to help. After witnessing a couple of botched attempts, I offered to roll them a spliff. They happily accepted.

We began talking and smoking.

The girls were flying back to Austria later that day and were having their last couple of smokes before they went to the airport. We chatted and laughed for about an hour. When they were ready to leave, they gave me the rest of their weed. They weren't going to take it onto the plane, and they wanted to say thanks for the help. An even better gift was the contact numbers they gave me if and when I ever came to Austria.

With two kisses on the cheek from both the girls, as was their custom, they said goodbye.

As mentioned, Austrians made a lovely first impression on me.

So with Stacey gone, Austria directly south of my current, chilly location and two beautiful women offering me a place to stay, my decision was easy.

I looked in my address book for their contact details. They lived in Wien. I'd never heard of Wien and couldn't find it on my map, but I assumed the ticket salesman at the train station in Prague would know. I called Sabine to ask if I could crash at her place for a few days. Her excitement to hear that I was coming reinforced my decision to visit.

I bought a one-way ticket to Wien, boarded the train destined for the Austrian city and had an uneventful, short journey.

A few hours later, I arrived.

They say that first impressions are important, and accurate perceptions of people or places can be determined during the critical first encounter. It was my second impression of Austria, however, that had me scratching my head in bafflement.

As I walked from the train into Wien's arrival terminal, I was struck with an overwhelming feeling of familiarity. It was the strongest case of déjà vu that I'd ever experienced.

Then it hit me. The train station in Wien was identical to the train station in Vienna.

The more I walked through the station, the eerier it became. The two stations were impossible to tell apart. The infrastructure was the same. The colour scheme was the same. The shops and restaurants were the same. I know I had been delirious when I had ambled through Vienna's station, but I could swear that even the woman who worked the flower stand looked similar to the flower lady here in Wien.

Still amazed at the similarities between the two stations, I went outside. My mouth fell open. I felt as though I stepped into some freaky episode of "The Twilight Zone." Even though I knew I was in Wien, the city in front of me looked identical to Vienna.

This was getting a little too weird. Maybe I could understand the Austrians using an efficient, established blueprint for all the train stations, but to duplicate an entire city plan? I couldn't decide if these people were bizarre or simply uncreative. I assumed that Austrians subscribed to the "if it ain't broke, then don't fix it" philosophy.

Still baffled by my surroundings, I got into a taxi and gave the driver Sabine's address.

It wasn't until we drove past the exact same pub that I had visited ten days earlier that I began to figure out where I might be.

There was the slim possibility I had either boarded the wrong train or got off at the wrong station. I didn't think this was the case, but to be sure, I asked the driver if I was in Wien.

As a taxi driver, I'm sure that he had been subjected to countless idiotic questions from tourists. This one was nothing special, and without taking his eyes off the road, he nodded yes.

I was now 99 per cent positive what was going on. However, to remove the iota of doubt, I swallowed my pride and asked the taxi driver another question.

I asked him if we were also in Vienna.

He gave me a look that suggested he wasn't completely sure I came from this planet. It was a gaze that said he had heard lots of stupid comments over the years, but these particular questions were up there with the dumbest.

He didn't need to answer. I was also in Vienna.

Wien and Vienna were one and the same.

I was ignorant that Wien is the German translation of Vienna. Being the clueless traveller that I was, I made the ridiculous assumption that the mad city planners of Austria had designed the blueprint for an "ultra city" and had implemented it throughout the country.

So it is not just Americans that represent the stupidity of North America. Canadians, as well, can be a wee bit slow on the uptake.

Mind you, I don't think I'm the only Canuck who would make that mistake. Quiz a hundred Canadians and find out how many know that Vienna and Wien are the same place. I would guess not too many would.

I keep coming back to the conclusion that there is a ton of information about our world that I know absolutely nothing about. The key is to learn from my mistakes and to broaden my knowledge from them.

At this point, I really didn't mind looking like a tit. I recognized trial and error was essential for my escape from the North American bubble and for my education about life and our planet.

In a way, I was looking forward to making my next mistake.

8
GET A JOB

DECEMBER

How much did I have left!?

I rubbed my eyes and reread my bank statement just in case my baby blues were deceiving me.

Unfortunately, my eyes weren't playing a cruel trick. Despite my desperate wish that I was somehow mistaken, I was reading the correct total.

There was practically nothing left in my account.

I started to sweat.

Could it be possible? Could my savings have depleted so quickly? I'd only been travelling for a little over two months. Could somebody have stolen from me? That seemed like the only possible explanation. It was inconceivable that I could spend so much in such little time.

Or was it?

I do remember buying more than my share of rounds whilst in Scotland, England and Ireland, countries where the currency is more than twice the strength of the Canadian dollar. I ate in a lot of restaurants. I smoked a pile of weed in Amsterdam. I also hopped on and off planes like some rock star, which was not the most economical way to travel on a backpacker's budget.

Fuck.

There was no theft or mysterious withdrawals.

I had spent my money.

I had always known this moment was inevitable. I knew that the money I had saved wasn't going to last forever. I knew that I was going to have to work at some point during my travels. I just hadn't anticipated it being only two months into the trip. I consoled myself by saying that I had learned a lesson about the value of planning and, more importantly, sticking to a budget.

With my bank account almost empty, my fear was that I might not have another opportunity to learn from my mistake.

It was time to focus and find a job.

There wasn't a chance in hell that I would spend the winter in a cold climate, which immediately eliminated a lot of possible destinations. And I wasn't sure that I'd have the finances to make it to Israel. Thankfully, I had a buddy from home that had family living in Spain, and I hoped that through him I'd be able to dig up some contacts and possibly land a job in that warm and sunny country.

So I departed Vienna on another epic train journey destined for Barcelona. I wasn't too bothered with the distance, for I love travelling by train. Between the comfort, the privacy of the cabins and the bar car, travelling by train was much better than travelling by bus, which was an often necessary mode of transportation that I despised.

I crossed Austria and Switzerland without incident. However, when we arrived on the French border, the steward informed me that there was currently a railway strike in France, and my train wouldn't, in fact, be heading to Barcelona.

So I asked the obvious question, "How do I get there?"

The answers I received from the steward, information booths and a variety of ticket salespeople steered me from one destination to the next where, inevitably, I was told that there wasn't a train destined for Barcelona.

Always, I asked, "How do I get to there?"

The train strike had me zigzagging across southern France. I went from Avignon to Lyon, then from Lyon to Montpellier. When I eventually arrived in Montpellier, I was told that all international trains had been cancelled.

So again I asked, "How do I get to there?"

I was told the only way to reach Barcelona was by bus, and the first one didn't depart until late that evening. My patience was vanishing. What began as a relatively simple and enjoyable cross-continental train journey had malformed into a frustrating and tedious merry-go-round of French train stations and bus terminals. Nevertheless, if all went to plan, I would be in Barcelona first thing in the morning.

The bus arrived in Barcelona at 3:00 AM, which was a far cry from what I would classify as "first thing in the morning." It was also amid a torrential downpour.

This was turning into a battle.

The fatigue of the lengthy journey and the hammering rainstorm was further compounded by not knowing where to stay. All the information booths, which could point me in the right direction, were closed due to the time of night.

Luckily, I caught up with two girls who I had talked with on the bus. They said they knew where a hostel was located.

Thankfully, they knew where they were going, and after I checked in, I was finally able to get dry and horizontal.

I slept like the dead.

I woke up the next day feeling refreshed and ready to tackle the world. I strolled around the city to get my bearings. The plan was to spend one night in Barcelona and then …

Okay. I need to stop right there.

Anybody who has been to Barcelona knows that it's impossible to stay just one night.

The nightlife of Barcelona is intoxicating, figuratively and literally. The clubs are massive, and the music is incredible. The people are friendly, the women are gorgeous, and the party goes all night long. There is no need to leave for the clubs until at least one in the morning, and even this time is considered early.

Another aspect of Spanish life that delayed my departure from Barcelona was the brilliant concept of afternoon siestas, or in my case, the "late afternoon until late evening" siestas.

The recipe in Barcelona was a simple one: party all night, sleep late, get some food, take a siesta, wake up at midnight, be at the club by 2:00 AM and repeat.

It was an uncomplicated recipe, but it certainly didn't motivate one to leave in a hurry. The taste of the vibrant city was addictive.

Therefore, it should come as no surprise that I had a week of fiestas and siestas before I finally escaped Barcelona.

Don't roll your eyes at me. I know what you are thinking. What the hell was I doing partying for seven days when I should have been looking for work, especially considering that I was so poor?

My uncomplicated answer is that life is too short, and Barcelona was too incredible to rush through. It needed to be experienced. Besides, I was practically broke. I wasn't *completely* broke.

But by the following week, I was as close to penniless as I wanted to be.

My job-hunt hadn't gone exactly as anticipated. I spoke to my friend, but he couldn't set me up with a job. He did suggest that I head south, though, to the Cos de Sol where I would have a better chance to find work.

Working in Barcelona wasn't an option, for I knew my weakness when it came to great nightlife and beautiful women. I knew I wouldn't save a dime in this festive city. So I took my friend's advice and travelled down the Cos de Sol to the coastal town of Malaga.

I spent two days searching for work. For two days, I was told there wasn't any work available.

From there, I travelled further down the coast to Marbella. It was the same story as Malaga. There was no work to be found.

The situation was looking grim.

I had a few obstacles hindering my success at finding employment. I didn't have the right clothes for job interviews or first impressions. It seemed that jeans, a clean T-shirt and hiking boots didn't portray the image of a reliable employee.

Then there was the snag that I was looking for work during the off-season, and the majority of resorts, restaurants and bars had either reduced their staff or shut down completely.

Finally, there was the small issue concerning my Spanish. The issue was that I didn't speak any. No hablo español, no work amigo.

The situation was looking desperate.

At the end of another jobless day in Marbella, I was at my breaking point. I must have been rejected at least 30 times, and my anger and frustration were starting to inflate. My hope was quickly vanishing. I plunked my unwanted butt down on the beach and contemplated my ominous predicament.

The same, terrifying conclusion kept surfacing, despite my best efforts to ignore it.

I was going to have to go home.

It was the low point.

How could this have happened? How could I have screwed up my plans this quickly? Was I really going to have to pack it in and go back to Canada? Was my timeless trip around the world only going to consist of seven European countries over the span of 10 weeks?

I wasn't ready to go home.

I tried not to think about the embarrassment of returning to Canada after failing miserably at global travel.

I sat back on the sandy beach and stared dolefully at the setting sun.

Then something incredible happened. As I watched the massive red ball of fire sink into the Mediterranean, an amazing feeling came over me. I wasn't worried about my money situation. I wasn't pissed off because I couldn't speak Spanish. I wasn't stressed about not finding work. I wasn't annoyed that I was an ignorant traveller. In fact, I was so at ease with absolutely everything that I began to smile. I realized that I, a Canadian, was watching the sunset on a beach in Spain.

It didn't matter that I was on the verge of being penniless. Why? Because I was sitting on a beach in Spain.

It didn't matter that I couldn't find a job. Why? Because I was sitting on a beach in Spain.

Call it a moment of clarity. Call it an epiphany. Call it whatever you want. My current predicament was suddenly and unmistakably put into perspective. I wasn't in Canada going through the monotony of life. I wasn't doing the same routine or looking at the same view. I wasn't on the same route to the same office to do the same shit, day in, day out, year after year.

I was sitting on a beach in Spain.

I was experiencing something new, fascinating and unique.

I was completely on my own. There wasn't anybody around who could help me.

The only way to get out of this dilemma was by myself.

I would not let myself down. I would not go home.

Words cannot begin to describe how these innovative and overwhelming feelings motivated me. I had recharged my optimism and positive energy. I told myself that tomorrow would be a new day filled with new opportunities.

I felt so revamped and confident that I sauntered into a pub on the way back to the hostel and asked the barman for a job.

"Sorry, amigo."

His refusal didn't diminish my positive outlook. Unfazed, I reminded myself that *tomorrow* would be a new day. No was definitely the word of this particular day. Truth be told, I wasn't expecting to find a job there anyway. I was certain I had been in that very pub earlier in the afternoon and had received the same answer.

My real motivation for coming into the pub was *cervesa*.

Even though I was counting pesetas, the re-evaluation of my predicament called for a well-earned pint. I began talking with the barman about my struggles to find work, and we got to the sticky subject of my lack of Spanish.

"Why don't you go to the Canary Islands," he suggested.

The Canary Islands?

I didn't have a clue where they were located. I vaguely remembered the Canary Islands from my university course on the history of slavery. However, the chances of me being baked during the monotonous lecture were quite high, no pun intended.

The barman explained that the Canaries were Spanish islands located off the western tip of Morocco, and that they were predominately a British holiday destination. He said that because the large majority of the tourists were British, English would be necessary for any job, which there would be plenty of as we were coming into the Christmas season. He said there were lots of bars, restaurants and hotels, and finding a job would be simple. He went on to say that it was easy to get there. There were cheap flights departing from Sevilla, which was a town located further down the coast.

The information had potential. The Canary Islands could be the answer to my economic woes. He did say *islands*, which meant there was more than one. I asked on which island I should look for work.

"Go to Tenerife. Then head to Playa de Las Americas. That is where all the tourists go, and you'll find a job, no problemo."

And that was all the advice I needed. I would go to Tenerife to look for work. I could tap into my emergency fund to pay for the flight. It was a meagre nest egg I had set aside to fund a failed return home or bribe my way out of imprisonment. I really didn't have much else going for me. Mainland Spain didn't hold too many career options, and the rest of Europe was getting way too frigid for my liking. It might have been a long shot, but it was the most encouraging news I had received in a long time.

Tenerife was warm, spoke English and was, apparently, dripping with seasonal jobs.

To avoid the unthinkable, a return to Canada, it was a chance I was going to have to take.

Without a doubt, it was going to be my last chance.

9
ACTUALLY, THE FLOOR WASN'T THAT BAD

DECEMBER

I met Pablo on the flight from Sevilla. He was sitting across the aisle from me and having an all around raunchy time on the short journey to Tenerife. I'll give him credit; he played the slick role well. Pablo was tall, dark and handsome, never without a drink and quite possibly loved women as much as he loved himself. He was heading to Santa Cruz, a town in the north of the island, to visit his girlfriend. Between drinks, he informed me that there weren't any buses running at this time of the evening. He said it would be impossible to get to Santa Cruz, Playa de Las Americas or anywhere else on the island tonight. The only people in the airport would be the hotel tour guides there to pick up the holidaymakers. As he undressed our leggy stewardess with his eyes, he indicated that my only option would be to sleep in the airport, which is what he would be doing.

I would have to wait and see.

Despite my inquiries, there was no way to get to Playa de Las Americas tonight. The buses had stopped running. The tour groups were heading to the big and outrageously expensive hotels, and none of the hostesses I spoke with knew of any hostels or backpackers on the island.

Unfortunately, Pablo was correct. I would be sleeping on the airport floor.

The terminal was deserted. I was on the last flight, so after all the holidaymakers departed, I virtually had the airport to myself.

Pablo and myself, that is.

I found a pillar to lean against, pulled out my sleeping bag, stretched out and was trying to find a comfortable position to sleep when I heard footsteps coming in my direction. It was Pablo. He sat against a pillar a few feet away and casually asked if I wanted to smoke a joint.

Under normal circumstances, when I am asked if I want to smoke a joint, the word no would never escape my lips. But being in the middle of an international airport was not normal circumstances.

I declined his offer.

Any suspicion that Pablo was an undercover narcotics agent disappeared when he sparked up and blazed away in the middle of the empty Tenerife International Airport. Granted, there was nobody in sight, but there had to be someone somewhere in the building. There had to be a flight attendant, a custodian or possibly even a security guard hanging around this massive building. Regardless of the person, chances were they would have a sense of smell. It was also probable that they would come running as soon as they detected the instantly recognizable scent of burning marijuana.

I shook my head in disbelief and tried to fall asleep.

Despite the spacious bedroom, my bed wasn't as comfortable as I had hoped. I'm guessing the inventor of linoleum floors didn't anticipate their use as a sleeping mat for grungy backpackers. It was, therefore, rather difficult getting comfortable enough to stay asleep for any length of time. I'd wake up, roll over then drift into a state of semi-consciousness. A few minutes later, I'd wake up, roll over and drift back into semi-consciousness. The third time I woke up, I didn't immediately fall back asleep. My eyes and brain were debating if they understood the outrageous scene unfolding before them.

They agreed. They weren't playing tricks on each other. Defying any form of common sense, they established that they were witnessing Pablo smoking heroin.

Smoking heroin?

Had Casanova completely lost his mind? Pablo was leaning against the pillar with a lighter in one hand. In the other was a square section of aluminium foil, on which lay the brown powder. He was casually burning the smack and inhaling its addictive fumes. The lunatic was actually smoking heroin in the middle of an "I don't give a shit if it's deserted" international airport! He looked over with glazed eyes and said, "Don't ever get into this shit, man. It'll fucking kill you."

Thanks for the tip.

With astonishment, I watched Pablo smoke another hit and slump back against the pillar. I took that as my signal, escaped to the opposite side of the column, closed one eye and forced myself to doze by using the "Christmas morning" philosophy: the sooner you go to sleep, the sooner morning will arrive.

Morning did arrive.

When I opened my eyes, the first thing I saw was luggage. To be more precise, it was luggage that didn't belong to me. There were masses of people everywhere.

I quickly deduced that in my haste to move away from Pablo, I had repositioned myself into what became a check-in line for passengers returning to Paris. The departing tourists had to detour around my outstretched sleeping bag to enter the roped-off corral that would zigzag them to the check-in counter.

I was bombarded with looks of annoyance, disgust and pity.

The second thing that caught my attention was Pablo. He hadn't moved an inch from the last time I saw him, and he was also caught up in the French blockade. He was lying on his stomach with his sleeping bag pulled up over his head, and he was propped up on one elbow. He poorly concealed what he was doing. Oblivious to being in the middle of a jam-packed international airport with people staring, Pablo was, once again, smoking heroin.

My eyes and brain had their little argument again. And again, they quickly agreed that they were on the same page. Regardless of the setting, people, environment and the obvious dangers, Pablo was smoking heroin. It appeared that the junkie had been smoking most of the night because his face was completely blackened with smoke.

I didn't have words.

The French travellers had words—outraged, demeaning, insulting words. Despite the enormous difference between someone waking up in an airport and someone smoking heroin in an airport, the French tourists were giving me the same irate stares and hurling the same angry insults they were directing at Pablo. It was a clear-cut case of guilt by association.

It was time to say adios loco … pronto.

I quickly stuffed my sleeping bag back into my pack and headed to the men's room to splash some water on my face and brush my teeth.

I don't know what became of Pablo, and I don't really care. Spending any more time in his general vicinity was asking for trouble. Why he wasn't arrested during the night is beyond my comprehension. And what about this morning when the airport was jam-packed with people and cops? Were they blind? Did they even care?

I couldn't spend any more time or energy on these curiosities or Pablo. I had my own problems, although they were not quite as detrimental. The hurdles I faced required getting my butt out of the airport, onto a bus to Playa de Las Americas and finding a job before I ran out of money and had to go home.

As I was cleaning up, another guy came into the men's room and started doing the same. He looked about my age and looked more like a backpacker than a package tourist.

Normally, striking up a conversation in a public bathroom with a total stranger isn't the most socially acceptable way to make a new friend, and it isn't something I do on a regular basis. Nevertheless, I had just slept on the floor and watched a guy smoke heroin; I figured social norms were temporarily suspended.

In spite of our setting, we began talking. His name was Tim. He had just arrived from England and was also in search of work. Much like me, he didn't have the slightest idea about the island or if there were any hostels there. We decided to put our non-existent knowledge together, and maybe we could find a place to sleep. We agreed that two empty heads were better than one.

Tim seemed like a safer bet than Pablo. Since Tim hadn't smoked, injected or snorted any narcotics (a feature that now seemed necessary when formulating my first impression of someone), he was the wise option.

Finding a bus to Playa de Las Americas was simple. There was an abundance of transport positioned outside the terminal destined for the tourist hot spot. We started the drive, and as the sun beat down through the bus window, I smiled and took in the volcanic countryside.

Despite my lack of sleep, I felt great.

Only a few days ago, I was sitting on a beach in Marbella, rejected for the umpteenth time that day, broke and without a clue where to go. The future of my trip had been at a critical, desperate point.

Then I watched the sunset.

Now I was sitting on a bus, heading to Playa de Las Americas, where I was told I could get a job without having to speak Spanish. Even though I had nothing to compare it to, Tenerife looked like a piece of paradise. The island was visually stunning and, more importantly, stinking hot. Without a doubt, it was the warmest this Canadian had ever been in December.

I was getting a good vibe.

As the bus pulled into Playa de Las Americas, I noticed a golf course built on the fringe of town. I began to smile. I had an overwhelming conviction that I would get a job on the course. I allowed myself to visualize working in the sun, sneaking in a few rounds and picking up a decent salary in the process. What more could one ask for in a travelling job?

Tim's economic situation wasn't as catastrophic as mine, so he decided to look around for a place for us to stay while I nabbed a job at the golf course. We got off the bus in the centre of town, decided to meet at four that afternoon and walked off in opposite directions. Dripping with optimism, I headed directly back to the pro shop.

I was positive that I was finally in the right spot and would salvage my voyage.

I was positive that the golf course would hire me, even though I was a grubby backpacker, still carrying my pack and looking as though I had slept on the airport floor.

I was wrong.

For the record, a grubby backpacker still carrying his pack and looking as though he slept on an airport floor isn't going to get a job at a golf course or, as I discovered during my frustrating walk back to Playa de Las Americas, in any other type of establishment.

I was hoping that Tim had better luck finding somewhere to sleep.

It was not to be. He had as much success finding accommodation as I did finding employment. With the sun getting lower in the sky, we decided to team up and focus our efforts on finding a place to crash.

We had no luck. There was absolutely nothing available.

Our search to find somewhere to sleep was getting desperate. Our packs were beginning to weigh us down. Neither one of us knew a soul on the island. There wasn't a single hostel in the city. And because it was Christmas season, every hotel room, bed and breakfast and pension, despite their exorbitant prices, was booked through New Year's.

We started to accept that we would be sleeping on the beach … possibly for awhile.

Then, as luck would have it, a guy walked by whom I recognized from the flight from Sevilla. I recognized him because he was the only other person on my flight who didn't look Spanish and who might be a backpacker. He got his gear and disappeared from the airport before I made it through customs. I assumed his quick exit meant he knew where he was going. I wasn't going to lose him twice.

I approached him and struck up a conversation. His name was Peter. He was from Poland and had been to Tenerife a few times. When I asked him if he knew of hostels, he laughed. Peter explained, as did the barman in Marbella and Pablo, that Playa de Las Americas was strictly designed for package tourists. Backpackers didn't bring in enough money. There was nothing built for us. Even the pensions, the least expensive and most basic rooms available, were high-priced and hard to find. If finding accommodation was such a nightmare, I asked, then where did he stay?

With a straight face, he answered, "In a cave."

With a confused face, I asked if he meant a hole in a rock.

Poker-faced, he replied, "Yes."

Peter looked relatively normal. He didn't carry a club. He wasn't dragging a woman by the hair. As far as I could tell, there was nothing remotely Neanderthal about him. So what the hell did he mean a cave? I looked at Tim for any sign that he was picking up something I was missing. His wide eyes and gaping mouth indicated that I had heard Peter correctly, and for the sake of curiosity, I should proceed with the next question.

Still confused but mildly intrigued, I asked where this cave was located.

"I'm going there now. Why don't you guys come along? I'm sure there is an extra cave to sleep in," he said without blinking.

An extra cave? Now I was definitely intrigued.

Besides, did we have a choice? The day was quickly disappearing, and the chances of Tim and I finding a place to sleep were slim and none. Peter was our last option before the beach. I glanced at Tim for his opinion, and he simply shrugged his shoulders in a "what do we have to lose" kind of way. What did we have to lose? Unless Peter and his mates were vampires, we would be cool.

We went with Peter.

As we walked to the mysterious cave, Peter confirmed what I had figured out from my short time on the island. Tenerife was, like all the Canary Islands, an extinct volcano. I noticed that the island was on a constant incline. From the moment you left the water, everything was on a slope upwards. Scattered across the abrupt, rugged, brown landscape were what I guessed to be little, once upon a time volcanic "spouts."

It was inside one of these spouts that Peter said he was taking us.

There was a small gap in the rocks at the base of one of the mounts, which Peter proceeded to lead us through. He guided us into the middle of the hollowed out, massive stone funnel. It looked much like what I imagined the interior of a non-active volcano would look like.

They were identical in all regards, except for the people living within the rock walls.

There were about ten residents when we arrived. A mishmash of seasoned travellers, they were all different ages and looked as though they had been living in a cave for a long time. They also looked like they had given up on society ages before that. The people had long, scraggly hair; they were unshaven, filthy and stunk of sweat and dirt. They wore rags for clothes. If you added up all their teeth, you'd have one full set among them.

However, as I've often learned, never judge a book by its cover, and this was most certainly one of those cases.

The cave dwellers were extremely friendly and welcoming and said we could use one of the caves for as long as we wanted. There were a dozen caves scattered along the interior of the wall, all set at different levels with different sized openings. There were even little gardens and porches built in front of some of the cave openings, indicating that people had been living there for awhile.

The cave they let us stay in wasn't massive, but there was more than enough space for two mattresses, which were already there, and our gear. There wasn't enough room to stand up, but the cave opening allowed a surprisingly large amount of light to enter. It wasn't ideal, but at least it wasn't the beach, and it was a step up from the airport floor. Maybe it was the kid in me dreaming of being Batman, but there was a part of me that actually found it cool sleeping in a cave. It was going to be a *temporary* part of my adventure. I wasn't worried about having to stay here too long. In spite of the afternoon's rejections, I was confident I would find a job in the morning and with it, a more accommodating place to live.

Things didn't go according to plan.

After my third day of unsuccessful job-hunting and, therefore, my third day of living within the earth, Tim came back to the cave smiling from ear to ear. I knew it was something good. We were both beginning to lose our sense of humour and adventure, and laughing was becoming a rarity. Although the cave initially had some comic book charm, the novelty of living in a hole was beginning to wear thin. The lack of space was one thing, and having to eat fast food continuously was another. But it was the lack of facilities that ultimately did me in.

Obviously, when you live in a cave, plumbing isn't a luxury one can expect. This meant we had no toilet, sink, shower or running water. For any of these basic needs, I had a 20-minute hike to the filthy, public facilities and showers located at the beach.

To make my mood considerably worse, I had been rejected by at least 50 potential employers who all said I had no hope of finding a job since I didn't have a working visa.

I was at the end of my savings. My emergency fund was now out of bounds since I had already tapped into it for the flight from Sevilla. There was just enough remaining to afford the flight of failure home. Even though I wasn't spending anything on accommodation, I estimated I had enough money to last for about a week at the most.

Then I'd be screwed.

I'd be flat broke and would have to take my pathetic ass back to Canada.

Tim's smile had better be justified.

"I've found us a sweet and cheap place to crash for a week," he said with a mixture of excitement and relief. "And best of all, we can move in now!"

With not much to pack, we left the cave. We thanked Peter and the rest of the cave dwellers for their generosity and helping us out of a jam. There was a small trace of sadness as we left the rock; however, the thought of a hot shower instantly destroyed any sense of lingering melancholy.

The place that Tim scored made me forget how to spell cave.

The Bahia Bontanico was a five-star condominium complex. Incredibly, Tim had come across the two-bedroom apartment through a housing agency after a last minute cancellation. We had the condo for a week, and we rented it for practically nothing. It was a steal.

Having come from a cave, anything would have been an improvement. This was why we felt as though we won the lottery when we moved into a two-bedroom condo with a large balcony overlooking the swimming pool. The apartment had a massive, self-contained kitchen and a living room complete with a TV and stereo. We even had a daily cleaning crew to tidy up the mess around our backpacks.

The first night, I didn't have a hot shower; I had a Jacuzzi.

The next day, things got even better.

We both found work.

Tim got a job as a barman in a little Irish pub, and I got work as a busboy in a restaurant that was a five-minute walk from the condo. I knew being a busboy wasn't my calling in life and that I might struggle with some aspects of my job description, which included clearing and setting tables, washing cutlery and dragging out the garbage, but *The Sunset Boulevard Restaurant* was the only place in Playa de Las Americas and Playa de Los Cristianos that would hire me without a work visa.

Despite being employed as the lowest of the low in the restaurant hierarchy, I was delighted.

Despite the ridiculous, striped uniform I would have to wear, I was ecstatic.

Despite the humiliating birthday songs I would have to sing, I was thrilled.

Despite the crappy pay, I was relieved.

My quest to find work had finally ended. I wasn't going to run out of money or starve. And more importantly, I wasn't going back to Canada. I was back in the travelling game. I had a job and a place to live.

That was, until the next week.

Our week living like kings in the five-star condo was over, but fortunately, Tim was able to pick up another cancellation. It was only a three-star hotel, which meant we didn't have a swimming pool or daily cleaning. This was a minor setback. I was just starting to get used to that pampering.

However, the real setback was that the hotel was located in Playa de Los Cristianos, the next city over. This move turned my five-minute walk to the restaurant into an hour hike across town. Taking a taxi wasn't financially possible, so I was looking at two hours of walking through shitty, dodgy streets and alleys to get to a job that was ridiculous, degrading and a pain in the ass. Nevertheless, beggars, something I was very close to becoming, couldn't be choosers.

They weren't ideal, but I still had a job and a place to sleep.

That was, until the next week.

We had to get out of the three-star condo. Moving was becoming a major annoyance, and to make things more problematic, it was now three days before Christmas. There were no more cancellation condos to snag. Thankfully, Tim was the master at scrounging. He found a reasonably priced place in Los Cristianos. And more importantly, the landlady said we could stay as long as we wanted.

We rented the room from this large, scary, old Spanish woman in a rather rundown pension, which is essentially a cheap bed and breakfast without the breakfast, in a rather rundown section of Los Cristianos. This particular pension was a dive, but it would have to do. We weren't on the beach or back in a cave. We each had a bed and the use of a bathroom that was only a few feet away.

Ultimately, the knowledge that I didn't have to move for awhile far outweighed any discontent about the filth of the apartment or the length of my walk to work. I thought I was finally going to settle into Tenerife.

That was, until the first night.

Following another undignified, inglorious shift cleaning cutlery and the lids of ketchup bottles, I made my way back to the pension. When I arrived at the apartment, I discovered three scantily dressed women sitting in the front room. Actually, they weren't sitting; they were posing. I took a step back and looked around to see if I had possibly entered the wrong building. No, I was in the right spot. I recognized the painting on the wall. I strongly doubted there could be two paintings that were so similar in vulgarity.

I was definitely in the right place.

However, the front room had been transformed into, for lack of a better word, a parlour. The place had been dowsed with lace doilies and ambience. The stench of perfume was thick, cheap and tacky. As I made my way across the lounge to the staircase that led to my room, the girls said something to each other in Spanish and began to giggle. Beginning to blush, I went to my room and found Tim lying on his bed and laughing like a fool.

Before I could ask what was going on downstairs, he told me to be quiet and listen.

I listened.

What I heard was moaning and groaning and the squeak of bedsprings being put to the test. It was the unmistakable and uncomfortable sounds of people having sex. Then my ear deduced that there was more than one rhythm being produced by the bouncing springs. There were, in fact, three distinctive beats. Things were beginning to make sense.

I looked at Tim in disbelief.

"This," he said, waving at the ceiling and the walls, "has been going on for the past two hours. We're staying in a fucking whorehouse mate!"

I thought the cave was uncomfortable.

Obviously, I couldn't fall asleep that night. Even with earplugs, the vibrating walls, floor and bed made sleeping unmanageable. As I lay wide awake, I considered alternatives to the obvious.

(thump, thump, thump, thump)

Maybe it was somebody's—excuse me—*everybody's* anniversary.

(Thump, thump, Thump, THUMP, THUMP, THUMP, THUMP, THUMP)

Maybe I was staying with a family of sailors on shore leave.

(THUMP, THUMP, THUMP, THHHUUMMMPPPP … thump, thump, thump)

Maybe, I wasn't ready to conclude that I was living in a brothel.

However, for the next 10 nights, I returned to the pension to find the same suggestive girls lounging in the same tacky parlour, waiting to be bought. For the next 10 nights, I had to endure their endless screwing.

Any doubt that I was living in a house of carnal pleasure had long vanished.

As far as I could gather, the old landlady was the madam of the establishment, and at least two of her daughters were labourers. Throughout the night, the place was filled with licentious sounds making it impossible to sleep. By the time the last client stumbled home and the grunting stopped I was delirious with exhaustion. However, just when I thought I could finally get some peace, the little, hyperactive brat of one of the daughters would wake up. Between this child and his domineering grandmother, the screaming was as endless as the humping.

Sandwiched between my crappy job, the long walk to and from work, fatigue and poverty, living in the whorehouse was becoming intolerable. Regardless, I had to stick with it. I got my first pay from the restaurant and felt as though things were back on track. I kept reminding myself that I still had my job and a place to live.

That was, until the grandmother madam kicked us out.

One morning, she barged into our room and screamed at us to leave. Tim shouted, "What the hell for?"

"You make too much noise," she shrieked as her grandson clutched to her leg and wailed for no discernable reason.

I thought she was joking. However, before I could laugh, Tim snapped. He screamed, "We're making too much noise? Are you fucking nuts? Take a look at the little bastard clinging to that fleshy mass of fat you call your leg, you old bitch. Or maybe it could be your slut daughters making all the fucking noise. One in particular is a right screamer!"

She stood there with her arms crossed, absorbing every single abuse Tim was shouting. Still, she wasn't willing to change her verdict.

Tim argued and insulted to no avail. We packed our stuff and left the house of lust. Getting kicked out of a brothel was the last straw for Tim.

"I'm leaving."

I asked where he was going.

"I don't know. I'll figure it out at the airport. I do know that this place isn't my scene at all. I fucking hate everything about it. My job sucks. The people suck. Getting kicked out by that ancient whore put the nail in the coffin. Don't take it personally, mate, but I have to go."

We said goodbye at the bus station.

I was sad to see Tim leave. We had gotten on great. We had spent Christmas together, my first major holiday away from my family, sitting on the beach drinking and smoking our gifts to each other.[1] But most importantly, we had been a fantastic source of support for one another. At least he was for me. If it weren't for Tim, I'm sure I would still be sleeping in a cave or, more likely, sitting on a plane back to Canada.

Nonetheless, like me, he was travelling alone. He had the freedom to do what he wanted. I didn't take it personally, and in a way, I understood his decision to bail. Tenerife was proving more of a struggle than I had anticipated. I couldn't quite discern what it was exactly, but something about this island and, in particular, this city was off. It would be easy to blame sleeping in a brothel or cleaning tables in a striped uniform, but it was much more than that. There was something ominous and still very unclear about Tenerife.

---

1. I gave him rum, and he gave me Moroccan hash. They were not the most traditional presents. However, waking up Christmas morning in a brothel wasn't customary for this Canuck either.

Regardless, I didn't have a choice; I had to keep struggling. Well ... I did have a choice. I could go home, but that wasn't an option I'd even consider. I was here now. I'd fight through any and all situations. One positive factor was that my current bout of homelessness wasn't going to be a dilemma.

The owner of *The Sunset Boulevard Restaurant*, a man named Rodney Tucker, was also the owner of several large condominium complexes, a number of clubs and other restaurants. Because accommodation was tough to find, and because a large majority of his staff of five thousand came from overseas, he put aside a small block of condos as temporary residence for those struggling to find a place to live. They had a strict policy regarding who stayed at the *Paradise Hamlet*. It was staff only, which is why Tim and I didn't abandon the busiest little whorehouse in Los Cristianos when I was first employed. However, with Tim gone, I could now take advantage of the condo.

I also reminded myself that I had a job. It was a shit job, but still, it was a job that this poor traveller desperately needed. And although it was a pittance, I was getting paid. Slowly, I'd be able to get enough together to finance my next destination.

I was hoping to eventually settle into life in Tenerife. I was hoping that despite the unpromising beginning, my time on this island would prove a rewarding and enjoyable experience.

That was, until I found out whom my boss really was ...

10
GANGSTER'S PARADISE

MARCH

I learned a tremendous lesson that December afternoon while sitting on the beach in Marbella. While I was contemplating the desperation of my economic predicament and the bleak future of my travels I grasped the significance of perspective.

It is perspective that keeps me going on my trip around the world. And the indispensable key that helps me find perspective is the glorious setting sun. I used this approach in Tenerife to trudge through the shit that surrounded me daily. Any chances I had, which due to my work schedule were few, I escaped to watch the sunset. Without fail, the setting sun reminded me of the distance I had put between Canada and myself.

Perspective is what had kept me going over the previous four months.

I never really settled into the rhythm of Tenerife, and at the end of the day, I believe this was a good thing. After the ninth and final move, I was finally able to unpack and call somewhere home. However, I was never able to feel at home. Call it a gut instinct, but when I first arrived in December, I detected something perplexing about the island. Initially, I couldn't determine which factor was bothering me. In any event, I wasn't in a financial situation to attempt another drastic move, so I forgot about it or possibly even blocked it out. Despite having spent four months in Tenerife, I was still not positive what aspect made it impossible for me to settle down and unwind.

There were many factors to consider.

Maybe I was disappointed with Tenerife because I wasn't getting anything Spanish out of my experience on the Spanish island. Knowing I would have to be in Tenerife for several months in order to make enough money to continue my travels, I assumed that I would pick up some Spanish. Unfortunately, Tenerife, and specifically Playa de Las Americas, was more English than Spanish. At least 90 per cent of the tourists were English. The English pubs poured English beer and cooked English food, and everything was served by an English staff. There was always English football on the English sports channel so that the English patrons could feel right at home.[1]

Tenerife was, essentially, England in the sun.

I didn't come across anything remotely Spanish. I didn't make any Spanish friends. I didn't eat any Spanish food. I didn't listen to any Spanish music, and I didn't hear the Spanish language ... zilch, zip, nada.

In fact, the only evidence of Spanish culture that I could uncover was in a taxi-cab, for all the drivers on the island seemed to be local. Sadly, the only Spanish expression I was able to pick up during my exhausted, early morning cab rides home, was "soy cansado," simply meaning "I'm tired." It was a far reach from learning a new language.[2]

I did, however, learn a lot about the English Premiership football league.

Maybe I didn't enjoy Tenerife because of the tourists. I was particular disgusted by their motivation for coming to the island and their mentality whilst here. I realize this isn't applicable to every Canaries visitor, but from what I saw, the stereotypical tourist was a 20-something Brit on a one-week bender with a pack of mates. They were not in Tenerife for the sun or the beaches. Their top priority wasn't the drinking, the music, the clubs or meeting members of the opposite sex. Even getting laid wasn't paramount. The main thrust was drugs. Cocaine and ecstasy were what everybody sought. That was all everybody talked about, and that was all everybody consumed. It was cocaine and ecstasy every night for the entirety of their vacation.

---

1. The other 10 per cent were German. The two were easy to tell apart. The Brits were dressed in their favourite football jerseys and white running shoes. They were dripping with gold jewellery and sporting bright, lobster-red sunburns. The German tourists, however, had socks and sandals, a bumbag, and their giveaway feature, Speedos. Due to their sheer numbers, one could assume that the godawful Speedos were handed out at the airport to every German traveller before their departure. For the record, there are very few people who should wear this overly revealing and unflattering swimwear. It certainly shouldn't adorn an entire nation.
2. I did have one taste of true Spanish culture, and that was during the Carnival in February. And what a taste it was. Tenerife hosts one of the biggest Carnival festivals in the world. It is even comparable to the party in Rio de Janeiro. For this one week on Tenerife, the music, costumes and atmosphere were authentically Spanish. I'd never seen so many happy and festive people in one place. You didn't walk from place to place. You danced. Unfortunately, I only experienced one night of the festivities, for I had my slave duties at the restaurant. Worse still, once the festival was over, the "English Invasion" was back in full force.

The rest, like the sex and the sun, were extras.

I don't mean to sound like a hypocrite, considering I have also experimented with a variety of drugs. However, the key word here is experimented. I have never let anything I sampled interfere with anything else I was doing. It was an additive to a party or a festival. The drug itself was never the party.[3]

This wasn't the case in Tenerife.

Drugs were why people came to the island. Sadly, it wasn't just the tourists. Most of the people I worked with were driven by their addictions. This included teenagers who had been on Tenerife, in some cases, for years. It was why they worked. It was their incentive. It was the reward. It is what drove them. And ultimately, it was why many of them had remained on Tenerife for years. They either couldn't or wouldn't leave. They were indebted to the drugs, often both physically and financially.

I once saw an 18-year-old kid snorting cocaine off a table in the middle of a crowded restaurant as casually as someone smoking a cigarette. Much like when Pablo smoked heroin in the airport, nobody seemed to notice or care.

Maybe I had a hard time adjusting to Tenerife because the few locals weren't the slightest bit friendly towards foreigners. In fact, the few I came across were downright rude. They were nothing at all like the Spaniards I had encountered on the mainland, who were some of the friendliest people I'd met to date.

That being said, I can't really blame the Tenerife locals for their loathing of the foreigners. They treated their island like a frat house toilet. I would be pissed off too if visitors treated my home the way these British tourists treated Tenerife.

Unfortunately, the locals weren't aware of my empathy. This meant that when they saw me walking down the street or standing in the club, they didn't see the harmless, friendly Canadian who was respectful of their culture and interested in learning their language. Instead, they saw an arrogant, obnoxious, drugged-up English hooligan who was trying to fuck their women. This was not the easiest stereotype to shake when trying to make new friends and immersing yourself into a culture.

Maybe I couldn't connect with anybody in Tenerife because everybody who lived and worked on the island seemed to be on the run. Nobody came to Tenerife for something. Instead, they came to Tenerife to *get away* from something. In some cases, my teenage co-workers were running away from their parents. In

---

3. You may be thinking, "Didn't you go to Amsterdam solely to smoke weed?" The answer is yes, but there is a vast difference between smoking marijuana and taking Class A drugs such as ecstasy and cocaine.

other circumstances, they were running away from relationships. Some were avoiding debts, and I worked with a few who were evading the British authorities. I worked with one girl who was trying to escape two physically abusive ex-boyfriends. She was living in the Canary Islands under an assumed name. She told me all this the day she fled Tenerife. It was the same day she received a call from one of her abusers who had finally tracked her down. She was 24 years old.

Like I said, everybody seemed to be on the run from something.

Maybe I loathed Tenerife because I had a despicable job. I didn't have a problem with the uniform or the menial chores, although both were undignified.[4] What made me despise my job was how I was treated by those I worked for and worked with. Busboys, being the lowest of the low in the restaurant industry (even dishwashers get more respect), are pissed on and treated like shit by absolutely everybody. The servers treated us like morons. The barmen wouldn't talk to us. And the cheap, British patrons thought that because we wore aprons, they had the right to bark ridiculous orders. They regarded us as colonial slaves who were there to serve their every, ludicrous whim.

And to make matters worse, we got zero support from management, who were themselves a bunch of coked-up, power happy pricks. They seemed to relish humiliating us and did so at any given opportunity.[5] It was bad enough scrubbing the insides of garbage cans. It was worse singing the crappy birthday songs to the pretentious guests. But the ultimate humiliation came during the holiday week when the entire staff was required to dress as a Disney character, for this was the ridiculous theme of the restaurant. To make matters considerably more embarrassing, we were forced to do a song and dance to a Disney medley in front of the entire restaurant on New Year's Eve. To fine-tune our pending humiliation, all staff was required to arrive 45 minutes before our shift so we could practice the choreographed degradation.

The bastards made us stumble through it three fucking times on New Year's.

---

4. The uniform consisted of black pants, a black and white striped shirt (much like a referee) and a black leather vest that was adorned with a minimum of five pins of a cartoon nature. We looked like a motorcycle gang of referees with Peter Pan complexes.
5. The labour camp, also known as *Sunset Boulevard*, had a variety of fines that they imposed on their staff for an assortment of infractions. These ranged from not having a pen (why a busboy would need a pen is beyond me) to not having enough Disney pins on your leather vest (a tacky part of the already tacky uniform). The worst of the fines was for snacking during your shift, even if you were out of sight from the customers. If caught by a manager, a mere bite would cost you a week's wages.

If I took anything away from my job, it was that I never want to work in a restaurant again. The pathetic, trivial disputes that take place within the walls of a restaurant were mind-boggling. There was backstabbing, badmouthing and pettiness. There was a continuous power struggle among the various groups of employees. Everyone tried to get ahead of each other, and they used any two-faced means necessary. Then there was the extra dynamic that everybody was trying to get into each other's pants, if they hadn't been there already. The place was incestuous. There weren't "love triangles." There were "love octagons."

Between teary-eyed waitresses, psychotic cooks, arrogant barmen and the power happy managers, all of whom banged each other, the place was a madhouse filled with quarrels and stresses that, in the big picture, were irrelevant.

I know working in a bar or nightclub would have similar, in-house controversies and dilemmas. However, the massive distinction between the two is the clientele. People are, more or less, in a good mood when they are drinking. This isn't the case in a restaurant. People get impatient, demanding and offensive when they are hungry. I imagine even the Dalai Lama is a right grumpy monk when his guts are empty.

Needless to say, the rude, obnoxious, dissatisfied Brits were a cantankerous nightmare.

Over and above these draining and frustrating conditions was another matter that made me edgy. It was a factor that literally stared me in the face every day. Yet, coming from my idyllic upbringing in Canadian suburbia, I was unaware that such notorious lifestyles existed outside fiction. That I somehow found myself in the middle of the seedy drama was even more unfathomable. My naïveté made me oblivious to the reality of the dangers that constantly lurked on Tenerife and within the walls of *Sunset Boulevard*.

Maybe I was finished with Tenerife because I found out whom I worked for. Or should I say, I found out who he actually was.

I was told the name of my employer, Rodney Tucker, the day I was hired at *Sunset Boulevard*. However, it wasn't until late February I found out the identity of Rodney Tucker and his notorious past. I had observed some strange and frightening occurrences at the restaurant, and I had heard several hearsay accounts of some rather violent episodes. They all revolved around Mr. Tucker and his friends.

One morning, following yet another peculiar incident in the restaurant, I asked one of my roommates who had been on Tenerife for awhile, if he thought there was a certain air of aggression and mayhem surrounding *Sunset Boulevard* and its employees.

"It has everything to do with Tucker and the rest of the Brutes," he said cynically. "They're all maniacs … a bunch of fucking gangsters."

I asked him what he meant by gangsters.

"They're gangsters … thugs, criminals. Call 'em whatever you want. The whole lot of them are dodgy. He has so much coin from the Hatton Garden Heist that he can do whatever he bloody wants," he continued resentfully.

The Hatten what?

"You've heard of the Hatton Garden Heist, haven't you?" He asked in a tone that suggested this robbery should be common knowledge.

I told him I'd never heard of it.

The story he proceeded to tell me about the Hatton Garden Heist and Rodney Tucker's involvement was unbelievable. I thought my roommate was talking shit and messing with my head. Yes, there had been some bizarre and unclear events over the past few months, but this story was a stretch. What he described was the plot of a gangster movie complete with a cast of bad guys.

It was such a tall tale that I decided to investigate further.

The next morning I went to an Internet café and Googled Rodney Tucker's name.

What I read about my employer not only confirmed what my roommate had said, but it added new dimensions of madness and danger to the already dubious setting of Tenerife.

I uncovered that in 1980 five teams of armed men simultaneously raided five separate jewellers in London's diamond district and made off with 32 million pounds in uncut stones. The Hatton Garden Heist, as it was labeled, was the biggest and most intricate diamond robbery in British history. Rodney Tucker, despite admitting his involvement in plotting the caper, slipped through a crack in the legal system and was acquitted of all charges, including handling stolen goods. Tucker quickly took himself and his fortune to the Canary Islands, where he established Tucker Enterprises and developed time-share condominiums, restaurants and nightclubs. He quickly became one of the richest people on the planet.

This, I thought to myself, is the man paying my salary.

This is the man … excuse me, gangster whom I work for.

However, just as alarming, if not more so, were some of the other people employed by Tucker.

It is alleged that when Tucker had a problem with competitors or disgruntled employees, all he had to do was mention that he would call security, and the predicament rectified itself.

One of the many "soldiers" Tucker employed, known to the restaurant's staff as "the Brutes," would ensure that all problems were resolved one way or another.

Even though I didn't know who they really were at the time, the Brutes were pointed out to me during my first week at *Sunset Boulevard*. I assumed that they were regulars or possibly friends of the owner based on how at ease they made themselves in the restaurant. It didn't take long to pick up some of the fearsome rumours concerning these beasts' behaviour. One of the scariest accounts of violence that I overheard involved a member of Tucker's time-share staff who had been beaten up at a rival's nightclub by an aggressive bouncer. As the story went, a gang of Brutes grabbed the bouncer in question, took him to a secluded section of beach, beat the living daylights out of him, buried him to his neck and, adding insult to injury, pissed in his face.

Despite having heard the identical story from several people, I couldn't say that this thrashing happened for sure. Mercifully, I didn't see that beating with my own eyes.

Nevertheless, I did witness something with my own eyes.

The Sunset Boulevard Restaurant, although a "family establishment" in the evening, was a scene right out of *Goodfellas* during the day. With all the tourists either on the beach or nursing a hangover, the empty restaurant had one or two tables continuously occupied by a rotating group of Brutes. The Brutes, dressed in their Bermuda shorts and tacky Hawaiian shirts, dripped with attitude. They invaded the restaurant, talked shit, ate and played cards, all while demanding the utmost respect and service from the poor staff that happened to be rostered during the day.

One incident I witnessed, although at the time I could only believe it was an overreaction, was when a waiter's sense of humour almost led to his demise. He was serving a table of Brutes when one of the thugs complained that his hamburger was overcooked. The waiter, who had worked in the restaurant for years and was friendly with the Brutes, jokingly replied, "I didn't cook it."

The Brute had the server against the wall by his throat before the upended chair hit the ground. I was amazed a man of that size and limited brain matter could move that fast.

The thug growled at the terrified employee, "Does your dumb, worthless existence not understand the meaning of respect?"

A satisfactory apology was squeaked, and the helpless waiter was thrown to the ground where he gasped for air.

The Brute sat down, as if nothing had happened, and continued to eat his overcooked hamburger.

A few days later, I overheard a one-sided conversation that added further validity to my trepidation. A different, yet equally intimidating, Brute came into the restaurant one evening during "family hours." He cornered one of the waiters on duty near the spot where I was cleaning cutlery. He asked, rather politely, if the waiter had the money that he owed.

The kid meekly replied, "No."

The Brute then said that if the waiter didn't have the money the next time he came, he would stand on his throat until it popped. The Brute said this in a calm and polite manner that added a dimension of horror and conviction that the monster would be true to his word. I had no doubt that the Brute had heard such pops and had probably enjoyed the sound.

When I saw the same waiter at the pub that night, I asked him why he didn't just do a runner back to the UK if he didn't have the money. It seemed like a better option than having your neck popped.

He looked at me as though I had a death wish. "Are you out of your mind? There would be fucking Brutes at Heathrow waiting for me with more than just a warning. Nah. No fucking way, man. I'm going to have to bide my time and figure out a way to get the bucks."

He did a runner two days later.

However, it was my own "close encounter with the Brutish kind" that initially made me wonder what the hell I had landed myself into. The incident also made me wonder who the hell I was in it with. The event occurred my first night at *Paradise Hamlet*. It was the day Tim left the island. I was jolted from my slumber at five in the morning by a violent pounding on the front door. When I answered it, my sleepy eyes discovered the biggest, scariest mammoth of a man they had ever seen. He barged in and roared, "Where the fuck is Bill!?"

I stuttered that I didn't think there was anybody here by that name.

The beast slammed me against the wall. "Don't fuck with me you little shit! Where the fuck is Bill!?"

I didn't have an answer. I didn't have the foggiest idea who Bill was. At that precise moment, I would have given my left nut to know the identity and whereabouts of Bill. Despite my inevitable beating, I saw the bitter irony in the fact that if I didn't figure out who Bill was, I would probably lose my left nut. I'd probably also lose my right nut and several other vital components to my body.

That was the point when my life began to flash before my eyes.

That was also the point when the guy I shared the apartment with, whom fortunately (or unfortunately) wasn't named Bill, woke up and joined the impending slaughter.

"Easy, man. Bill isn't here," he bravely intervened, trying to pacify the psycho. "I haven't seen Bill in five days. I don't have a clue where he is."

The heaving, raging maniac slowed his breathing. He had a puzzled look on his face that suggested his brain was having difficulty comprehending what to do in a non-violent situation. However, he released his grip, and the vein on his forehead returned to its place of origin within his oversized cranium.

But his voice still carried a point.

"Tell that little prick that he owes money, and I want it last week!"

And with that final command, the humanoid stormed out and slammed the door.

I swallowed.

I looked at my roommate. My eyeballs were safely back in their sockets, and I asked if he could possibly explain why a raging lunatic had threatened me and who, for the love of Christ, was Bill.

"Bill used to work in the kitchen at *Sunset's*, but he split last week. I really haven't seen him since. I guess he owes somebody some money. It's best not to ask questions in these situations."

He yawned and went back to his room.

In these situations? At the time, I didn't know what that was supposed to mean. Was there a right time to inquire about the actions of a raving madman who had woken you in the early morning hours to beat information out of you?

That near-death experience should have been a massive alarm that something was dangerously awry in Playa de Las Americas. However, having lived in a cave and a brothel, being dead tired and in desperate need of money, the magnitude of the threat (and the man delivering it) didn't register as a warning. I failed to grasp that Tenerife and the people around me were, to say the very least, dodgy.

Nevertheless, now that I had confirmed Tucker's criminal background, that confrontation, along with the others, made startling sense. The violent rumours became painfully verified. There was terrifying truth to the far-fetched fiction. I sometimes wonder if my indebted co-worker made it safely back to the UK, or if the Brutes had, as promised, popped his throat. I never found out what happened to that poor, stupid bastard, otherwise known as Bill.

I can only imagine the worst.

But as I've learned, it's best not to ask questions in these situations.

I realized I was working for a British mobster. No, I wasn't extorting or throwing my muscle around intimidating people, but I played a small part in their money laundering process. My labour was the soap. So was the labour of all five thousand employees of Tucker Enterprises, who were, not surprisingly, paid weekly in cash. His restaurants, clubs and time-share condos were the washing machines. It was all one big laundering scam. Looking back, I asked for work at hundreds of locations, and *Sunset Boulevard* was the only place that didn't require a working visa. They never even asked if I had one.

Crooked people in a shitty and hazardous environment engulfed me. Sure, the weather was sweet, but life in Playa de Las Americas was intensifying my anger and frustration back to their previous and detrimental Canadian concentrations.

I'm not sure what straw it was that broke the camel's back, but I decided to leave Tenerife.

Maybe it was the locals.

Maybe it was the tourists.

Maybe it was the job.

Maybe it was the gangsters.

Maybe, just maybe, it didn't matter.

The bottom line was that I wasn't enjoying myself. In the end, that was all the reason I needed to leave the Canaries. I had the bucks. Thankfully, during my four months in Tenerife, I avoided the lifestyle, the drugged up pace of the city and, most importantly, the vengeful eye of Rodney Tucker. By doing so, I saved enough money to get out of gangster's paradise and on to my next destination.[6]

It was time to continue the trip around the world.

The question wasn't why I was leaving. It was where I was going.

---

6. When I gave *Sunset Boulevard* my two-week notice, I asked them to write me a letter of recommendation. I wasn't planning on using the reference in a job interview or putting it on my CV. Experience as a busboy wouldn't get my foot into too many doors. The only reason I asked for the letter was to find out if I was in their good books or if I'd have Brutes waiting for me.

Puerto Colon,
Adeje 38860
Tenerife South,
Canary Islands

March 1999

Dear Sir/Madam,

Reference Mr Matthew Hamilton

This is to certify that the above named was employed by ███████ Restaurant from 19th December 1998 until 8th March 1999 in the position of Busser.

During his employment he proved himself to be a very reliable and conscientious member of staff who was willing to do anything asked of him. He was punctual and held an excellent attendance record.

I would not hesitate to recommend him to any future employer and I believe He would be an invaluable asset to any Company. I would be happy to re-employ Matthew if the opportunity presented itself once again.

Yours Faithfully,

GENERAL MANAGER

> This was my inconspicuous way of finding out if there would be Brutes waiting for me at Heathrow. By the glowing words of recommendation, I believed that my safety was secured. I didn't think that they would break the legs of "an invaluable asset."

11

A NAME FROM THE PAST

MARCH

When the plane took off from Tenerife International Airport, a wave of relief swept over me.

I finally let out a long, deep breath. Holy shit, I thought. Was I insane? What the hell was I doing in Tenerife?

With the brilliant vision of hindsight, I can honestly and accurately say that Tenerife is one screwed up island. I certainly didn't belong, and I was not capable of adapting to the hazardous surroundings. My four months on Tenerife would not be remembered as a highlight of my trip, and I would not return to the out of control island anytime in the foreseeable future, if ever.

In hindsight, I'm thrilled I was so naïve about what was going on in Tenerife for so long. I'm not sure I would have mentally survived the island if I had known about Tucker and his associates' history when I first arrived. Yes, I was looking for an education on the road, but learning how to launder money, pop necks and work coked off my head wasn't the schooling I had in mind. Being continuously surrounded by gangsters, drug addicts and people on the run inevitably takes its toll on you in one way or another.

The nefarious environment of Tenerife was not where I wanted to settle. When I eventually clued in to the insanity around me, I made sure to remain focused on the task at hand: making enough money to continue travelling. This determination to save money kept me out of the clubs and the drug scene, which wasn't easy on this island that seemed to snow cocaine. In the end, I was able to stay out of debt. I was as confident as possible that I would arrive at Heathrow without one of the Brutes waiting for me. I made sure that my rent and meagre bar tab were square and that I left the restaurant on good terms.

It may seem like an insignificant detail, but being oblivious to what was going on also prevented me from lying to my parents about the dodgy cast of characters I was living among (Lying is something that my family never does to one another). Not completely sure why things were so insane, I didn't want to speculate on the phone and add justified concern to their already worried minds. I don't think my folks would have been too comfortable with the idea of their kid working and living with a bunch of established and successful criminals. Christ, my mom forbade me to skydive or bungee jump during my travels. If she knew her baby was working in the company of British mobsters, it would have sent her to an early grave.

With hindsight's 20/20 vision, I realized that in a very twisted way, I was lucky. I was lucky to have escaped Tenerife without acquiring an addiction, falling into debt or being beaten to a bloody pulp. However, my physical well-being had more to do with keeping my head in the sand and out of harm's way than being fortunate.

Where I got lucky was finding a job at all.

Sunset Boulevard hired me even though I didn't have a work visa. This documentation was something I never contemplated since the question was never raised on the Spanish mainland. For whatever clueless reason, I assumed that work visas were only required for professional jobs such as lawyers, doctors, accountants and so forth. I figured restaurant and bar work could all easily be found under the table. Besides, I was Canadian. I had an unsubstantiated belief that because everybody loved Canadians, they would also be more than happy to give a happy Canuck traveller a job, work visa or not.

At least so I thought. But I was very wrong.

Consequently, if it wasn't for *Sunset Boulevard's* desire to pad the books and clean some cash, I probably would have never found work in Tenerife. I would've returned to Canada a frustrated and failed traveller.

In a strange way, a gangster saved my travels.

Tenerife served its purpose. It was a job in the sun. For the first time, I stayed warm and tanned for the entirety of winter. It was an enthralling experience, which fortified my belief that cold weather is for suckers. I promised myself that the following winter, assuming I was still travelling, would be spent in a similar climate.

In addition, Tenerife also helped me shed some of the Canadian naïveté that I dripped with before leaving home. Thanks to the cast of hookers, addicts and criminals, I toughened up and fine-tuned my ability to assess people and avoid conflict. Ultimately, I shed some of the boyish gullibility that draped me like a wet blanket.[1]

Nevertheless, the most important accomplishment on Tenerife was that I made enough money to finance my next destination. Now the question was where my next destination would be.

With money in my pocket and my safety relatively secured, my next priority was to figure out where I was going. I was on a flight back to London, but I did not intend to stay in England or anywhere in Europe for that matter. Europe was expensive and it was too easy to get around.

Being a poor, young backpacker, I felt I didn't get everything out of my European experience that I should. I couldn't afford to eat in the good restaurants and sample vintage wines. I ate McDonald's and drank Coke. I couldn't afford to sleep in a chateau or villa. I stayed in international hostels.

It was also effortless getting around Europe. Between Euro-rail and quick, cheap flights, there was no hassle travelling from one country to another. Even if it was time-consuming, Europe was a comfortable and uncomplicated continent to negotiate. I was too young and adventurous for the simplicity of European travel.

Now wasn't my time for Europe.

Now was my time to endure endless, bumpy journeys in shitty vehicles on shittier roads.

Now was my time to experience these hardships while I still had the patience, energy and youth to do so.

Now was my time to rough it.

Then, whilst sitting on the plane and daydreaming about the Third World possibilities the globe had to offer, a name popped into my head. It was a name I hadn't thought of in almost six months. In fact, the last time I saw her was through red, swollen eyes the day she dumped me unmercifully in the armpit of Ireland.

---

1. Despite their limited numbers, there were some good people on Tenerife. The most interesting was Lady Lola. Lady Lola was, without a doubt, the most flamboyant individual I had ever come across. Imagine the gayest person you've seen in the movies, up the mannerisms and dialect by ten, and you are somewhere near Lady Lola. His real name was Bruce, but he would bitch slap you into next week if you ever called him that. It was Lola during the day, but at night, when the glam and glitter made their appearance, it was always Lady Lola. I don't think I had any homophobic tendencies before meeting Lola, but if I did, they were destroyed after partying with this transvestite. I have never laughed as much or as hard as I did when I was with Lady Lola in the clubs.

For whatever obscure reason, I thought of Sabrina. With the recollection of her name came a potential destination.

Why not South Africa?

Even though we hadn't kept in contact, I thought we had a strong connection that night in Cork. Regardless, Sabrina had made a fantastic impression on me. For once, it wasn't a woman's beauty or knowledge of *Star Wars* that had me considering a drastic move. Instead, it was her ability to sell the merits and splendours of her country that had me contemplating flying to the other end of the planet. Due to the excessive amount of Guinness consumed in the Cork pub, I don't recall exactly what she said that was so special about South Africa. What I do remember though was her glowingly positive attitude about that distant land, which was in contrast to any media report I had previously heard.

I pulled out my pocket map. My geography of Africa, like most of the world, was basically shit. I knew South Africa was in the southern tip of the continent, and I was pretty sure that Johannesburg was its capital. But that city's location within the country or, more imperatively, Cape Town's location was still unknown.[2]

My trip was supposed to be around the world, and, as far as I knew, Africa was a major part of the planet. I was going to visit the continent at some point, so why not now? After staring at my African map for about 10 minutes, I came to the decision to embark on a Cape Town to Cairo journey.

When I decided to attempt a Cape Town to Cairo excursion, all I meant was I would start in Cape Town and would somehow end up in Cairo. I decided not to research any logistics of such an expedition. I was enjoying the bliss of ignorance that, despite a few bumps and hurdles along the way, had proved advantageous in the enjoyment and continuation of my travels. Therefore, the when, where, why and how of this epic voyage would be established as the venture unfolded.

Although I did make a couple of inquiries once I arrived in London.

I had learned an imperative lesson in Tenerife regarding working visas—check them out. I wasn't planning on working in South Africa, but nonetheless, I still called the South African embassy to find out if any documents were required. I was told I would be issued a three-month holiday visa upon my arrival in Cape Town. They said the only required item would be proof of either a return or onward flight. I had no intention of returning to London, so once again I con-

---

2. Actually, South Africa has three capital cities, none of which is Jo'burg; the administrative capital is Pretoria, Bloemfontein is the capital of the judiciary, and Cape Town is the legislative capital.

sulted my trusty, invaluable map. I discovered that a place called Namibia, a country I knew even less about than South Africa, was the closest neighbouring nation to Cape Town, and Windhoek was its capital. It was good enough for me. I booked a flight to Cape Town and an onward flight to the Namibian capital for three weeks after my South African arrival. It would be step two on my trip up the continent.

Before I could think things through or change my mind, I found myself sitting on the 12-hour flight and heading for the southern tip of Africa.

When the captain announced that the plane was beginning its slow descent into Cape Town, a wave of anxiety swept over me.

I sucked in as much air as I could and thought to myself, "Holy shit! Was I insane? What the hell was I doing in South Africa?"

Other than Sabrina, I knew nothing about the country.

Well, I knew almost nothing. I knew there had been something called apartheid, which was a racist regime in which black South Africa was essentially stripped of all rights. I also knew that this racist policy had ended thanks in part to a man named Nelson Mandela, who had become the president of the country. I'd been told by the media that South Africa is plagued with crime and violence. In spite of being highly suspicious of the liars ... excuse me, *media* ... deep down, I believed there was a good chance of getting mugged at some point on the African continent. I would consider it a part of the travel experience.

I had no idea what there was to see or do in South Africa.

I had no clue what the cultures, peoples and climates were like.

I didn't even know if there would be hot water.[3]

Details of Sabrina, my African contact and so-called "inspiration" for coming to South Africa, were sketchy. We hadn't stayed in touch over the past six months because we hadn't exchanged contact details. This meant there was no way of letting her know that I was coming. All I knew about Sabrina was her first name, that she was from Cape Town and she worked in a bar called *The Den*. Whether she still worked there, lived in Cape Town or was even in the country was unknown.

As far as I knew, she could have changed her name.

Oh shit ... what had I gotten myself into?

---

3. This is no joke. The day I departed London for Cape Town, I spent a little longer than normal in the steamy shower. I honestly wasn't sure if there would be the possibility of a hot shower while in Africa, so I relished every warm drop that much more. I was going to the "Dark Continent" after all.

I felt a bit panicky, so I looked out the window and hoped to find some inspiration. All I could see was the Atlantic Ocean. There were acres and acres of dark water stretching into nothingness. It lasted as far as the eye could see. In terms of inspiration, the black, endless ocean failed miserably. Instead, the prospect of my African travels seemed hopelessly bleak.

Cape Town to Cairo? Travelling the entire African continent by my ignorant self? Was I out of my mind? How did I expect to pull this off when I didn't even know if there would be hot water in Africa?

The plane did a half turn. I glanced out the window again to see if I could find any indication that I hadn't, as usual, put myself up shit creek. I was searching for some sign that I, for a miraculous change, had made the correct decision in coming to Africa.

And there it was.

As the plane made its final descent into Cape Town, I was transfixed by the overwhelming vista of the city and what loomed above it. Looking in from the ocean, the city was engulfed by a massive grey mountain. It was a giant, stone plateau, and the sprawling metropolis stretched up to the base of the awe-inspiring mass of rock. The sight was one of the most beautiful spectacles I'd ever seen.

Looking over my shoulder at the breathtaking view, the lady sitting next to me said, as if reading my thoughts, "Isn't Table Mountain beautiful?"

So that was what the masterpiece of nature was called. My impression of the city had exponentially improved, and my wave of anxiety was replaced by a wave of anticipation. Much like the sunset in Spain, Table Mountain served as an immediate and incredible reminder that I was in the middle of a phenomenal adventure of which most Canadians can only dream.

I was about to explore Africa.

I couldn't wait to get off the plane.

To my pleasant surprise, the South African officials spoke an easy to understand, accented English, and getting through immigration and customs was a piece of cake. To make my arrival that much easier, I found that the currency exchange counter and the information centre were side by side. After changing money, I headed to the adjacent information booth and asked the woman behind the desk about hostels in the city. The friendly and helpful South African not only recommended a hostel, but she organized my shuttle into town. Everything was falling into place.

"It'll be 100 rand for the taxi," she said politely.

I hadn't had a chance to examine my new currency, the rand, and I didn't know what denominations I was carrying. Playing the role of the newly arrived tourist, I slowly turned my bright, new currency in my fingers, oblivious to which note represented 100 rand. The reason for the delay in finding the correct bill was because I wasn't looking at the numbers, which were clearly displayed. My eyes were, instead, captivated by the designs featured on the notes.

"It's the one with the elephant on it," she said with a smile.

I knew I was in Africa.

During the entire ride to the city, my eyes were transfixed on the quickly approaching Table Mountain. It was enormously hypnotic. The only time I looked away from the mountain was when I caught striped movement out of the corner of my eye.

It was a pack of zebras.

There was no doubt about it; I was in Africa.

We drove into the heart of Cape Town, and as the view from the plane suggested, the mountain towered over the entire city. I was the only one dropped off at the hostel, which was a place called *The Traveller*. What I first noticed about the place was the amount of security. There was a high, cemented wall lined with barbed wire as well as a gate with buzz through entry. Despite my hatred and mistrust of the media, these security measures were strong indicators that perhaps CNN had reported the news accurately. Crime did appear to be an issue. The level of security added validity to the belief that I would, at some point, be robbed during my African adventure.

However, with Table Mountain dominating the background, my attention to the barbed wire and my impending mugging was temporarily distracted.

After checking in and grabbing a quick nap, I decided to walk around the city. I did this in every new town in order to get my bearings. I wanted to know what was around the hostel and, more importantly, how to find my way home if and when I got drunk.

I got about 200 metres from *The Traveller* when I saw my first signs of life outside the gated, barbed wire protection of the hostel. It was a gang of young, black guys who were loitering on a corner. Apparently, they were doing nothing except watching me walk in their direction.

I stopped.

The very little I knew about South Africa revolved around Nelson Mandela, apartheid and crime. None of the guys lurking on the corner looked like Mr. Mandela. From what I knew about apartheid, I was pretty sure those lads had taken the brunt end of the stick. And that stick had been wielded by a dude with my skin complexion. If that were the case, it would be understandable if those guys were still somewhat pissed off about the whole thing. And as far as crime, I knew that in order to have crime, you needed a victim.

Call it paranoia, or call it ignorance.

I call it me turning around and going back to the gated safety of my hostel to look at the animals on my money.

I knew that my fears were probably exaggerated and unjustified. However, having spent four months on an island surrounded by violent bastards, my nerves were frayed, and my brain anticipated the worst from people. As mentioned, I was half expecting to get robbed during this African mission. However, I imagined my mugging would be at the hands of rebels somewhere in the middle of the Congo or possibly by Somalian bandits.

I didn't want to be robbed in broad daylight by a bunch of teenagers after only three hours on the continent. That setback would be too disheartening.

However, that night I mustered up some courage to venture from the safety of the hostel. After my initial panic attack, I talked to the other travellers. Everyone had only amazing and positive words to say about Cape Town and all they'd seen on their South African journeys. And to my pleasant surprise, *The Den,* was situated on Long Street, which was only a few blocks from the hostel.

I had no idea if Sabrina was working, but I was going to find out.

Long Street was a party. There were cars and people cruising everywhere. It was Saturday night, and everybody was dressed to the nines for their appearance on the main drag. The number of beautiful women I passed had my neck muscles working overtime. So much so that I would have walked right past the entrance to *The Den* but for the very loud and funky music pouring from the club's door.[4]

I paid the entrance fee and made my way up the dark and narrow stairwell to the main floor. The club wasn't too big, and it was packed with people. The large, boisterous Saturday night crowd was dancing to the groovy music pumping out of the speakers. It had the makings for a great first night in South Africa.

To my relief, Sabrina, who was even more beautiful than I remembered, was working away at the main bar.

I made my way there and found an empty spot so I would have an easier time catching her attention. I had no idea if Sabrina would recognize me. She was as drunk as I was that night in Cork, if not more so, and who knew what she

---

4. As I would later discover, Cape Town is the movie and model heart of Africa. This cosmopolitan capital of the continent had leggy, drop-dead gorgeous blonds everywhere.

remembered of the evening. Not to mention it was half a year ago. I wouldn't be surprised if she didn't remember me.

Sabrina, busy pouring a drink, did a quick scan of the crowd waiting to be served. When our eyes met, she paused then continued making her drink. A moment later, she took another glance in my direction and looked a second or two longer. Again, she went back to her drink. I began to smile. She recognized me but was having a hard time figuring out from where. From the puzzled look on her face, I knew she was more focused on where she knew me from than the brandy and Coke.

Then, to my complete surprise, she looked at me with an "I know it's you, but is it really you" expression.

My gigantic smile answered her question.

She raced from behind the bar and gave me a massive and welcoming hug. "Holy shit, bru! What are you doing here?"

I answered honestly. I reminded her that she had told me Cape Town was an amazing city and that I must visit. What more reason did I need?

She laughed. "Unbelievable, bru … unbelievable."

She turned to the other barman and said, "Andre, I'm going to take a 10 minute break. The brandy and Coke is for that guy over there. Is that cool?"

"Ya. Lekker," replied her colleague in a thick, deep accent.

We went to the second storey patio that looked down upon the thriving and bustling Long Street. As I took in the Cape Town night, which was packed with young and beautiful people, all Sabrina could say was, "I can't believe you are here. I can't believe you actually came. It's so kiff, bru!"

I felt very welcome in this new country.

I felt even more welcome when Sabrina pulled a massive joint from her bag and sparked up.

She detected my delight and surprise about the openness of her smoking the gigantic cannon and laughed. "I told you Cape Town was a very, very chilled place."

She took another deep, long drag of the burning bud and passed me the spliff.

I was feeling good. I was feeling relaxed. I was feeling at home. It was the first time in a very long time that I felt this at ease with a place. I certainly didn't feel this way in Tenerife between the brothel, cave, gangsters and whores. Only Sinead's hospitality in Cork could compare to what I was feeling here.

But there was more.

I was feeling something I couldn't place. It was like an energy radiating into me. Cape Town had a similar presence to the energy I first detected in Tenerife.

There were deeper levels to the place than were initially apparent. However, unlike Tenerife, the power I was detecting wasn't ominous. It was inviting, alluring and captivating.

Without question, I was hammered that alcohol-sodden night in Cork half a year ago. I'd barely registered a thing Sabrina had said. However, despite my insobriety, I remembered that she had told me something important, almost a warning, regarding Africa.

She had proclaimed, "Something happens to you when you are in Africa. Something gets inside you that will make it very difficult to leave. And if you are somehow able to get away, you'll have an overwhelming urge to come back."

Time would tell if her prediction would prove true.

Table Mountain. Cape Town, South Africa.

The over-the-top security measures of a residential home in Cape Town, South Africa. In Canada, one might find these precautions at a maximum-security prison ... certainly not somebody's house.

12
EXPECTATIONS

APRIL

Expectations are remarkable phenomena. They exist everywhere, are created by people from all walks of life and are applicable to all aspects of life. Parents have high expectations of their kids' education and success in life. Employers have expectations of their employees' performance. People have expectations of the behaviour, love and support from their friends and family. We even set expectations upon ourselves. There are expectations of the food we eat, the teams we support and even the movies we watch. In most case, those expectations are high and rarely met. The food tasted as though it was from a can. The Cubs blew another season. Tom Cruise's acting in his recent self-glorifying film was, once again, diabolical. This frequent failure to meet high expectations often results in bitter disappointment. Just talk to a Chicago Cubs fan.

Therefore, the philosophy that I decided to incorporate into my travels was to not have any expectations.

If I didn't have any expectations, then it was impossible to be disappointed. If I expected a country to have electricity or hot water and it didn't, then I would be pretty pissed off about the situation. However, if I didn't expect these basic amenities anywhere in the country, and they did exist, then I would be pretty happy and overwhelmingly surprised about the state of affairs.

I'm not saying that setting high standards is a bad thing or that we shouldn't strive for the best in life. I'm simply suggesting that sometimes it can be beneficial to not have high expectations. For instance, when you are travelling to a completely unknown part of the world, it is my recommendation to leave all expectations at the gate.

When I arrived in South Africa, I had zero expectations. Well … I did expect to get mugged at some point, and I expected to not be able to wash off the blood because there wouldn't be any hot water.

Thankfully, and to help prove my point, those expectations weren't met. Not only did I avoid being mugged and enjoy long, hot showers, but I also found a spectacular city with a beautiful climate, stunning scenery, a great nightlife and a diverse and friendly people. All this was set amid a country that had incredible pride despite its dark past. Despite juggling two jobs and a boyfriend (yes, I was secretly disappointed), Sabrina managed to spend some time with me and provided a local insight to Cape Town and South Africa. The more she talked about her country and its peoples, the more I wanted to see it with my own eyes.

I wasn't expecting any of it.

I was intrigued by the country and wanted to see more of it.

Unfortunately, my desire to extend my stay exposed the downside to not having expectations. Sometimes you aren't in a position to take advantage of the new-found discovery. This was the situation I now faced in South Africa, which was a country that had captivated me from the moment I arrived. My dilemma was that I had an onward flight to Namibia set to depart in two days. It was a flight that would take me away from this enchanting country with its unexpected beauty and intrigue. I'd only been in South Africa three weeks, yet I knew this special and diverse land had much more to teach me.

Three weeks?

What was I thinking? Three weeks was barely enough time to take in Cape Town, let alone explore the rest of the immense country. When I had booked my onward flight to Windhoek, I didn't have any perception of the magnificence and size of this exquisite land. I assumed that the rest of South Africa was as astounding as Cape Town. I based this assumption on the vibe from the city and countless enthusiastic stories from travellers who, unlike me, had had a chance to explore the country.

I needed to stay longer.

However, in order to do so, there were two issues that required my time and attention. I had to extend my visa and change my flight's departure date. It was a "which came first, the chicken or the egg" situation. I didn't know if I could extend my visa without first changing my flight, and I didn't know if I could change my flight without first having documentation saying I was allowed to stay longer.

I decided to head to the Department of Home Affairs (Immigration) first for no other reason than it was closer to the hostel than Air Namibia's ticketing office.

When I arrived at the government building, I immediately became disheartened. The mass of people congregated in the visa department was mind-boggling.

It wasn't the number of individuals that had me feeling cynical. Rather, it was the apparent lack of organization that had me shaking my head.

The waiting foyer was, in a word, chaotic.

South African lines differ from Canadian lines in several ways. African lines are much, much longer and much, much slower. The other noticeable distinction is the width. In South Africa, it's as if people are waiting five abreast in some invisible funnel, squeezing their bodies towards the one open service window. The daunting queue wound through the entire office and continued well out the door and into the corridor. I wasn't even sure where it began.

I moved to what I thought was the back of the line and decided to give this bedlam 20 minutes. When I hadn't moved forward an inch but, instead, seemed to have been pushed back further into the corridor, I gave up.

Getting my visa extended was going to be a full day event, and this was something I didn't have the time or tolerance for. There was no sense wasting an entire day amid this bureaucratic nightmare when I didn't know if changing my flight was even possible.

Therefore, Air Namibia's Cape Town office was my next stop. I hoped I'd have better luck there.

Regrettably, this wasn't the case.

Even though there wasn't another customer in the entire office, I didn't get the assistance or answers that I needed. The three, uninterested employees barely lifted a finger to help answer my inquiries about changing my flight. The only explanation I could pry out of them was a vague statement that they couldn't (or wouldn't) help me because the ticket hadn't been booked in that particular office.

I walked back to the hostel frustrated and disillusioned. I guessed staying in South Africa wasn't meant to be. There was no sense returning to Home Affairs. I was sure the line hadn't moved a speck, and the bureaucratic day was drawing to a close. And I wasn't going to waste my last day in South Africa running between the inefficient and disorganized offices.

Fuck it.

I decided to continue with my original plan. I'd fly to Windhoek, and then I'd have to wait and see. I didn't have an onward flight from Windhoek, so I wouldn't have a time restriction if I felt the same way about Namibia as I did about South Africa. I could stay in Namibia, continue up through the continent or come back to South Africa. I could do whatever I wanted.

Even though I made the most of my final 48 hours in Cape Town, it was with much dismay and hesitation that I checked my bags onto the plane. I felt even more reluctance going through immigration. When the officer stamped my passport and I was officially out of South Africa, I had an overpowering desire to stop and go back.

It didn't feel right.

I wasn't ready to leave South Africa.

Sabrina was bang on in her assessment of what happens to people when they first visit Africa. There is an overwhelming urge to stay. I really didn't want to go. Even though I knew that I could and most certainly would come back, I still felt this pulsating force screaming at me not to get on the plane to Windhoek. It wasn't an "I think this plane is going to crash" kind of suspicion. It was more of an "I haven't finished with this place" intuition.

I felt I shouldn't leave South Africa.

Nonetheless, my bags were being loaded onto the plane, I had cleared customs and my passport was stamped goodbye South Africa. I was as good as gone.

I wandered aimlessly around the departure lounge. I thought about buying a drink. I decided I wasn't thirsty. I wandered some more then sat down in one of the terminal's uncomfortable chairs. I tried to mentally prepare for Namibia, which was the next destination that I knew nothing about.

Then, while sitting there thinking of nothing, wild and miraculous events began to unfold.

It began with a simple tap on the shoulder.

I broke from my thoughts and looked up to find a woman in an Air Namibia uniform smiling at me. "Excuse me, sir. Are you by any chance travelling alone," she politely inquired.

I answered that I was.

She continued, "Sir, I work for Air Namibia, and we have a small problem that I hope you can help us resolve. It seems that our flight to Windhoek is overbooked, and we need to find somebody who wouldn't mind staying an extra night in Cape Town and flying to Windhoek tomorrow. Might you be interested?"

Was I interested? Does a Canuck put maple syrup on his pancakes? Damn straight! Of course I was interested! Another 24 hours in Cape Town might give me enough time to scheme my ass into uncovering a way to extend my stay in South Africa.

Before I could agree to help, the woman, who was quickly becoming my hero, proceeded to say, "For your inconvenience, we will pay for your ride back into town and your hotel accommodation. We will also give you 800 rand spending money."

I wasn't waiting to find out if the deal got any sweeter. As far as I was concerned, the extra day in Cape Town was sweet enough. To the woman's relief and my exultation, I accepted her request and had another day to experience South Africa.

As we were leaving the departure lounge, the woman profusely thanked me for being so helpful. She said she had asked three other people before me, all of whom had said no. I was baffled. Who wouldn't want to stay in Cape Town? I laughed and explained the banalities of trying to prolong my stay.

The next few words out of her mouth changed my destiny once again.

"You know," she proceeded, "If you want to stay more than a night, you're most welcome to. Your ticket is open for one year."

I asked if she was joking.

She assured me she wasn't.

She thought, however, there might be a small hitch with immigration. Because I had technically departed South Africa, I now had to re-enter the country and have my passport re-stamped. She thought immigration officers were only allowed to issue two-week extensions when a passenger got bumped. She wasn't positive and said I'd have to ask the individual official.

Since I wasn't on an arriving flight, there weren't any other passengers trying to clear immigration when I arrived in the hall. I approached the only open window. The immigration officer took my ticket and passport and asked when I was leaving South Africa.

I decided to run with my luck and confidently said, "In three months."

He looked at my plane ticket, shook his head and replied, "I'm sorry. I'm only supposed to issue two weeks, maximum ..."

The way he said "supposed to" caught my ear.

He said it in a way that indicated there might be more to say on the matter. I decided to ask again. The worst-case scenario was him saying no. Regardless, I had an extra two weeks in South Africa. It was better than one night and a hell of a lot better than sitting on a flight to Windhoek. What did I have to lose? So I asked the immigration officer in the most sincere, polite, borderline ass-kissing voice I could muster if there wasn't anything I could do to receive the three-month extension. He looked at me for a moment then asked a question that caught me a little off guard. "Do you smoke?"

Luckily, I had half a pack of cigarettes in my pocket.

Without answering, I took them out and slid the Stuyvesant Extra Milds across the counter.

He grabbed the smokes and quickly put them into his pocket. He proceeded to rubberstamp my passport with a three-month South African tourist visa.

I wasn't sure if half a pack of cigarettes would be considered a bribe, since no actual money was exchanged. However, bribe or no bribe, I had received my visa. I had another three months in South Africa.[1]

I was on cloud nine.

Once I was officially back in the country, the Air Namibia representative, who had my easily identifiable backpack removed from the plane, found me and handed me an envelope containing 800 rand (the equivalent to 200 Canadian bucks), a taxi chit and hotel voucher.

Although the prospect of staying in a hotel was appealing, I much preferred to return to *The Traveller*. I was positive that the social atmosphere of the backpackers was more of a party than any hotel lounge. Despite the exterior security, the hostel was relaxed, comfortable and friendly. *The Traveller* and the people staying and working there were big reasons why I didn't want to leave South Africa in the first place.

I wasn't in South Africa to eat room service and watch hotel movies by myself. I was here to experience South Africa and meet people from across the globe.

I suggested that I could save Air Namibia a few bucks by returning to *The Traveller* as opposed to staying in a pricey hotel. My words and tone insinuated that it was *me* doing *them* the favour.

The Air Namibia representative, who looked as if she had already endured a very long and problematic day, didn't hesitate. She handed me another 100 rand and asked, "Will that be enough for the hostel?"

I told her it was too much.

"Then buy your first couple of beers on Air Namibia," she offered, wanting to be finished with the whole situation.

Done and done.

The ride back to the city was … magical. Table Mountain isn't the biggest mountain in the world, but it is hard to beat in its setting and the positive effects that it radiates over Cape Town and its population.[2]

When the taxi came around the bend on the N1 and I caught the first glimpse of Table Mountain, a sight I thought I might never see again, I was overwhelmed.

---

1. Bribe: offer to give something to someone to gain favor, influence, etc. There was no doubt about it. The pack of smokes was definitely a bribe.
2. To put this stunning piece of nature into perspective, if you looked at a piece of dog shit with Table Mountain looming in the background, I promise you would be amazed how photogenic the turd had become.

I believed that the miraculous events that had just transpired were meant to be. They certainly helped support my belief in the existence of the tremendous sensation to stay that I was feeling. I obviously wasn't supposed to leave South Africa yet. If this indescribable force actually existed, which I believed it did, it had the power to pull me off the plane and get me back in the country for at least three months. There was even another potential nine months to play with thanks to the Air Namibia ticket being open for a year. And, to further sweeten the deal, this energy threw some extra cash in my pocket.

I was obviously ecstatic when I arrived at *The Traveller*.

I checked in, put my bag in the small dorm room and made my way to the backpackers' funky bar to begin spending my new-found beer money. As mentioned, I was in a fantastic mood. How could I not be? I felt as though the South African gods had pulled some strings to keep this goofy Canuck around a bit longer.

I was smiling from ear to ear when I ordered my beer.

There was a guy sitting next to me at the bar. I didn't know his name, but I had seen him around the backpackers the last couple of weeks. I was in a generous mood, so I offered to buy the stranger a drink, which he happily accepted.

I introduced myself, and we began talking. I recounted my day's adventure and the incredible luck that had befallen me. I told him how I planned to take full advantage of my time and properly explore South Africa. Vince, an English lad who had been living and working in Cape Town for four months, asked me what my plans were from here.

I hadn't given it any thought. The drastic and fortunate change of my circumstances hadn't yet sunk in. I glanced at the clock on the wall. At that precise moment, I would have been landing in Windhoek if the Air Namibia representative hadn't found me. If I had gone to buy a drink or slipped into the bathroom for a piss, I wouldn't be in South Africa right now.

What were my plans? I didn't have a clue, but I knew I could do pretty much anything I wanted. South Africa was my playground.

Vince informed me that he worked for an adventure company that abseiled people down Table Mountain. He told me that he, his brother and a co-worker were going on a two-month promotion run.

He mentioned that the trip started in Cape Town, went across the entire country and ended in Swaziland.

He said that his company paid for the car and that we would have discounts along the way in backpackers, bungee jumps and so forth because he worked in the tourism industry.

He revealed that there was an extra spot in the car, and he wondered if I would be interested in taking it.

Maybe my generosity in buying him a couple of beers led to the offer.

Maybe Vince felt there was something lucky about me and wanted to keep me around as a type of rabbit's foot.

Maybe it was the mystical South African power working through Vince and ensuring that I got out of Cape Town and properly explored and experienced all this enthralling land had to offer.

Regardless of the reason, I jumped at his invitation and happily accepted the free ride across South Africa.

I looked at the clock again. If my day had gone according to plan, I'd probably just be clearing Namibian immigration.

Auspiciously, things didn't go according to plan,

With the power of the "African pull," I think, deep down, part of me wasn't expecting that they would.

13

WHO KNEW?

MAY

The first time I arrived at *Smuggler's Cove Backpackers* was on a moonless evening. Vince, his brother James, Charles and I had been driving most of the day, and were having an impossible time finding the tiny coastal village of Chintsa and the secluded hostel in the dark. When we eventually arrived, we were not only tired but also a little stressed.

However, within two minutes of our arrival, all signs of the day's fatigue were eliminated. Even though it was pitch black, I appreciated that I had stumbled upon something special. This may sound a little "out-there," but the place immediately massaged a soothing calm into my body and soul.

It was a transcendental moment.

When we walked into reception, we were welcomed by a cute blond girl with a brilliant smile. She was drinking a beer at the desk with her boyfriend, who I would describe as the stereotypical white African bushman: long-haired, bearded and barefoot. He was sprawled across the counter. The serenity of these two further added to my belief that *Smuggler's Cove* would be an advantageous stop for many reasons.

We checked in. As Kate, the English girl from reception, walked us down the hill to one of the little beach cottages, we small talked. I could hear waves breaking out in the darkness, so I asked Kate how close to the beach we were. She gave me a knowing smile and said, "You'll have to wait and see."

When I awoke the next morning, I was quite hungover. The *Smuggler's Cove* pub, which was the best backpacking bar I'd seen to date, was having a party which carried on well into the early morning hours. I stumbled to the toilet. I was barely able or willing to expose my eyes to the light. On the way to the washroom, I passed a window. I took two steps past the glass and stopped. My brain began processing the information that my eyes were slowing transmitting.

I took two steps backwards and forced my eyes open to look again.

What I saw made my mouth fall open and my eyes, despite the pain, pop from their sockets.

We were a couple hundred metres from the edge of the sea, but it wasn't the proximity to the ocean that had me staring in utter amazement. It was the glorious setting. Our cottage, being set on a hillside, provided me with an elevated, unobstructed view of the picturesque landscape. There were lush, vegetated dunes, a sprawling, deserted beach and the seemingly endless Indian Ocean.

It was the most beautiful place that I'd ever started a day.

My hangover disappeared and was replaced by a blissful smile.

My initial assessment of Chintsa's power was accurate. This little chunk of coastline had an overwhelming, natural energy that splashed you like a bucket of water.

You couldn't help feeling rejuvenated in Chintsa.

Unfortunately, due to Vince's time schedule, we could only stay three days. As we drove away at the end of the third day, I had a deep suspicion that this wouldn't be the last time I experienced Chintsa.

A month later, my trip across South Africa with Vince came to an end. Our last stop was in Mbabane, Swaziland, and all my travel companions had different directions they were now heading. Charles was travelling to Zimbabwe. Vince's brother was flying home to England, and Vince, without telling anyone, took off with the car to see a girl in Cape Town.

For me, it was time to continue with the rest of my African adventure.

After almost three months in South Africa, I felt as though I'd finally seen and explored it properly. I don't feel that I have been to England; I've only been to London. I haven't been to the Netherlands; I've been to Amsterdam. The same can be said about Greece, the Czech Republic, and Austria. I've only spent time in some of their cities.

However, this wasn't the case in South Africa. I'd had a proper chance to explore. I could move on with a sense of satisfaction.

I contemplated heading into Mozambique from Swaziland and then travelling up the east coast of Africa. However, with my plane ticket to Windhoek sitting in my wallet and not wanting to waste it, I decided to head back to Cape Town. I wanted to take my time and retrace my steps through places that I wished I had stayed longer.

Specifically, I wanted to spend more time in Chintsa.

Although I saw some truly beautiful parts of the country and stayed in some amazing backpackers, *Smuggler's Cove,* situated in a part of South Africa known as the Wild Coast, was hands-down my favourite spot. In fact, it was my favourite place that I'd seen anywhere on my travels.

I journeyed from Mbabane to Durban, where I got my tongue pierced, then quickly hopped on a bus destined for the tiny coastal village. When the bus drove down the bumpy dirt road entrance and the magical view of Chintsa Bay made its first appearance, I knew that I had made a wise decision. *Smuggler's Cove* was just the place to put my feet up and chill out for a couple of weeks.

I needed to rest both my body and mind.

Smuggler's Cove was ideal to do just that.

The hostel complex was quite large, and it spread out across a lush, forested hillside. The bungalows, breakfast house and main bar blended magically into the indigenous bush as if camouflaged by Mother Nature. There was also the endless beach at its doorstep. Having come from the ridiculously packed beaches of Tenerife, the infinite amount of sand guaranteed that I would have enough space to relax in privacy. The place had tons to do. There were free activities, tours, surf schools and an amazing bar. But if you chose to do nothing, not only were there countless places to hide, but the staff didn't hassle you one way or another. If you wanted to spend two weeks sitting on the beach, resting and thinking, it was fine with them.

In a nutshell, there was loads to do or nothing to do.

That was exactly what I needed.

My body was understandably tired from the past two months of travelling. It had been an incredible but hectic trip across this beautiful land whose diversity was beyond compare.

One has to look no further than South Africa's 11 official languages to fully appreciate the variety this country has to offer. I find this remarkable considering Canadians struggle with only two. When you further consider the countless tribes and the varying histories of the South African people, it is easy to understand why South Africa is considered the "Rainbow Nation."

In addition, South Africa has an environmental multiplicity that is equally captivating. The country possesses pristine beaches, subtropical jungles, winding rivers, dry savannas, forests, deserts, rugged coastlines and mountains.

What was truly amazing was how fast the scenery would change. If I fell asleep in the car for an hour, I would wake to a completely different landscape and could have believed we were in a different country.

Yet, it was South Africa's diversity of activities that really had my body in need of some rest and relaxation. Within the space of a few months, I'd partied in Cape Town, broke a promise to my mom and survived the world's highest bungee jump off Bloukrans Bridge (216m), witnessed a herd of several hundred ostrich being shepherded down the highway, hiked around rocky peninsulas, climbed through caves and saw ganja plantations in the heart of the Transkei. I'd gone on game drives and glimpsed all of the magnificent beasts that adorned my South African money. I cruised up rivers in search of crocodiles and hippos. I'd climbed Mount Sibebe, which is the second biggest rock on the planet, jumped off waterfalls and swam in the powerful Indian Ocean.

There was no question. I needed to rest my body.

I also needed to rest my mind. Despite the advantage of travelling in a car, spending that much time in close proximity with three strangers can test one's patience, as it did in my case several times. We were very different people who were exploring South Africa for very different reasons. Don't get me wrong. I loved the trip. Getting bumped off my flight and meeting Vince was the best piece of luck I'd had on my travels. I had a great time with the guys, but after two months, I needed some space.

In addition to space, I also needed time to process everything that I had learned and observed during my time in South Africa as well as the 10 months that I had been travelling away from Canada.

It didn't take long sitting on the beach to conclude that I had made some inexperienced and ill-advised choices along the way.

Beginning my trip in Glasgow, for example, could have been better researched. Blowing through my savings on airplanes and rounds of Guinness was uneconomical, and working in Tenerife among gangsters was not the safest of living environments. Nevertheless, these mishaps were important lessons. And at the end of the day, I was able to further add to my education about the world. This made my mistakes worthwhile.

I proved to myself that I had an ability to adapt, improvise and overcome.

All things considered, I attributed my finely tuned survival instinct and the ability to "jump ship at whim," to travelling alone.

Without question, my decision to tackle the planet by myself was the best choice I made. Travelling alone allowed me to do the runner from Brian in Glasgow. Travelling alone allowed me to follow Stacey to Prague. Travelling alone led me to and, more importantly, away from Tenerife. Travelling alone put me in a position to get bumped off an airplane and into the extra seat on Vince's South African promotion run.

Travelling alone provided me with the opportunity to be selfish.

I almost cringe when I call myself selfish. It isn't a word I would normally consider a positive characteristic. According to the Coles English Dictionary, the word selfish is defined as "too concerned with one's own welfare or interests, with little or no thought or care for others."

However, if I'm honest, being selfish is exactly what I had been doing the previous 10 months.

I hadn't been concerned with the interests of others because there hadn't been others, such as family and friends, to be concerned about. Sure, I'd met tons of people on the road, and some were great. But most of them were simply passing through my life just as I was passing through theirs. Those people were probably being just as selfish on their own voyages as I was on mine. They too had little or no interest for others.

The people I had met on the road were just that—people I had met on the road.

Don't get me wrong. I don't want to give the impression that just because travellers are often solitary, they are self-centred, cold, lonely, secretive, miserable bastards. When I say that travellers "have little interest in others," I don't mean that we have little interest in knowing who a person is, where they are from, where they've been or where they are going. What I'm implying is that travellers' selfishness is based on making decisions regarding their own travels. They go where they want, and they go for their own reasons.

I'd like to further clarify that my selfishness wasn't about taking advantage of others. Rather, it was a selfishness that focused on the development and understanding of who I am and what I wanted in life. I wasn't hurting anybody. I wasn't stealing or hanging people out to dry. I wasn't stopping anybody from doing what he wanted to do. Everybody is entitled to his own freedom, and I'm included in that.

I used to think I knew what the word freedom meant, but it wasn't until I began my travels that I actually understood it. I've been told my whole life that I come from a "free country." We're a nation that isn't under the thumb of a foreign dictator, and we're a place where beliefs and ideas can be freely expressed. However, with our affiliation to the United States, governmental constraints and the blinding power of the media, I'm not sure how much "freedom" we actually have. Commitment and responsibilities such as families, friends, jobs, bills and debts are forms of chainless constraint. We are willing slaves to the system.

As a result, Canadians, unlike Australians and people from many other countries, find it very difficult to drop everything and go.

Despite the financial freedom to explore the planet, many North Americans are restricted by a mental barrier. They are almost phobic about abandoning the safety of a Canadian life and escaping the velvet rut. We are seduced into thinking this is the only way of life and that the alternatives aren't worthwhile.

Whether the desire to explore the world had been quashed by family, friends, work, the government or society as a whole, it is often difficult to reject the velvet rut and experience what the rest of the world has to offer. We are afraid to give true freedom a chance in case we lose what we already secured.

To be brutally honest, I was terrified as well.

Leaving Canada was the most difficult choice I ever had to make. Yet once I made the decision, everything else came almost naturally. When I began my travels, I realized it was the first time in my life that I was truly free. It was like being born and raised in prison. I believed that was how life was supposed to be. Then all of a sudden, I was released and tasted actual freedom for the first time.

For this Canadian ex-con, the flavour of freedom was delicious.

I don't mean to sound like a hypocrite. I'm fully aware that despite my criticisms, Canada was a great place to grow up. I know I was extremely fortunate to have been provided with opportunities of which many kids on the planet could only dream. If it weren't for my Canadian upbringing, education and prospects, I wouldn't have been in the position to travel the world and compare and properly assess where I'm from.

I am fully aware of the irony. But so what? The entirety of my travels have been dripping in irony, and frankly, I love it.

Of course, there are downsides to travelling alone. Being a solo traveller, I don't have the unconditional support system of my trusted family and friends to watch my back. I always have to keep my wits about me, or as my dad would say, keep my head up. Con artists, the good ones anyhow, won't show any inclination that they are trying to scam you.

Another downside to travelling alone is that I won't have anyone to reminisce about my adventures with later in life. There won't be any opportunity to sit back and talk about the once upon a time travel days. There won't be anybody to say to, "Hey, do you remember that night in Amsterdam?" All the memories will be my own. In fact, even recounting my tales to my closest friends would be pointless. I can't imagine they would be too interested because they would have zero point of reference to the story, people and setting. Not to mention describing every detail of every aspect of the tale would probably come off as boring if not arrogant.

Mind you, these drawbacks really aren't drawbacks at all. Having to look out for my own ass has fine-tuned my ability to assess the character of the countless people I've met on the road. The minor setbacks have also helped strengthen my independence. I spent most of my life being spoiled. With my mom cooking dinner and doing my laundry, I was the true definition of a "mama's boy." The proof that I could survive on my own was a beneficial and necessary lesson for me.

And as far as not having people to share my memories with, I'll just have to wait and see how it all actually unfolds. Regardless, one's memories are one's own. I know that wherever I end up, I'll be able to sit back and smile remembering my adventures.

Who knows? I have no idea where I'll eventually settle in life and who that will be with. I've met hundreds of people travelling from the four corners of the planet, and one of them just might end up being a neighbour. In fact, I've met more people the past 10 months than I had in the past 10 years.

This is one of the biggest misconceptions about being a lone traveller—that you are alone.

I hate to break it to you, but you are never alone.

Let me clarify. You are never alone unless you choose to be.

This planet is packed with a few billion humans. There are always people around. Whether they are locals or travellers, they are always there. In fact, it's very difficult to find yourself completely alone. There have been many times on my trip when I would have loved absolute solitude, but I found it next to impossible to find a quiet place to chill.

When I did find a peaceful escape from the distractions of others, I discovered that I quite enjoyed the time to myself. Those moments of seclusion have been some of the few times in my life that I have been able to sit and be deeply reflective.

So as it turned out, my concern that I'd be alone on my travels actually became one of my greatest pleasures. Okay, there have been times when I missed my family and friends. But I realized after several phone calls home that they weren't going anywhere and neither was their love. I'd almost bet that I'd be able to find my mates at the *Sergeant's Pump*, our local pub, whenever I decided to return to Ottawa and that I'd get hugs from all around.

I realized that loneliness, like all emotions, is a state of mind and can be controlled. If I wanted to be alone, I could be. If I didn't, then I could strike up a conversation with the person sitting next to me. It might lead somewhere very interesting.

In one particular instance, chatting with a stranger led me across South Africa to Swaziland.

And in this particular instance, while sitting on the 17-kilometre beach in Chintsa, chatting with a stranger provided me with some inside information that could lead to a job.

Well, she wasn't a total stranger. Kate was the first person I met and connected with at *Smuggler's Cove*. My tongue was extremely swollen from having it pierced in Durban the day before my Chintsa return, and as a result, I wasn't talking with too many people. Kate and her boyfriend Simon, who had scored me some weed, were really the only people to whom I subjected my garbled conversation. In the end, Kate provided me with some insider information that would ignite an amazing ride.

She told me that the barman was planning on leaving *Smuggler's Cove* and that there would be an opening on the staff. She suggested that if I was keen on working, then I should talk to Scott, who was the son of the family who owned *Smuggler's Cove*.

I gave the idea some thought.

For the first time in a very long time, even before I left Canada, I finally felt at home. I felt welcome in all of South Africa, but I felt particularly comfortable in Chintsa. Whether it was the location, the climate or the people who owned the hostel, the extremely friendly and generous Crosby family, I knew there was something magical about *Smuggler's Cove*. Because I just re-entered South Africa from Swaziland, I had a brand new three-month tourist visa in my passport, and my flight to Windhoek was valid for another nine months.

I had the time.

Although I still had money from slaving in Tenerife, I knew it would eventually run out. I would inevitably have to find work somewhere on the African continent. *Smuggler's Cove* seemed an idyllic place to live and save. It was a great job, surrounded by great people and set amid a great lifestyle. And depending on how long I stayed, it might be possible to put enough aside to finance my travels the rest of the way to Cairo.

I had the economic motivation.

At the end of the day, I had loved every minute of my time and education in South Africa. I saw no reason why that would change. One of the promises I had made to myself before I began my travels was that I would spend as much time in a place as I wanted. I wasn't on an itinerary. There was no need to rush through anywhere if I was still enjoying it. I knew that South Africa had much more to offer and much more for me to discover.

Ultimately, I had the freedom to do what I wanted.

I wanted to stay.

I found Scott the next morning and told him if they needed anybody to work their bar that I'd be more than interested in the opportunity. With a touch of obvious reservation, Scott said he would discuss it with the family and let me know.[1] Despite being a smiling mute the past fortnight, I must have made a good impression on the Crosby family because Scott got back to me the next day and offered me the job as the barman at *Smuggler's Cove*. I, of course, happily accepted.

I could once again unpack my bag.

I believed it was that African pull that Sabrina had warned me about that was making it next to impossible to leave South Africa. It can also be argued that this incredible energy bumped me off a flight and led me back to Chintsa at a time when a job was available. I presumed this powerful African force had put me in the right place at the right time.

Whatever the reason, I understood that it wasn't my time to leave this exceptional country. I obviously wasn't finished with South Africa. Or maybe South Africa wasn't finished with me.

Time would tell.

---

1. As I would later learn, Scott's hesitation had nothing to do with my wardrobe. Although surf shorts, a T-shirt and being barefoot won't get you a job in most places, it was haute fashion on the beach in the Wild Coast. No, his reservation had everything to do with being unaware that I recently had my tongue pierced and couldn't talk or eat. Up until that point, he knew me as the fasting Canadian mute who walked around in red-lensed sunglasses, wore a hemp hat and who smiled a lot. So in addition to his image of me, when the first words he heard me speak sounded like I had marbles in my mouth, it came as no surprise that he was wary of offering me a job. I'd have been wary too.

A black and white photo cannot begin to capture the beauty of a sunrise over the Indian Ocean. If you can visualize a splattering of purples, reds and oranges painting the sky and reflecting off the water, then you can appreciate the spectacular view that I had from the warmth and comfort of my bed in Chintsa. It was not a bad way to start the day.

14

MONDAY

JULY

Sunrises are just as glorious as sunsets. However, one of the big problems with sunrises is the time that they insist on rising.

I've never been a morning person. Actually, I'm a miserable bastard first thing in the morning. I always have been, and I probably always will be. Although I may desire to see a sunrise and may even ask to be woken up, one must be a brave soul to consider interrupting my slumber. If I should happen to wake up at that godawful time of the morning, I guarantee that I will not be in a sociable mood.

The other issue I had with catching the sunrise was that I was never in a location to actually see a worthwhile daybreak. Growing up in a city, I had suburbia and buildings serving as a weak excuse for a view. If I wanted a natural, unobstructed vista of the sun breaking the horizon, I would have had to actually get up even earlier, get dressed and physically "go somewhere."

Consequently, because of location, bad timing, my grumpiness and others' justified fear of waking me, I slept through most of the sunrises in my lifetime and did not have a chance to truly appreciate their beauty and inspirational powers.

In spite of these factors, this particular morning in Chintsa, I watched yet another sunrise. It was spectacular. The deep reds, oranges, pinks and purples that coloured the sky as the sun cracked the horizon of the Indian Ocean cannot be justly described with words. Sounds such as "oooohhhh" and "ahhhhh" are probably more appropriate and to the point.

Mind you, the true beauty of this sunrise, as was the case with all sunrises I had witnessed in Chintsa, was that I was able to watch Mother Nature showcase her masterpiece from my bed.

To say that I landed on my feet at *Smuggler's Cove* would be a gross understatement.

Not only did I land on my feet, but I landed in a comfy double bed with an ocean view.

When a new member of the *Smuggler's Cove* crew moved into the staff cottage they began on the bottom rung of seniority. The person who had been employed at *Smuggler's Cove* the longest was entitled to the double bedroom. The next two on the rotation shared the twin room, and whoever was left fought over the lounge that had next to zero privacy. Therefore, when I first joined the *Cove's* crew, I was assigned the living room couch as a bedroom.

Nevertheless, within three weeks, there was a changing of the *Cove's* guard, which left me sitting atop the staff castle. I moved straight from the lounge into the double bedroom. It was a room with complete privacy, space and, above all, an unbelievable view of the Indian Ocean, which was a vista that was best appreciated from bed.

My new-found comforts now put me in a position to kill two birds with one stone. I was in a beautiful location to watch the sunrise, and I didn't have to subject others to the terror also known as my morning mood.

Now all I had to do was wake up.

This dilemma was, fortunately, taken care of thanks to the aging process. As I've gotten older, I've noticed that I have to wake up early in the morning to take a piss … desperately take a piss. Not that long ago, I could sleep through any pressure my bladder imposed on me. Now, in spite of my fatigue or the previous night's party and subsequent hangover, I have to leave the warmth of my bed to take a squirt. I would have found this bodily necessity an extreme annoyance if it weren't for my morning piss coinciding with Mother Nature waking up.

After a quick flush, I would get back under the warm blankets, prop my back against the pillow and watch the brilliant colours decorate the sky. Once the sun had breached the horizon and the colours faded into a vibrant blue, I would slide all the way back under the covers and fall easily and peacefully into a blissful sleep. An hour or so later, the sun would reach a point where its beams would enter the room and tickle my face, providing me with a gentle and warm reawakening.

Life was good.

I don't think I'll ever be a "morning person." I'll never be all chirpy and singing in the shower. In spite of this, adding a sunrise to my daily routine had mellowed my mood considerably. It was extremely difficult to have a bad day after watching Mother Nature do her thing.

Mind you, this serene and peaceful beginning to my day was the complete opposite of my bustling and hectic nights. I was living the life of a professional party maniac. My bar job at the backpackers was undoubtedly one-of-a-kind. It was a one-man show in the pub, which meant it was my job to serve drinks, play the music, keep the vibe and be responsible for all the hammered, rowdy backpackers crammed in the bar every night. What made the bar particularly unique was that it was located in the bush. It was essentially in the middle of nowhere, which meant, unlike city pubs, there weren't any rules, and there certainly wasn't anybody to enforce them.

As a barman, I could drink and smoke behind the bar. This was restricted in most establishments, but it was a privilege that I took full advantage of here in Chintsa. However, the most appealing aspect of my job was my clientele. It was this clientele that ultimately led to my nightly festivities. These strictly international travellers tended to be, on the whole, very chilled out, open-minded, young men and women who were ready to party for no other reason than they were on the other side of the world and away from their homes. There wasn't any grief, stress or aggression within the walls of the pub. This was another glaring difference between this and most bars I'd been to. Everybody simply wanted to have a great time before ambling down the hill to bed.

I was no different. I was a Canadian living and working in South Africa. I had every right to celebrate. In fact, I had more reason. I was getting paid to party.

My closing time was when the last person wanted to go home. There were many nights that turned into mornings sitting on the pub deck, gazing into the Indian Ocean, watching and listening to the world wake up.

It didn't matter if it was Friday, Wednesday or Sunday night. Every night was a bender. The crowd may have changed, but their energy and desire to party remained consistent.

Life was very good.

Following Mother Nature's gentle and motivating awakening, I would combat any signs of a hangover with a greasy breakfast and my morning spliff. Assuming I didn't regurgitate my bacon and eggs, in which case I would hit the sack for another couple of hours, I would commence my daytime responsibilities. This primarily consisted of re-stocking the bar in preparation for the upcoming night's binge. This task was normally accomplished within an hour, leaving me the rest of the afternoon to do as I pleased.

However, every now and then, my afternoons lounging at the pool or sitting on the beach were interrupted by other little chores or responsibilities. Some days I had to unload the booze delivery. Some days I had to help with dinner. And some days we had, as rare as they were, staff meetings.

Staff meetings are something I normally despise. I understand the importance of everybody being on the same page, but it has been my experience, regardless of the job, that staff meetings are a waste of time, and they painfully drag on. Back in Ottawa, the insurance brokerage I worked for conducted a staff meeting in a stuffy conference room first thing every Monday morning. I became an expert at sleeping with my eyes open and concealing the mini-head nods.

In Chintsa, staff meetings were a little different. There was still a lot of oxygen wasted rehashing points and discussing irrelevant details, but the massive distinction between this meeting and any other I had been subjected to was the location and time of the gathering. That particular day's meeting was to begin at two in the afternoon underneath the sun on the deck of the Crosby's house with the Indian Ocean as the backdrop.

It was definitely better than a conference room.

The downside was that it was easy to become distracted by the beautiful setting. This meeting was no different. My daydreaming took me out into the ocean.

Then something caught my eye.

There was a mysterious, large ripple in the bay that grabbed my attention. Upon further inspection, I concluded that the ripple was, in fact, a pod of dolphins. From where I was sitting, the pod appeared to be enormous and swimming just on the other side of the break.

There are many things I hope to experience in my lifetime: jumping out of a plane, trekking the Himalayas and viewing Earth from outer space to name a few. However, near the top of my wish list was swimming in the water with dolphins. To be clear, I'm not talking about frolicking in a tank at some marine park with trained dolphins that do back flips and shoot through hoops on request. Rather, my desire was to be in the open sea with wild dolphins.

Shortly after my arrival at *Smuggler's Cove*, while sitting on the beach, I enviously watched surfers play in the waves with half a dozen dolphins. The surfers and dolphins were sharing the waves. Together they cut left and right as if the display was choreographed. As much as I wanted to be out with them, the dolphins were too far out for me to swim safely. As I sat there watching man and beast play, I vowed to learn how to surf for no other reason than to be able to swim with dolphins one day. Unfortunately, learning to surf was a tough gig. By the time of the staff meeting, I still wasn't anywhere near talented enough to paddle out to the pod.

Still, they were so close.

Then I remembered that Grant was on the beach. Grant was the *Cove's* surf school instructor and the true definition of beach bum. He had a passion for dolphins that surpassed even mine. I knew that his surf lessons were ending and that he had his two-man sea kayak stored halfway down the hill.

I needed to get out of this meeting.

I looked at Mike, who was conducting the discussion. He was knowingly smiling at me. As a true lover of the ocean, he too had spotted the pod of dolphins and knew what I was thinking. On more than one occasion, I had expressed to Mike my desire to be in the water with dolphins. A surfer and champion wave skier, he had been lucky enough to experience this sensation on numerous occasions. He knew the rush far too well.[1]

We had already covered the bar on the meeting's agenda, so there was really no need for me to stay. Mike knew I wanted to bail. I knew it, and he knew I knew it. From his cheeky grin, I knew he was messing with my head and building up my anticipation. I felt like a kid on Christmas morning waiting to get the go ahead from my folks to start tearing into the gifts. Mike winked at me and said, "Have fun, bru."

Being dressed in baggies, I was ready to go. I sprinted down the hill and onto the beach to get Grant. A bit breathless, I managed to spit out that there were dolphins awaiting our company in his kayak. He didn't take too much convincing. He was amped. Hoping to catch up with the dolphins, we raced back up the hill, grabbed the kayak and ran back down to the sea. However, a good 15 minutes had passed since I first spotted the pod in the meeting.

It was possible that the dolphins were gone.

The swell was big, and we were struggling to get through the white water and over the first break to the back line where I thought the dolphins were. From our sea-level position, it was impossible to see over the rolling waves. We had no idea if the dolphins were still around.

There was the strong possibility that they were long gone.

However, I wasn't going to give up.

---

1. Mike and I had attempted to "catch" dolphins on a previous occasion. He was talking to me as I was stocking the bar. I looked out the window and saw a pod that was virtually swimming on the shore. Swimming out to them was possible. The two of us sprinted down the beach and into the sea, yet the dolphins had vanished. I realize this is a bit anti-climatic, but the point is that I tried. That I could even attempt to swim out to a roaming pod of dolphins blew my mind. How many people can say that they can look out of the window at their place of work, spot dolphins, leave what they are doing and try to swim out to them? I would guess it's not too many.

We persevered, we battled, and we were knocked back by the powerful waves and white water. Yet we were determined not to quit. After what seemed like an eternity, we finally managed to overcome the first break, and our kayak came down smack dab in the middle of several hundred dolphins.

We were surrounded. They were everywhere.

Grant and I began laughing and screaming at the magnificent sight.

The pod seemed to have a purpose. They would swim a kilometre or so, turn around as a group and then swim back in the opposite direction. Grant thought they were hunting and feeding. They could have been making a ham sandwich for all I cared. What mattered was that these amazing creatures were all around me. In fact, they were so close that I could actually stare into their eyes. Maybe I should say that they were so close that *they* could stare into *my* eyes. It really felt as though the dolphins were checking us out. Their curiosity seemed as keen as ours. They would surface a foot from the kayak, give us a quick glance and then disappear beneath the water.

Making eye contact in close proximity with an intelligent yet wild creature is a mind-blowing experience. By staring into their eyes, I felt as though I had made a connection with nature. I realized that there wasn't too much difference between these wonderful animals and myself. We were both living creatures, and we were essentially neighbours sharing this remarkable chunk of rock called Earth, which was a place we both considered home.

The exhilaration can only be compared to, and I hate to say it, sex.

However, much like getting caught in the act by your girlfriend's parents, my joy quickly turned to panic when I heard Grant shout, "Oh fuck, bru. Paddle … PADDLE!"

My first thought was shark … big shark. Part of the reason I was hesitant about swimming far out to sea with dolphins had nothing to do with my swimming abilities, which were fairly strong. I was tentative because I had heard, "Where there are dolphins, there are sharks," once too often. This may have been an "ocean myth," but I had heard a couple of tales first-hand about people being in the water when dolphins had, in a way, come to the rescue.[2]

---

2. I once met a French guy who had told me that he had been surfing when he saw the unmistakable and terrifying shape of a shark's fin carving through the water. He said at that exact moment, two dolphins appeared from nowhere and began circling his surfboard. He said they were so close that they would actually brush against his board. They swam next to him and seemed to protect him as he paddled back to the beach and safety. He told the story with such sincerity and passion that I couldn't help believing him.

Whether dolphins were protecting people from sharks or whether dolphins and sharks both hunted the same prey was irrelevant. Enough people had stated their association as fact for me to be somewhat cautious. Not to mention, it was the Indian Ocean, which had an abundance of sharks.

In addition, I knew that Grant was more shit-scared of sharks than I. His phobia was so severe that he didn't even like to say the word "shark." So when Grant screamed, "Oh fuck, bru. Paddle," my first thought was that we were about to become lunch.

Being in the front of the kayak, I wasn't able to turn around and see how big the beast was. I was too fearful that I might tip us into the monster's awaiting jaws. Although it wasn't much, I felt a million times safer on this piece of fiberglass as opposed to treading water with my appetizing legs. I shouted over my shoulder and asked from what direction the creature was making his attack.

"It's not a sh-sh-shark. Look at the fucking wave!"

I barely had a second. But in that second, I realized we had been so captivated with the dolphins, we hadn't noticed that our kayak had drifted into the oncoming wave's breaking point. This particular wave, which was massive, was sucking us up and over.

The angle of the wave and gravity launched me from the craft. The last thing I saw before the wall of water drove me beneath the surface was Grant clinging to the back of the kayak as it was catapulted into the air by the mammoth wave.

I was dragged underwater and tossed like a rag doll.

The moment before we flipped, dolphins had surrounded us. As far as I knew, they hadn't gone anywhere, and they should still be there. In fact, they were everywhere. They were swimming all around me. I could feel them swoop by, skilfully avoiding my floating body. The dolphins swam under my legs, over my head and past my outstretched arms. Feeling their energy race past me was overwhelming. When I surfaced, I was facing the oncoming pod. Countless fins ducked and dived past my bobbing body.

I stuck my head back underwater to watch the grey blurs dash past.

Although the shadowy outlines of the darting dolphins were spectacular, it was the noise of these creatures that had me locked in a state of amazement.

The sound wasn't your typical dolphin noise, and it was not at all what I was expecting. It was nothing like the high-pitched, chirpy banter on "Flipper." Flipper was only one dolphin. Beneath me, there were 300 or so Flippers communicating. The sound was deafening. The best I can describe the noise would be to compare it to a bowl of Rice Crispy cereal the size of a swimming pool. Then imagine the "snap, crackle and pop" that it would create when you poured milk onto the big bastard. That is the sound of 300 dolphins.

Grant, who had miraculously held on to the kayak, snapped me out of my trance and got me back onto the craft.

We paddled with the mammals for another hour.

It was three o'clock on a Monday afternoon.

I noticed the time and day because, like many other moments during my travels, I realized how fortunate I was to be experiencing what I was experiencing. I also thought of what I would have been doing if I hadn't built up the courage to leave Canada.

At that moment, it was nine in the morning in North America. Most of my Canadian friends were just arriving at work, or worse, they were stressing because they were stuck in traffic and late for work. Either way, they were at the very beginning of the five-day stretch.

At that moment, it was three in the afternoon in most of Europe and the United Kingdom. These friends were probably staring at the clock and thinking, "Damn. This is another long-ass Monday that doesn't ever want to end."

At that moment, it was eleven at night in Australia. My friends down under were perhaps getting ready for bed after a long, tough, draining Monday on the job. It was feasible that as they drifted off to sleep, they were thinking, "Fuck. I've got four more days of this shit before the weekend."

At that moment in time, I was swimming with dolphins in the wild.

At that moment in time, I was living out a dream.

Life was very, very good.

Dolphins swimming in Chintsa Bay a few hundred metres from the beach and my South African home. Regardless of the numbers, it's hard to beat the natural rush one gets when seeing even one dolphin in the wild.

15

A TRANSKEI BUY

SEPTEMBER

I was awoken by the sound of roosters, which served as the Transkei's alarm clock.

There wasn't a snooze button for these persistent buzzers, so I got up and stumbled into the kitchen to put on the kettle. As I waited for the water to boil, I grabbed a few healthy buds from the bowl of weed on the table and rolled a joint. With a coffee and spliff in hand, I strolled to the top of the hill, which dropped steeply onto the rugged shoreline of the Wild Coast.

I sat down, took a sip of coffee, lit my spliff and waited.

I didn't wait long.

A pod of about 20 dolphins came into sight a couple of kilometres away. The section of the coastline that I sat upon was on the edge of a tectonic plate, and as a result, it had extremely deep water close to land. Therefore, the marine life often swam close to shore. This was the case with this quickly approaching pod. In addition, sitting on the edge of a cliff provided me with a vantage point to stare down upon the dolphins. These creatures were currently displaying their skills by surfing the last breaking wave before the shore.[1]

Since my close encounter with dolphins, I felt a bond with them. It was not the trendy kind of connection where I rush out and have a dolphin tattooed on my body. Rather, it was an inspirational relationship, which motivated me to seek their presence and energy whenever possible. As far as I was concerned, where I was currently sitting was the best place in all South Africa to dolphin watch.

---

1. They say that dolphins are reincarnated surfers. One has to make some religious assumptions in order to believe this divination, but after watching dolphins surf with grace, expertise and enthusiasm, conversion is a possibility.

This was how most of my days in the village of Mpande began: sitting atop a cliff, drinking coffee, smoking a spliff and watching pods of dolphins surf the massive waves. The overwhelming energies absorbed from this type of start ensured that a blissful afternoon and evening would ensue. Today, however, I was replenishing my reserves of caffeine, THC and Mother Nature so I would be in shape to embark upon my mission.

Maybe "mission" isn't the right word. A mission implies hard work. Although I had a long walk ahead of me, my task would be beautiful, educational and inspirational. In truth, I was excited about the undertaking and couldn't wait to get started.

One of the most pleasant surprises about South Africa had been discovered on my third day in the country. There seemed to be a lot of weed floating around *The Traveller* in Cape Town. Everybody seemed to have a stash and was more than generous in sharing the social plant. However, I preferred to be in control of my ganja. I wasn't a fan of patiently waiting for someone else to skin up then swooping in to mooch a toke or two. So I asked the barman at the backpackers' pub if he could score me some weed.

"Ya, bru. How much do you want?"

I had no idea how much weed cost in South Africa. Being a tad wary of spending too much and not wanting to sound completely naïve, I confidently asked for 50 rands worth, which was equivalent to 10 Canadian bucks. I couldn't imagine South African weed costing more than Canadian gear, which was 10 bucks a gram. One gram would barely last me the night, but I figured, to be on the safe side, I'd start low. If the weed was quality, I'd buy more the next day.

The barman came back about 15 minutes later with a clear, plastic bag full of ganja. It held about 20 grams worth. It was the most weed I'd seen in a very long time. I gave the guy a curious look. I asked if all that was for me. He nodded that it was. There had obviously been a miscommunication. He had brought me way too much. I apologized and clarified that I wanted *50* rands worth.

"Hey, bru, that bankie is lank packed. That is a lekker deal for 50 rand," he said defensively.

I got the impression he believed I was challenging the amount and that I thought he was ripping me off. In actuality, it was the complete opposite. I thought I was ripping him off by only paying 50 rand for such an obscene amount of ganja. I expected a bag of weed that size to cost at least 10 times the price. It certainly would have back home or anywhere else that I'd travelled so far.

I took the big bag of weed.

I was dumbstruck.

When I first arrived in South Africa, I never contemplated that marijuana might be cheap. In fact, with the prospect of cold showers and muggings dominating my thoughts before my arrival, the possibility of getting stoned in South Africa was never even a vague consideration.

Once again, my lack of expectations had led to another pleasant surprise. Not only did South Africa have an abundance of quality weed, but this potent bud was dirt cheap.

I can, at times, smoke enough weed to subdue a small elephant, so the revelation that marijuana was inexpensive was yet another factor that made South Africa that much more alluring.[2]

I encountered the next size available when we arrived in the Transkei. "Arms" are tubes of compressed weed that are then wrapped and sealed with newspaper. The length and width of the ganja cylinder is about the same as a forearm, hence the name. The quarter pound package of marijuana would set you back a meagre 150 rand. When Vince and I first visited Port St. Johns in the Transkei, the part of the country famous for its ganja, we toured several marijuana plantations.

We walked away with an arm each.

We had so much weed that it was humanly impossible to smoke it all, although we tried throughout the rest of South Africa. The morning we drove from St. Lucia, our last South African destination, into Swaziland, we rolled continuously, and we smoked throughout the two-hour journey to the Swazi border. As hard as we tried, we couldn't get through it all. Five kilometres from the border, we still had about four ounces left. There wasn't a chance in hell that we were going to try and smuggle the plant across the border, especially when we knew that the legendary and equally cheap "Swazi Gold" was waiting on the other side.

I did the only thing I could.

I threw the remaining weed out the window.

If I was at home and lost even a half gram of ganja, I received a slap upside the head from my mates and rightly so. In Canada, weed is hideously expensive. To lose half a gram would be depressing. Yet, here in South Africa, due to the cost

---

2. As I continued my travels across South Africa, I learned that weed wasn't sold by weight as it was at home. Grams, eights, quarters and even ounces don't exist in South Africa. Instead, you asked for what the weed comes packaged in. For example, in Cape Town I bought a "bankie." Being the smallest and most common quantity, the three-quarter ounce bank coin bag was the most popular and convenient for travellers. For most, that amount of dope was enormous and more than sufficient to satisfy one's habits. I was going through bankies as if they were going out of style.

and availability, throwing ganja out of the car window as we approached the Swazi border was not only the correct and safe decision, but it was also incredibly fun.

It was a novelty.

In every single guest house that I visited in South Africa, there were smokers. There was always somebody to help score the weed, and many of the hostels even had designated ganja-smoking areas. I'm not suggesting that every traveller visiting South Africa was a smoker. However, there was a common level of tolerance and acceptance that created a relaxed setting.

Smuggler's Cove wasn't much different. Although smoking dope wasn't officially condoned, a blind eye was turned to the countless backpackers and staff, namely me, who enjoyed a toke by the pool, on the beach or as the evening's festivities got going in the pub.

I had access to plenty of Arms in Chintsa, yet I rarely bought the local product. I am a bit of a ganja snob, and the Chintsa weed, although cheap, wasn't the best quality. There was the added motivation of buying weed elsewhere because I lived right near the section of South Africa renowned by ganja smokers worldwide … the Transkei.

Most white South Africans that I had met had never been to the Transkei. In fact, many warned me to avoid the Transkei at all costs. They even said to drive around the massive province in order to avoid the dangerous land. There seemed to be a lot of fear and apprehension when it came to the Transkei.

During apartheid, the government relocated millions of the black population to designated "homelands" across the country. Although they were supposed to be self-sufficient and self-governing, homelands were simply apartheid's way of keeping the blacks away from the whites. They were on their own with no access to white South African resources, which resulted in massive poverty and all subsequent maladies. The Transkei was one of those homelands. In the eyes of the world, the Transkei was a part of South Africa, but as far as apartheid South Africa was concerned, the Transkei was a different country. South Africans had to show their passports to enter or leave the Transkei, and to this day, the empty immigration office is still present on the edge of the Kei River, which is the border of the Transkei.

Today, the Transkei is a part of South Africa, but many white South Africans continue to believe that the area is a dangerous, barbaric and backward land.

How wrong they are.

What most of the white South Africans failed to realize was that they had "dumped" the black population into some of the most stunning landscape that

I'd seen anywhere in the world. However, it was more than just the unbelievable scenery that captivated one's mind when arriving deep into the heart of the Transkei. There was a sort of strength. Despite the overwhelming poverty, the beauty and raw energy of the environment was obvious, formidable and almost indescribable.

Part of me understands why the white South Africans fear the Transkei. The local people, the Amapondo, are an extremely proud and strong tribe with a rich history. I don't doubt that if someone entered their land today with the attitudes, prejudice and fears from yesteryear, that individual would be quickly identified and harshly dealt with. However, it was my experience that if you visited the Transkei with an open mind and heart, then the friendliness and hospitality was some of the best the planet has to offer.

This section of the country is truly special and extremely addictive. One could spend a lifetime exploring the Kei and its magical coastline, and many do. There is a condition in the Transkei known as "Pondo Fever." Pondo Fever isn't a disease but a state of mind. Pondo Fever is the condition that simultaneously drains and replenishes one's energy. Pondo Fever is the force that brings people back to the Kei or never allows them to leave. This wonderful affliction was much like the African pull Sabrina mentioned and I knew existed. But in the case of Pondo Fever, it strictly referred to those stuck in the Transkei.

I caught a serious dose of Pondo Fever when travelling through the Transkei with Vince, and I knew I would return to this stretch of land to further explore what it had to offer. Nevertheless, despite the Kei's endless beauty, I discovered one spot in particular that found its way into my heart and soul and kept bringing me back for more.

I initially discovered *The Kraal* when a Dutch friend, Robert, and I made a get-away from *Smuggler's Cove*. He had recently ended a six-year relationship with his girlfriend, and because his ex was currently employed at *Smuggler's Cove*, he felt he should leave Chintsa. Robert needed to clear his head and decided that he was going to take off for a few months and hike around the Drakensburg Mountains and then possibly travel to Zimbabwe. Worried about my friend, I decided to travel with him for the first leg of his journey. We decided to check out this eco-friendly, rustic and unique hostel situated in the Kei, which was a place that countless travellers had recommended.

It was a long, slow journey down the bumpy back roads to *The Kraal*. In fact, the last 20 kilometres took well over an hour. However, despite the difficulties of riding in the back of an overcrowded bakkie, both Robert and I suspected that we were being transported to somewhere very different and very special.[3]

The one thing that caught my eye was that people chose random spots on the roadside to sit and apparently do nothing. It was difficult to determine where they had come from or where they might be going. It was a very long walk from somewhere just to sit underneath a particular tree. However, this was exactly what many did all day long.

This sight made me smile.

It displayed an understanding of what it meant to stop and smell the roses. Whether it was to sit back and think, ponder, observe, reminisce, pontificate, debate or relax was irrelevant. Whether it was because they were old, unemployed or had nothing better to do was equally irrelevant. To me, that they took the time to stop wasn't irrelevant. One of my biggest concerns at home was that we really didn't stop to appreciate how good our lives were. We didn't take the time to let our minds disengage from the hectic pace of the velvet rut and enjoy a simple vista.

However, what I loved most about the drive through the hills and valleys was that, regardless of whom I passed, if I waved, they would wave back. In fact, this was one of my favourite observations throughout South Africa. It didn't matter if people were driving a car, walking down the road or sitting beneath a tree, my greeting was returned with a genuine wave and a genuine smile.

If I waved at strangers in the Western world, the reaction would be very different. More often than not, the response would be a hesitant "who was that" wave or possibly a much ruder gesture. Either way, I would wager that it wouldn't be friendly. For some reason, at home we have a hard time accepting that people can be naturally friendly without sinister, ulterior motives. For some misguided reason, we are suspicious of random acts of kindness.[4]

This wasn't the case in South Africa. A wave and smile are returned with a wave and smile, especially in the Transkei.

There was no question that Robert and I were being transported somewhere very different and very special.

After having our view obstructed by the thick forest that canopied the road, we finally arrived in the coastal village of Mpande, and the expansive Transkei shoreline left us awestruck. With kids chasing after us, waving and asking for sweets, we drove through the village and eventually up and over a steep hill. We looked down upon the much-anticipated hostel. With a secluded beach, subtrop-

---

3. A "bakkie" is what South Africans call a pick-up truck.
4. Don't believe me? Go ahead and try it for yourself. Wave to strangers and count how many genuine, friendly waves you receive in return.

ical jungle and a winding river as the backdrop, we gazed in amazement at the tiny backpackers, which itself was nestled into a natural amphitheatre that directly faced the ocean.

As far as location, on a scale from 1 to 10, *The Kraal* scored about 37.

It was 280 kilometres from Chintsa to Mpande, but this trip couldn't be measured in distance. It took four and a half hours to drive from place to place, but again, this voyage couldn't be measured by the time spent in a vehicle. The best way to describe the journey to *The Kraal* was saying it was like travelling back in time 100 years or more. I could stand in one spot in the village, turn 360 degrees and be hard pressed to find a single indicator of the year 1999. It could have been 1899 or 1799 as far as I could tell. There wasn't any electricity. There weren't any telephone lines. There were thatched huts made with mud. There was livestock grazing freely. There were women walking with buckets of water on their heads. There were countless kids laughing and playing with nothing but each other.

The village population, structure and lifestyle seemed to be locked in a simple, beautiful and traditional time.

The Kraal, to its credit, blended into the village perfectly. Built in the same traditional way as the rest of the Mpande, *The Kraal* didn't have modern amenities such as electricity or telephones. Other than being non-existent in Mpande, they weren't necessary. Dillon, the rather eccentric owner of *The Kraal*, took the simplicity one step further. If you were wearing a watch when you arrived, he made you take it off and locked it in the safe until you departed.

Time was irrelevant at *The Kraal*.

You ate when you were hungry, slept when you were tired and woke when you were awake.

It was that simple.

Despite his idiosyncrasies, Dillon had done an amazing job ensuring that his hostel didn't offend the locals in any way and that it remained consistent with the style and traditions of the village, environment and culture. After first receiving permission from the local chief, Dillon began building his backpackers in 1997. He learned the local language, Xhosa, which, by the time I met him, he spoke fluently. He employed local labour. He built a primary school for the community. When constructing *The Kraal*, if he had to transport wood from Village A to Village B to Village C, he would hire workers from all three communities.

As a result of his patience, hard work, respect and determination to follow a dream, Dillon had created in *The Kraal* something very rare and very special.

On my first day at *The Kraal*, I went exploring for the Jack Astor shipwreck. Over the years, hundreds of ships had succumbed to the awesome and unforgiving power of the Indian Ocean, and many of their steel skeletons remained visible. The hike took me along the rocky coast that suddenly turned into secluded beaches. The thick, lush jungle served as a continuous backdrop and further added to the sense of isolation. My walk was occasionally interrupted by dolphin watching or snacking on smoked mussels. The local kids would pull the mussels from the rock pools and cook them right on the beach. It doesn't get any fresher than that.

For me, the hike was extraordinary, but for the locals, it was just another typical Transkei day. At the end of the hike, I found myself sitting atop a cliff, staring down upon the dramatic shipwreck while pods of dolphins swam by. Southern right whales breached off in the distance. Two 10-year-old boys, who had joined my journey and guided me to the shipwreck, began to sing in Xhosa under the warm African sun.

I sat back and deeply inhaled my joint. I asked myself if life could be any better than this.

I couldn't know the answer for sure, but I felt as though I was on the right track to finding out. At that exact moment, many things came into perspective. The simplicity and happiness that I had witnessed during the past 24 hours in this peaceful and poor village made me question if we, in the Western world, really understood what was important in life.

Yeah, we may have electricity and running water in every home, but had we lost our sense of community?

Life was an exquisite gift, and I'd be damned if I was going to let it slip by while sitting in an office, watching the decades disappear and not knowing or caring who my neighbours were. Fuck that.

The fascination of the Transkei had imprinted itself on my soul.

To give you an idea of the Kei's power, let me tell you about what happened to my Dutch mate. When I had to go back to *Smuggler's Cove* after a couple of days, Robert decided to stay at *The Kraal* and ended up getting a job working with Dillon.

When I left him in Mpande, Robert, a Dutch computer programmer, looked ready to go on safari. He owned and wore khaki shorts, khaki shirts, khaki socks, khaki boots, and he even had the matching khaki hat. He looked like the poster boy for African safari adventures. When I found Robert again, a mere three weeks later, he had changed.

He had lost all of his "Crocodile Hunter" attire.

He had grown a beard, wore a sarong and was barefoot.

He had Pondo Fever, and it was a remarkable sight.

For me, *The Kraal* became the idyllic weekend destination. Mpande's proximity to Chintsa made the journey, by African standards, quick and painless. In addition to having my friend there, and over time, Dillon too became a great mate, it was the perfect escape from Chintsa. Not that life was stressful at *Smuggler's Cove*, but it was a high-energy job. Therefore, from time to time, a break from the hectic pace of the nightlife was required. In these times, I would disappear for a few days to the seclusion and serenity of *The Kraal*.

Furthermore, Mpande was, from what I had seen, the best place to experience black, rural South Africa without feeling as if I was imposing. I was just there. People continued with their daily functions and traditions not because I was paying to see it but because that was the way it was done. I was a fly on the wall observing Transkei village life. Although my presence was known, it didn't change anything or anyone.

As a Canadian, it was astonishing to discover places of such natural beauty, which were completely unspoiled by commercialism. To have an electricity-and plumbing-free mud-hut village splattered with million dollar ocean views was way beyond unique. If situated anywhere in North America, this location would be overrun by five-star hotels and golf courses. The untarnished culture was a rarity that I valued and most certainly appreciated.

And if this weren't enough reason to come to Mpande, this specific section of the country was famous for its weed.

In the end, my visits to *The Kraal* were for relaxing, appreciating and restocking.

This particular visit to *The Kraal* was unfolding as expected. I'd had my peaceful sleep. I'd absorbed the morning energies of Mother Nature. Now, it was time to restock.

With a final sip of my coffee and a last drag of my spliff, I grabbed my empty day pack and began my search for the best ganja the Kei had to offer.

I strolled barefoot across the beach and made my way through the village and over the hill to the next beach and village. Once there, I found the mud hut that I'd been to many times in the past. I poked my head in the door and found four smiling faces.

The two young boys smiled at me and sprinted off into the fields. The mother invited me inside and offered me a cup of tea, while the daughter continued to play. Within minutes, the breathless father ran into the hut with his two boys in tow.

We shook hands and said hello.

The father, seeing that his wife had provided me with tea and a seat, wasted no time and pulled a potato sack from underneath the bed. The bag was overflowing with freshly picked marijuana. He handed me a large bud and some papers. He indicated that I skin up and sample his crop, which was a request that I enthusiastically obliged.

They were plump, sticky heads of ganja, and I only required a few tokes to know that this weed was potent. There was no need to search further. I asked the man how much it would cost to fill my day pack.

He looked at my bag. After some consideration, he held up six fingers.

I smiled and shook my head. Bargaining was part of the process in the lalies when it came to many items, including marijuana, so I countered with five fingers.

He thought about it for a moment, smiled and nodded yes.

He took my bag and began stuffing it with weed. I sat back with my cup of tea and spliff and took in the scene. In front of me was a family man who happened to have a plot of land on which he grew cash crops. He grew tomatoes. He grew spinach. And he grew marijuana. All three plants brought him money. The man was not a drug dealer. He was a farmer. This father knows nothing of the drug industry and its nefarious culture. He was not living a flashy, drug dealer lifestyle. He didn't have a BMW parked in the driveway; there wasn't even a driveway, let alone roads. He hadn't spent the money on home entertainment units because there wasn't electricity.

He was simply trying to feed and clothe his family.

One of the problems with buying marijuana at home was from whom I bought it.

Your typical Canadian drug dealer is often some little gangster wannabe who struts around with too much attitude and possibly a weapon. Usually the buy is made in the dealer's home, and it's a home littered with the spoils of his drug money. It's displayed in the form of large-screen TVs, stereos, video games and other such trivial luxuries. For me, it was a get-in and get-out situation. I didn't want to spend one second longer with the little punk than I had to. As far as I knew, the police had the drug den under surveillance and were going through their final preparations before the raid.

I was certainly not going to sit down and have a cup of tea.

But here in the Transkei, buying weed was conducted in a safe and peaceful atmosphere. I never felt the slightest bit uncomfortable. The possibility of a police raid was laughable because we were in the middle of nowhere. The chance that the farmer would rip me off or hurt me was ridiculous because his entire family was there with us. The wife was cooking dinner, and I was playing peekaboo with the boys. It was the most harmless setting one could imagine.

The real magic came when I handed him the money. The smiles on his face and those of his family were phenomenal. Five hundred rand would be food for two weeks for the family, if not more.[5]

I was smiling too.

Initially, these prices seemed fantastically insane. However, when I gave the cost further consideration, I thought why the hell shouldn't marijuana be this cheap? After all, it was just a plant or even a *weed*. No plant should cost 10 dollars a gram. Christ, asparagus doesn't cost as much. What am I talking about? *Gold* doesn't cost as much!

Nonetheless, I didn't give it too much thought. I'm a firm believer in living for the moment. And at that moment, I was far away from Canadian drug dealers and their exorbitant costs. At that moment, I was strolling back across the beach and returning to *The Kraal* as the proud and astonished owner of roughly 2000 grams of Transkei bud.

My only stress of the whole mission, and it was a sizable one, was transporting the weed the 280 kilometres back to *Smuggler's Cove*. There were numerous road blocks between Mpande and Chintsa, and despite the cops searching primarily for illegal weapons, getting caught with two kilograms of weed would get my ass thrown in jail for a big chunk of time.

There was never a point in my life where I thought that prison would be the lifestyle for me, but after the past year, I valued my freedom more than ever. Even if it were the Hilton of prisons, I didn't want to spend one minute incarcerated. I had a deep suspicion that the Transkei jails were a far cry from the cleanest and safest prisons the world had to offer.

Not wanting to find out first-hand, I thoroughly researched, pondered, debated and contemplated my means of transportation. When I decided on a course of action, I felt confident that the journey would be as safe as possible, for I had a few elements working in my favour.

Other than not being that interested in finding drugs, the police had, thankfully, even less interest in tourists. Because foreign tourism was new and such a vital component to the country's rebuilding, the police seemed either hesitant or

---

5. 500 rand, or 125 Canadian dollars, had bought me something in the neighbourhood of two kilograms of some of the best marijuana that I'd ever smoked. That's 2000 grams! In Canada, one gram is 10 bucks. Let me say that again to emphasize my point. In Canada, 10 bucks gets you one measly gram of dope. Here in the Transkei, 125 bucks gets you 2000 grams!

unwilling to search foreigners. It was believable that the South African government didn't want the groundbreaking tourists to return to their home countries with tales of police harassment fresh in their minds. The smiling police often waved tourists, who were in their distinctive rental cars, through the roadblocks.

Nevertheless, the sure way to avoid all obstacles was travelling by bus. However, this wasn't your everyday, ordinary bus. It was a heavily labelled and immediately recognizable mini bus designed to carry *only* backpackers from hostel to hostel. While other cars were being searched, our bus would barely slow down. It would pass through the roadblock and safely to the other side with its passengers (potential positive advertising for South African tourism) and, more importantly, my massive bag of weed.

The way I analyzed the danger, the police would have to first stop the bus (not likely), then decide to search the travellers and trailer (even less likely), then find the hidden weed (I became excellent at stashing my gear) then establish to which of the 20 travellers the bag belonged. Of course everyone would deny ownership (with me declaring my innocence as loudly as the rest). To further muddle the unlikely investigation, I travelled with two bags. One held my clothes and passport, so I could obviously claim it as my own. The other just had the ganja. It was the one I would avoid like the plague. I have affectionately named them my "decoy bag" and the "Mother Load."

However, in spite of my scheming and plotting, I knew that my plan wasn't foolproof by any stretch of the smuggler's imagination.

Understandably, there was always a tremendous sense of relief when the bus turned off the N2 and onto the back road to Chintsa. I could let out a sigh of relief, for I knew that there wouldn't be any more roadblocks the rest of the way. This was pretty much a guarantee. The beautiful drive down the coast back home to *Smuggler's Cove* was one filled with a sense of accomplishment.

At *Smuggler's Cove*, I'd always get a nice welcome back from my friends. Sadly, their thrill in seeing me back safely to Chintsa had nothing to do with them missing my wit, humour or personality. I had only been away two nights. Alas, their excitement was strictly self-indulgent. They were happy to see me home safely because they knew that, coming from the Kei, I would have a big, big bag of weed with me.

This time was no different. Like vultures, they swept in to get their fix, which I gladly accommodated. They were friends after all. And besides, I too had self-indulgent motives for dishing out handfuls of the Transkei's finest.

The sooner the weed was gone, the sooner I could do it all over again.

The real danger of the Transkei was the roads and their many hazards. It was best to expect the unexpected while travelling on the South African highways, especially in the Transkei.

The Kraal. Without electricity or telephones, this hostel was still the most unique guest house I came across on my travels. Set in a natural amphitheatre with an unobstructed ocean view and a secluded beach, the tiny piece of timeless paradise became my South African refuge.

A seasonal waterfall adds to the already incredible subtropical beauty of the deserted beach at *The Kraal*.

The Transkei's rugged and unspoiled coastline. Look closely. There are more cows on the beach than people.

A young girl stands in the doorway of her family's rondavel, which is the traditional thatched home of the Transkei. Despite its simplicity, the hut, which is a combination of mud and cow dung, retains heat during the cold winter evenings and remains pleasantly cool when the weather is stiflingly hot. It is African architecture at its finest.

The treacherous currents of South Africa's Wild Coast have claimed countless ships over the years, many of which are still visible. The wreck of the Jack Astor, a two-hour hike from *The Kraal*, is a chilling reminder of Mother Nature's unforgiving power.

The Jacaranda was another casualty of the Wild Coast's perilous waters. The ship's captain was miraculously able to avoid the rocks and beach his vessel on the thin patch of sand in a remote section of the Transkei.

Laundry day in the Transkei. Two girls make their way to a rock pool to tackle one of their many daily chores. The sight of the barefoot girls carrying laundry on their heads acted as an enchanting reminder that there were places that had remained, in many ways, locked in time.

A time to clean and a time to play.

In search of the Transkei's best ganja. It was another successful mission.

16

WERNER

DECEMBER

"Do you have any triangles?!"

I had been asked some strange questions during my time at *Smuggler's Cove*. "What time do they feed the whales?" was a good one. "Are there any sharks in the ocean?" was a classic. "If I started walking down the beach in one direction, how long would it take me to walk all the way around?" was still one of my personal favourites.

However, "do you have any triangles?" took the cake.

The other questions may have been more idiotic, but this particular query was certainly the most unusual.

Werner was frantic. This time he shouted.

"Do you have any triangles?!"

It was three in the morning. The bar was winding down. I was drunk, stoned and tired. My wits were a far cry from their capabilities. Under normal circumstances, I might have looked at the individual asking such a question and say, "Okay. What's the punch line?"

However, this wasn't a normal circumstance.

Or should I say, this wasn't a normal person.

Werner was a 42-year-old German who had been staying at *Smuggler's Cove* the past five days. Werner was a tad, and I'm being polite in saying this, weird. He rarely opened his mouth. In fact, the only time I heard him speak was when he ordered a Coke from me. He would sit at the bar in complete silence and sip his soft drink. He seemed completely oblivious to anyone around him. Occasionally, he would burst into spontaneous, uncontrollable fits of laughter. Those sitting around him, including myself, had no clue what the man found so hilarious. Then, as suddenly as he started, Werner would stop and return to his semi-comatose state of absolute silence.

The other bizarre aspect about Werner was that while he never really was anywhere, he gave the impression of being everywhere. You wouldn't see him on the beach or at the pool, but you would find him standing under some obscure bush or detect him standing in a random corner of some random room.

Consequently, being asked such a strange question by an even stranger man warranted a bit of apprehension on my part.

I hesitantly asked if he meant a "ding-ding," musical triangle.

"Any triangle, man!" he anxiously yelled.

His nervousness made me curious. I asked him why he needed a triangle.

"Defence!" he responded. He was growing more aggravated.

This was getting more bizarre by the moment, but I was very much intrigued. I decided to pursue my inquiry. I asked him what he needed to defend himself against.

"Aliens," he answered with a look of true sincerity and deep fear.

I wondered if I should stop my questions right there and just help the poor, crazy bastard find a triangle. But answers like that and people like this didn't come along everyday. Curiosity forced me to venture even further with my inquisition.

I asked if he had been having problems with aliens.

Werner glanced guardedly over his shoulder. "Yes," he said straight-faced. "I've been abducted many times."

I was now well past intrigued. I asked him when he was last abducted.

"Two nights ago," he answered fretfully.

There were so many people that came and went through *Smuggler's Cove* that it was sometimes difficult to remember how long somebody had been staying there. Werner stood out and was by no means easy to forget. If he had been abducted two nights ago, that would mean the aliens kidnapped him from the Red dorm. To confirm this highly improbable scenario, I asked if he was abducted from the dorm just above the bar, which was continuously filled with a dozen semi-conscious backpackers every night.

"Yes," he solemnly replied.

I had asked odd questions, and I had received odd answers. I didn't know what to say to this poor, desperate, crazy man. There was no sense in trying to calm him down or talk any sense into Werner. He was dead set in his conviction that aliens had gotten to him, yet again. And now he needed a triangle, of all things, to ward them off.

I gave the terrified man the racking triangle from the pool table, and he hurried off to bushes unknown.

Although brief, my exchange with Werner was the most abnormal conversation that I've had while travelling … possibly ever.

Nonetheless, it was moments like these that were the little extra bonuses associated with a traveller's world. They were moments that I savoured.

I've met all walks of life travelling. The stereotypical, ponytailed, dirty, lost soul backpacker is just one of hundreds of types of people exploring the earth. Hippies, punks, geeks, jocks, losers, scumbags or angels can all be found travelling. The smart and dumb, thin and fat, rich and poor, short and tall, gorgeous and pig ugly all float around the globe with a pack on their backs and various agendas.

Every manner of character imaginable is out there discovering the planet. And that includes, as rare as they are, people who have discovered other planets.

The exposure to the variety of people that life on the road offers can't be encountered within the velvet rut. Friends, family and co-workers tend to be cut from the same cloth, so styles, interests and backgrounds have little variety. The few mates who were a bit different stood out and were rarities. It's been my experience that the Western world is a clique environment, and any attempt to deviate from your established social box is not something often done without consideration and consequence.

On the road, however, I was not only exposed to the multiplicity of characters, but I also had an excellent opportunity to interact with this diverse group of people. Even the mohawked punk was easy to approach because, no matter what, I knew that we shared at least one thing in common. We were both travelling through a foreign land. That was all the connection needed. A goth and a computer geek might live next door to each other in London and never acknowledge the presence of one another. Yet in the backpacking world, they were having a beer and sharing a laugh the way lifelong friends might.

Meeting new people is just as exciting and educational as discovering a new country.

Yet of all the thousands of people I've met, I've never come across someone who was abducted by aliens.

Even though the aliens knew of his whereabouts in the Red dorm, Werner decided to stay in Chintsa. In fact, he stayed another four weeks.

Over the month, I spent a lot of time with Werner and got to know the space traveller very well.

Following the "I need a triangle" night, Werner spent most of the evenings in the bar. Because it was peak season, I would rarely close before four or five in the morning. Werner would sneak into the pub around midnight and sit at the bar drinking his soft drinks until I closed. This happened every night for the next four weeks without fail.

It was over this time that I got to know Werner.

He was a very interesting individual.

The first thing that surprised me about Werner was his extreme intelligence. He could discuss history, politics, religion, literature and science. You name it, and he had something enlightening to say on the subject.

Werner may have been crazy, but he wasn't stupid and crazy.

There was no doubt that in the eyes of German society, Werner was a few cans short of a six-pack. He did confess that he had been institutionalized as a youngster in Germany. He had vivid memories of the shock therapy that he had been subjected to along with the other horrors he witnessed during his time in the insane asylum. Most of his family had disowned him. He told me that the only person who still cared for him was his grandmother. For obvious reasons, he hated Germany, and if it wasn't for his grandmother still living there, he would never return.

Yet despite the therapy, barbaric treatment and tough love, he remained firmly resolved that aliens had abducted him on numerous occasions.

He explained that the aliens were not the little, green, bug-eyed lizard types that science fiction had created. Instead, they came in the form of a super advanced mathematical equation from another dimension. I'm not a mathematician, and I had a hard time understanding what Werner was trying to explain. But I doubt Einstein could have followed the complexity of Werner's description of the equations from beyond.

Apparently, the angles and symmetry of the triangle would confuse the alien equation. He told me that the aliens had subjected him to a battery of tests, but he couldn't properly describe them other than saying it was more "virtual" than physical. (This was a form of advanced math that we were dealing with.) He did remember that the pain was unmistakable, unforgettable and torturous. This accounted for his terror. He had been abducted many times, and nobody ever believed him.

I'm not saying that I believe or don't believe Werner.

I'm saying that Werner made me think.

Imagine for a moment that aliens suddenly abduct you, dear reader, obviously a very intelligent person, while walking one day in the park. You are thrown back on earth with a lot of pain and some serious questions. You know with certainty that aliens have abducted you. What do you do? Do you tell anybody? Possibly not, but let's assume that you do tell somebody, and that somebody is a family member or a best friend. You muster up the courage and tell them that aliens abducted you. What do you think their reaction might be?

I know how my best friend would react. Initially he'd laugh. Then he'd say something along the lines of, "Yeah. Sure thing, buddy. Whatever. How much did you smoke last night?"

He would definitely make fun of me. The more I persisted, the more he'd laugh. Eventually my determination to make him believe me would turn his laughter to annoyance. He'd say, "Jesus, man! Enough with your fucking alien shit. You're doing my head in!"

Remember, you know you are an intelligent person. You know you still have your sanity. You know that everyone is laughing at you or calling you crazy, and it's no longer behind your back but to your face. Your friends and family, completely fed up with the whole alien business, would inevitably turn their backs on your psycho ass or have you committed.

That type of rejection would be dreadful.

Werner wasn't a stupid man; there was no debating his intellect. But as preposterous as it may sound, he'd swear on his grandmother's soul that alien equations had snatched and experimented with his body and mind.

Whether aliens had abducted him or whether they were all demented figments of his warped imagination, Werner believed the experiences were true.

That was the fear that Werner was living with.

Aliens have never abducted me. I've never seen an alien. Nonetheless, just because I haven't seen something doesn't mean it doesn't exist. There are countless items that I accept even though I have never seen them. I remember trying to explain what a snowy landscape looked like to some of the Chintsa kids. Many had never even heard of snow. I told them to imagine ice cubes piled to their waists and spread as far as the eye could see. After a few seconds, the kids could put together a visual of the white countryside, and then they looked at me as if I was crazy. Their stares suggested that they thought I was from another planet.

Yet even though they had never seen snow, and many probably never would, I expected them to believe in the existence of arctic climates just because I had seen it with my own eyes.

Was Werner's appeal about aliens that much different? Was it that much more of a stretch of the imagination?

Okay, it was. Accepting Werner's belief would be a quantum leap of faith.

Catching a glimpse of an alien life form would be extremely rare and unique. But so too is witnessing a blue whale. I know that we have video footage of the gigantic beasts that prove their existence. But if we didn't have that footage, and you tried to tell me there was a whale that big cruising through the ocean, it would be difficult to believe. Without the video, how many people have actually seen a blue whale? Not that many I would venture. I wouldn't be surprised if there were more people who have seen aliens, than there are who have seen the blue whale.[1]

The universe is massive. No, it is much, much bigger than massive. It's so big that I can't even begin to get my head around the magnitude of the gigantic, endless, infinite sprawl of space. I won't pretend for a moment that I know everything that may be out there. In fact, it is safe to say that I know absolutely nothing about it, as do most of us living on Earth.

Maybe Werner really had been abducted. Who am I to say otherwise? What I did know was that Werner was a very kind, gentle man. I also know that his fear was very real.

Never judge a book by its cover. This important lesson had been reinforced through my encounter with Werner. He may have been a little strange, or maybe he wasn't. What wasn't in question was the goodness in his heart.

Werner also taught me to open my mind even more to the possibilities that this world, and perhaps others, had to offer. Who knows what's out there? I barely know anything about the items we already know exist. And we continue to make new discoveries and advancements in all fields every day.

Who knows what we might find?

Who knows what might find us?

Maybe, just maybe, Werner was laughing because he knew that he would have the last laugh.

---

1. I once read on the back of a Bill Bryson book that 3.7 *million* Americans believed that they had been abducted by aliens. Even if 99 per cent of those Yanks are off their rocker, that still leaves a shitload of intelligent, sane people who believe they have been in a space ship. I bet you *that* number is much higher than those who have been lucky enough to see a blue whale.

17

THE CHASE

JANUARY

As I was chasing the thief through the pitch-black bush, it dawned on me that I didn't have the slightest idea what I was doing.

What the hell was going on?! Why was I chasing a robber into the darkness?!

Not five minutes ago, I was sitting in the pub, rolling a joint and chatting up a lovely English girl. I was playing my "get the fuck out now" playlist, a compilation packed with mellow tunes, in a sly attempt to get the half dozen or so remaining backpackers to leave so that I could close up and make my move on the gorgeous English traveller. I could tell from the way she was looking and smiling at me that she was waiting for them to leave as well.

Regrettably, my plan of seduction and passion vanished when a backpacker came running into the bar and shouting that he had just seen a black guy rummaging around the communal kitchen stealing food.

Over the past month, *Smuggler's Cove* had been having some problems with petty theft. With the holiday season in full swing and Chintsa jam-packed, the criminals were taking advantage of the excessive number of tourists and their inviting and accessible wealth. The bright side was that it wasn't violent crime but rather the theft of food or the occasional backpack. In the latter case, it would often show up on the beach with only the cash missing, that being the only unidentifiable item worth taking. In fact, our staff cottage had been broken into a few times, though in each instance the only thing stolen was spare change.[1]

---

1. After the second break-in, I hid my real change dish in the back of my closest behind some folded clothes and kept a "decoy dish" with only a few coins sitting out in the open in case there was a third robbery. I came home one night a couple of weeks later to find the decoy dish empty. I opened my closet and discovered that the thief had located and emptied the real coin dish as well. My passport and camera were sitting next to the bowl, but the only item stolen was the change. Believe it or not, the guy who stole my coins even put my clothes back into the closet...neat and folded.

Regardless of the nature of the crime, theft was bad for business.

Therefore, I wasted no time and ran upstairs to the kitchen only to find nobody there. The windows, which dropped 12 feet to the bush below, were wide open. I thought this was how the thief had made his escape, so I raced back downstairs and around the side of the bar that was attached to the kitchen. I looked, but in the darkness, I couldn't see anybody.

As I was trudging out of the bush and back to the bar, a collection of backpackers had gathered on the deck above me. One cried out, "Shit, man! He's right there!"

The shrub directly behind me rustled. The thief jumped out and sprinted off in the opposite direction, down the dirt path and into the thicker brush. Surprisingly enough, my initial instinct was to run after him, which was exactly what I did. However, initial instincts are at times irrational, and I didn't get 20 steps into the darkness before I realized that this was one of those times. It has been my experience that in these moments, especially when that moment is leading me into the darkness, it is best to stop and reconsider whether or not the current move is the wisest.

I stopped running.

I thought to myself, what the fuck am I doing?!

Why in God's name was I chasing a thief into the night? I wasn't a security guard, bounty hunter or Bruce Lee. I was a backpacker working as a barman in a little speck of peaceful paradise with zero training for this type of confrontation. I poured drinks. I played music. I talked to people. I wasn't supposed to be chasing them. How was I going to subdue the thief if I caught up to him? Use the Vulcan death grip? Wing Chung kung fu? Barrage him with harsh words? I had never thrown a punch in my life, and honestly I didn't know what I would be capable of doing to detain the burglar. And that was assuming I was even able to catch the guy, which in the darkness would prove next to impossible. The night was so black I couldn't even see my hand in front of my face.

As I was contemplating my limited options for apprehension, another notion crossed my mind.

What had this thief actually thieved? Some food … nothing more. Part of me was sympathetic to this poor bastard. The hungry soul was not one of those gun-toting criminals. He was stealing bread and butter from wealthy European backpackers in the middle of the night.

Was this theft of nutrition really a crime?

Was this really a bad guy?

I re-evaluated the situation. I, an untrained, non-violent Canadian, was running blindly into the African darkness to chase a guy whom I actually felt sorry for.

The hungry bastard was on the run and on the defensive. I'm sure that this guy had received his share of beatings over the years and had possibly seen the inside of a jail. If that was the case, then I was positive that he would have no desire to return anytime soon. In fact, due to the violent nature of South Africa, he probably thought there was a high likelihood that I, a white man, would shoot him in the back and then call the cops.[2]

This theory meant the guy would do whatever necessary in order to escape and survive. If he was trapped in a corner, he could hit me on the head, stab me in the back or even worse. I couldn't know for sure how frightened, willing or capable he was. I did know how frightened, willing and capable I was.

I was terrified, reluctant and had never been in a fight.

What was stopping this petrified guy on the run from using his knowledge of the terrain and the camouflage of the night to get the upper hand on me? The answer was nothing at all. Christ, I had walked right next to him and hadn't seen him in the darkness. If he needed to take me out, he could easily hide in the bushes and wait for me to walk by. What was stopping him from eliminating me from the chase?

Again, the answer was nothing at all.

I was decidedly finished with the manhunt.

I walked back to the bar and told everybody that I obviously had to close up. I apologized to the English girl for having to go and went to wake up Scott. I told him what had happened. He quickly dressed, and the two of us did a token search around the property in case the thief was still lurking about. Going back into the bush with Scott, I was no longer worried about cornering the man. I had no doubt Scott would handle that situation. He was as mad as I'd ever seen him. He was definitely willing and able.

However, after about a half hour's futile search, Scott told me to pack it in and go to bed.

Not surprisingly, I had a hard time sleeping that night as I wrestled with the deeper significance of the night's events.

One of the promises I had made to myself before I left Canada was that the moment I became unhappy or uncomfortable in a place, I'd leave. Again, that

---

2. Although not as common as it was during apartheid, there are still those who pull the trigger first then ask questions.

was one of the main advantages and freedoms of my decision to travel alone. It was the reason that I lived out of a backpack. Ultimately, I could be gone from a place as fast as it took me to pack my bag.

The freedom to go on a whim proved beneficial in my runner from Glasgow, and it was advantageous in my escape from Tenerife. Was it, once again, applicable to my time in South Africa?

I kept asking myself the same questions. Was it time to leave? Was I unhappy in South Africa?

There was no debating that Africa had captivated me. I thoroughly relished every chance I had to learn something from my time in this special land. However, there was a massive distinction between experiencing the intricacies of Africa in a car on the way to *The Kraal* and chasing it into the bush. Watching it from a car would, at worst, have me shaking my head. Chasing it into the night could result in me losing my head … literally. Becoming a victim over a piece of bread wasn't what I signed up for when I began my travels or work at *Smuggler's Cove*. Was I risking my life working in this environment?

In addition, as much as I loved the bar, I knew that the party lifestyle was slowly taking its toll on my body and brain cell count. It was a party night every night, regardless of the day of the week.

The lack of sleep combined with the excessive drinking was a ticking bomb waiting to explode. I knew that my body could only handle so much abuse before something broke. My major concern was that my tolerance level to the countless toxins was growing stronger by the day. I could drink like a fish all night and still be sober enough to run the pub. Regardless of my ability to handle the booze, I knew that the copious amount of alcohol entering my system was doing damage.

Part of me, namely my liver, thought that maybe it was time to leave Chintsa.

I struggled with my predicament throughout the sleepless night. The thought of what might have happened if I had caught the thief, or if he had caught me, genuinely disturbed and frightened me. I was not, nor ever wanted to be, a violent person, and I was afraid living in South Africa was going to force me into a confrontational situation. I was honestly torn between the two options.

I had reached the point where I thought it was time to leave Chintsa.

I spent the good part of the next day walking around like a zombie. I was solemn and pensive, and I didn't say a word to a soul. Everybody, very wisely, kept their distance from my brooding temper. That afternoon, Scott braved my mood and came down to the cottage where I had been hiding and stewing. He knew from my silence, as did everyone else, that I was bothered by the previous night's events. He asked if there was anything he could do that would address my concerns and snap me out of my funk.

I opened up. I told Scott what I thought. I told him I was troubled that I had to act as a security guard. I told him that I thought it was pretty fucked up that a guy would have to resort to stealing food in a country that seemed to have so much. I told him that I thought South Africa was a long way from being where it should be with its incredible and embarrassing division of wealth. I told him that I wasn't sure if it was time for me to move on and continue my travels.

Scott listened and didn't say a word throughout my tirade. However, at the end of my spiel, he attempted to answer my questions. Some of my concerns were resolved. *Smuggler's Cove* would be hiring a night watchman, so hopefully I wouldn't have to chase anyone into the darkness ever again. Other concerns, such as my distress about the division of wealth in South Africa, were not resolved, but they were further explained in an attempt to help me understand why this country was the way it was. Scott talked of Nelson Mandela and his vision for the future. And regarding my decision to stay or leave Chintsa, he said that only I knew the answer, but if it meant anything, he and the family would hate to see me go.

He was able to calm me down and convince me to stay.

However, even before Scott came to the cottage and brought me out of my pensive shell, I knew deep down that I would be staying at *Smuggler's Cove* for awhile. I recognized that there was still much more for me to discover in this crazy yet enchanting country. I had decided that, at the end of the day, the chase was a good thing. The pursuit into the darkness yanked me back into South African reality. It reminded me that what was happening in the rest of the country wasn't as perfect as it was within the Utopian "*Smuggler's* bubble." The chase was further evidence that there was still a massive division of wealth in South Africa and that there were many who needed to steal food in order to survive.

Crime and the economic inequalities were tragic aspects of the country that I was going to have to accept and address if I wanted to stay in South Africa. If I couldn't handle these problems, my other option was to pack up my three T-shirts and leave. The freedom was mine.

Nevertheless, despite the struggles and problems this country faced, I was enthralled and excited about being in South Africa. These dilemmas were part of the battle that this changing nation had to undergo. I was sitting in the middle of a country that was redefining itself. There were positive and negative forces at work in the country's reconstruction. However, despite the frustrations and setbacks, I honestly believed that, over time, the good would prevail over the bad.

This country was packed with promise, and I was hoping that South Africa would reach its maximum potential.

By staying close to the scene, I could watch how Mandela's vision would unfold over time.

I wanted to find out if my belief would prove accurate.

There was no question in my mind that travelling was a great lifestyle. It was certainly the best one that I had discovered so far in my journey through life. Life as a traveller was undoubtedly more appealing than life as an academic or a participant in the nine-to-five, velvet rut. Nonetheless, as with all lifestyles, there were ups and downs. I've come to realize that the secret to happiness is finding a lifestyle where you experience more ups than downs and that the downs, because there will always be bad times, aren't too draining.

I believed I had found that easygoing and enlightening lifestyle in Chintsa.

In Canada, my ups were few and far between, and the downs would usually send me off the handle in fits of rage for days at a time. In Chintsa, my days were overloaded with the positive, and the negative would, more often than not, be nothing more than educational. Even the chase, although an experience I wouldn't want to repeat anytime soon, proved in its own way informative and eye-opening.

I knew I wasn't ready to leave South Africa.

At the end of the day, the determining factor in my decision to stay was the love that I had received from the owners of *Smuggler's Cove*, the Crosby family. From the moment I arrived in Chintsa, the Crosbys had made me feel welcome. And as time went by, they made me feel as if I was a member of their family. They were caring yet not imposing. They were supportive. They were open-minded and non-judgemental. They were a big reason why I initially found *Smuggler's Cove* appealing and found it even more so when I decided to stay and work.

This amazing family had provided me with a home away from home and a family away from family.

I knew that if I left Chintsa and South Africa now the sense of loss I would feel would have nothing to do with missing the African lifestyle, the great bar job or even the excessive amounts of ganja. My real loss would be because I wouldn't be able to spend the holiday season with a family who treated me like a son.

I wasn't going anywhere.

I wanted to stay in South Africa for as long as I possibly could.

Besides, I knew my liver could handle a few more drinks.

18
SHIT HAPPENS

MARCH

Some things change.

For example, I used to love TV. There was a time not that long ago when my schedule, like so many other North American schedules, was influenced by the television set. My Thursday nights were reserved for NBC's "Super Thursday Comedy Lineup." My Sundays were set aside for NFL football. I watched "The Simpsons" five times a day. Television was such a major part of my life that leaving it behind was one of my biggest anxieties before I began my travels. I thought, how would I survive without my TV? What would I do without Homer's brilliance and guidance five times a day?

As I said, some things change.

These days, I never watch television. I've grown to despise it … immensely. I've come to realize that it's littered with news programming exploiting human suffering, game shows and American dribble from sitcoms to soap operas, which are designed to numb the brain.

You could almost say that I was raised on TV. At times, it served as a parent. Other times, it was an educator. It certainly taught me more than some of the dolts who called themselves my university professors. I prided myself on my excellent knowledge regarding the entertainment world and those living within it. Whether it was movies or music, I was on the ball when it came to the lives of celebrities. I knew of their romances, breakups and drug habits. I was aware of the scandals and conspiracies. I was up-to-date in sports. I knew who was playing where, who was hot and who was not. Through television, I was able to tap into a little bit of everything.

Nowadays, I knew absolutely nothing about all of these pop culture arenas that I had once deemed important to my life and general well-being. I was completely out of the entertainment loop.

Don't get me wrong. I didn't mind being out of the loop. Actually, I quite enjoyed it. The entertainment loop was a loop that, ironically, isn't even the most entertaining one on the rope of life.

However, despite my new-found distractions, there were times when I wanted to get a feel for what was happening in my old world.

This particular night was one of those sometimes.

It had been a dead night in the pub, and everybody, for a change, had gone to bed by midnight. Thanks to the excessive partying over the past four months, my sleeping pattern wouldn't allow me to even attempt sleep before three. To kill the time, I decided I might as well stare at the boob tube for a little bit of catching up in my old loop.

The last thing I expected to see was a friend from home on television.

Tom Green wasn't exactly a friend. He was more of an acquaintance whom I met through a mutual friend in high school. My first impression of the guy told me that he was a complete and total idiot. Any other time I came across Tom, his behaviour only confirmed my initial suspicions. He was always overacting and looking to get a laugh from whoever might be around and paying attention.

Some said he was talented and had an amazing, original yet warped sense of humour.

I thought he was a moron.

As life moved on, Tom utilized his "talents" and slowly rose through the celebrity ranks of the greater Ottawa area. He first broke onto the scene as a rapper with a group called Organized Rhyme. Later, he became the host of his own cable TV talk show originally named "The Tom Green Show." He was still hosting this brainless program when I left Ottawa. So it should come as no surprise that a mere 18 months later, when I saw Tom Green on "The Dennis Miller Show" overacting as usual, I was a little freaked.

I rubbed my eyes.

Tom Green appearing on this show didn't make any sense. "The Dennis Miller Show" wasn't the biggest late night talk show in the States, but it was still considered a popular one. I would have thought that Dennis Miller, the one-time "Saturday Night Live" anchorman, would still have had enough clout in Hollywood to draw a couple of fading "A" celebrities or, at the very least, some "B" actors for his show. I was baffled why he would have to scour the Ottawa Valley to dig up some talent. I was mildly surprised that he, as a Yank, had even heard of Ottawa, let alone Tom Green.

I couldn't think of any possible reason why Tom Green would be on "The Dennis Miller Show."

Despite my bewilderment, I noticed that I was, in fact, not watching "The Dennis Miller Show" after all. What had disturbed me was merely a clip taken from "The Dennis Miller Show." The program that I was actually viewing was a show called "Talk Soup." From what I could gather, the program seemed to be a talk show about talk shows. It was the type of uncreative slobber that was being mass-produced in the United States. Essentially, it was a program that stole highlights from other shows, edited them together in a tidy little package, wrote in some unfunny commentary and distributed it into our living rooms. With Generation X as the target market, a group who required a never-ending flow of brainless dribble, there was sadly no question that "Talk Soup" would be a success.

Regardless of the program I was watching, I kept returning to my initial question. What was Tom Green doing on "The Dennis Miller Show"? Even if I understood why he was on "The Dennis Miller Show," which I didn't, why on earth would the producers of "Talk Soup" consider Tom's appearance to be a highlight of the week?

Tom Green was not a highlight. Yeah, Tom was a bit of a local celebrity in Ottawa, but so what? He was a *bit* of a *local* celebrity. Most people in Ottawa didn't even know who Tom Green was, so why would Dennis Miller sink to this level of guest? I realized that his "Saturday Night Live" glory days were well behind him, but surely times couldn't be that desperate for Dennis and the rest of the television world.

Then, as if my mind didn't have enough to contemplate, something happened that completely sent me off the rails of sanity.

"Talk Soup" returned from commercial and proceeded to its next clip, which so happened to be a segment from "The Tom Green Show." My eyes didn't bulge because "Talk Soup" was aware that "The Tom Green Show" existed. Although that oddity did create a moment of puzzlement, for "The Tom Green Show" was, as far as I was aware, only broadcast in the Ottawa area.

No. That wasn't the mystery that spun me out.

It wasn't what Tom was doing or saying either.

What sent my marbles rolling was with whom he was being his idiotic self.

For those of you who don't know, "The Tom Green Show" is essentially a program packed with clips of Tom behaving like a fool. He would hit the streets with a video camera and confront random bystanders with one of his many absurd questions or acts. Two of his biggest targets were his own parents. He had no shame or respect for their privacy or property. For example, his folks would go away for the weekend, and Tom would do something stupid like paint the exterior of their house the colours of the rainbow or fill the living room with popcorn. He would then film his mom and dad's honest, genuine reaction the moment they stepped out of the station wagon, fresh from a weekend at the lake.

Worse still, he and a cameraman would storm into his parents' bedroom at some godawful hour of the morning and wake them from their tranquil slumber with a host of idiotic schemes and questions. This invasion of privacy was pathetically done in the name of not-so-funny television.

The clip of his show that I was watching happened to be one of those "bust in on the sleeping parents" acts. He wanted to show his guest a quilt that his mom had made. Earlier, while out prowling the freezing winter streets of Ottawa with Tom, his guest had answered his ridiculous question of whether she liked quilts with a yes. The two of them then barged in on a peacefully sleeping Mom and Dad Green at four in the morning. After waking them, Tom demanded that his guest be shown the quilt.

Want to know who his guest was?

Monica Lewinski.

Clinton … cigars … the stained dress. Yeah, that Monica! My head was so disoriented that I thought I might have been having an acid flashback from my experimental university days. Hallucinating made more sense than Tom Green and Monica Lewinski, one of the most infamous and media-hounded women on the planet, hanging out in Tom Green's parents' bedroom.

This had to be a figment of my imagination.

Monica Lewinski?! There was no fucking way.

If my memory served me correctly, practically every news organization on the planet would have paid top dollar to get an interview with her. Everybody wanted a piece of Monica. Everybody knew her name. If you looked up "infamous" in the dictionary, you would see a picture of her. It was this global notoriety that made it impossible to understand why she would be chilling with Tom Green in his parents' bedroom at four in the morning and looking at a homemade quilt of all ridiculous things!

Was there any doubt in my mind that I was looking at the real Monica? Any uncertainties were removed by the reaction of Mom and Dad Green. Normally, when Tom disrupts their sleep, they respond with anger, aggravation and frustration. Typically, they would roll over and shield themselves from the prying eye of the camera. They usually screamed something along the lines of, "Get the hell out, Tom. It's four in the god dammed morning! This is the last time you try a stunt like this. I don't care if it's for your show … enough is enough!"

That would be their normal response.

But on this occasion, here were Mom and Pop Green patting down their hair with fluttery hands, smoothing their rumpled linen, modestly adjusting their night attire and rearranging their stunned faces into welcoming smiles as they politely introduced themselves and said how pleased they were to meet her. It was celebrity ass-kissing at its finest.

It had to be the real Monica.

Forget "The Dennis Miller Show" quandary. What was Tom Green doing with Monica Lewinski?

Showing her a quilt for a sketch in his rinky-dink, not-even-that-funny talk show?

I didn't buy it for a second.

I needed to get in touch with Nikki.

Nikki was an ex-girlfriend from high school with whom I continued to stay in touch after university. She was also Tom Green's first love, and they too maintained an excellent relationship after their breakup. If anybody could clarify whether these unbelievable events involving Tom were real or a hallucination, it would be Nikki.

Nikki confirmed the unbelievable but true. Tom had been on TV with Monica Lewinski.

However, she had a lot more to say about the "Tom Situation."

She said that Tom had become rather ambitious and had sent tapes of his show to the big networks in the States, hoping that one might see the humour and originality of his program and decide to pick it up.

Guess what?

One did.

Incredibly, it wasn't even a small network. MTV, "the nation's music station," saw a potential winner in the "The Tom Green Show" and picked it up for their late night programming. This time slot, once occupied by programs such as "Ren and Stimpy" and "Beavis and Butthead," was designed to appease the stoned and simple.

Guess what?

The show became an instant hit.

Actually, it became an instant phenomenon, and amazingly, so did Tom. Tom became so popular that Pepsi signed him on to be the spokesman for their extremely expensive Super Bowl commercial time slot. It's estimated that over a billion people worldwide watched that Super Bowl. Therefore, an estimated billion people worldwide watched Tom Green endorse a soft drink. It was more disturbing to think that a billion people had been subjected to Tom's lunacy.

What happened next to Tom was even more difficult for me to accept.

Apparently, one of those billion faces watching Tom behave like a tit took quite a fancy to him, and through her influences and connections, she arranged to meet, in her words, "the funniest man on the planet."

Guess what?

They hit it off.

Guess what?

They hit it off so much that they got engaged.

Guess who the woman was … Drew Barrymore.

Tom and Drew Barrymore being engaged was too much for me to stomach. She was on my "Top 5 List" for Christ's sake! (My Top 5 List was my fantastical list filled with the names of stars who I most desired to sleep with yet knew I would *never* have the chance of meeting, let alone shagging). Along with beauties such as Madonna, Salma Hayek, Pamela Anderson and Barbara Bach, the name Drew Barrymore adorned my list.

Tom Green, the idiot from Ottawa, was going to marry one of my Top 5 girls.

Nikki further elaborated about Monica's special guest appearance on Tom's show. She said that one of Tom's co-writers had approached Monica at a party in Los Angeles, and they had hit it off. They started dating. It was therefore relatively easy to convince the Washington tart to go on the wacky "Tom Green Show" and flirt up a storm with Tom, Mom and Dad. Since she was rarely seen, Monica's appearance on the program drew media attention from across the planet, and as a result, Tom's popularity skyrocketed.

All this happened in a little over a year.

I was having a hard time getting my head around what I was hearing. I trusted Nikki, but the notion that Tom's rise to fame and fortune could all transpire in a little over a year left me doubtful and unsure if the conversation had even taken place. As improbable as it was, there was still the possibility that I was dealing with an LSD flashback.

However, a couple of weeks later, all uncertainties were removed.

I had gone to the movies in East London. As with watching television, I didn't get to the movies that often. But when I did go, I liked to be there early, so that I could watch the trailers for the soon-to-be released films. I used to be a movie buff, and again, much like watching television, it was nice to sneak a glimpse of what was going on and what was coming up.

Unfortunately, this wasn't one of those times.

As I was quietly sitting in my seat, enjoying the trailers and happily shoving greasy popcorn into my trap, a massive, gaunt, pale, bug-eyed face filled the screen.

It was Tom Green.

Greasy popcorn fell from my gaping mouth.

This wasn't a flashback. I was 100 positive that I was watching Tom Green promote his new movie on the big screen.

It confirmed everything Nikki had told me.

I don't remember if the movie I saw was good or bad. For that matter, I don't remember what movie I saw. I was dazed and spaced. My mind was racing. I might as well have been on acid the way my mind and body were tripping on the harsh reality that was, literally, staring me in the face.

Later that afternoon, after I had settled down, I reflected on the events from the past couple weeks concerning Tom Green and his rise to Hollywood stardom. I had learned two very important lessons. The first and most reassuring was that I hadn't lost my mind. Tom Green had been on television. Monica Lewinski had been Tom Green's guest. My brain was still intact. There was a point during my reality roller coaster where I seriously doubted my sanity. It was a relief to know that I still had a bit of a grip.

The knowledge that I wasn't insane helped the second lesson, or realization, come to light.

Things change.

I used to say "things change," but I don't think I ever really believed that they did. At least I didn't think that things could change for those still living in Canada. I assumed that because I had left a stagnant and predictable life behind, it would remain stationary in my absence. I thought that because I was encountering so many new experiences that it would be impossible for anyone from home to change on a pace with me.

I was wrong.

I started to see the velvet rut with new eyes.

People do change. Life does move on. Tom Green is quite an extraordinary example, but his story made me appreciate that my friends and family were also moving on in my absence. They had new careers and were climbing the corporate ladders. They had new girlfriends. Some were getting married. Some were having children. Buddies were buying homes and building their portfolios.

The list of changes went on and on.

And it wasn't going to stop.

Things would continue to change. These changes could come about by encouragement and determination, or they could just happen without our say or control. For me, my friends and even probably Tom and Drew Green, change will be a part of our daily existence.

I'm kind of reassured by this knowledge.

Who knows?

Maybe I'll get a chance to meet Pamela Anderson.

19

BLAME CANADA

JUNE

I've mellowed.

I've noticed the change in my demeanour and so have the people around me. There is no question that living on a beach with my simple lifestyle has been a contributing factor to these positive adjustments.

I smile and laugh more.

I have more energy.

I watch the sunrise.

I watch the sunset.

I don't get stressed, and I don't get angry.

As I said, I've mellowed.

Going hand in hand with my tranquillity has been a re-evaluation of the fundamental priorities and perspectives by which I want to live my life. The best gauge of my new-found serenity is in regard to my opinions of my home country.

Much of my anger stemmed from the way Canadian opinion had been shaped by misconceptions and downright lies. The North American way of life and institutions—the rat race, the media, the government, taxes, sitcoms, the way we prioritized, the value-inflated luxuries—were all driving me towards the brink of an explosion of rage. Even after I had escaped, I still felt that fury for the first few months. I had hated where I was from, and I had badmouthed North America at every opportunity.

Thankfully, my negative attitude has changed. Through countless experiences, I've come to realize that Canada is quite a fantastic place to live. When all is said and done, life is pretty good. In fact, the Canadian lifestyle is so appealing that hundreds of thousands of people from the four corners of the planet flock to Canada every year. I don't think they are coming for the winter weather. Foreigners are immigrating because they know that they will be able to raise their families in a safe, hospitable and prosperous nation. They will raise their families in a country that values and protects the rights of its citizens.

Having said that, it's not anger that I feel but sad bewilderment.

Although I no longer carry a rage-laced outlook about my home, there are still many aspects of the North American lifestyle that I'm convinced are flat out insane. Just as my travels made me appreciate how good we've got it, the experiences have also made me realize how crazy we are.

An example would be our annual holidays. In North America, we are legally entitled to a mere two weeks of paid holiday per year. I never thought about this. I just accepted this scam as the way it was because I had nothing to compare it to. However, when I began my travels and started meeting Europeans, my eyes were opened to the alternatives. I almost had a stroke the first time I heard that the Dutch and Germans were entitled to six weeks off annually.

We were getting royally gypped.

All the same, this little titbit helped explain a lot.

It explains why I haven't met that many North Americans on my travels and next to none in South Africa. The restrictive 14 days serves as an invisible chain, which prevents us from venturing too far from North America. With only a two-week break, who has the time to travel to Southern Africa? A person would be looking at three days of travelling to get there and back. That's not including the days of inevitable jet lag, acclimatization and the culture shocks that one is subjected to. Before one would have the chance to take a photo, over a third of the holiday will have vanished on travel and recovery time.

Who wants to waste a third of a vacation sitting on a plane and recovering from the aftermath? Nobody. That's who.

So what do we Canadians do instead? More often than not, we hit the lakeside cottage or visit a nearby North American city. Anything within a half day of distance is acceptable. A two-week, all-inclusive trip to Mexico or Cuba would be considered exotic and lengthy.

In fact, it is rare that Canadians use all of their two weeks at once. They would rather break it up, using random days here and there to create long weekends or to take what we call "personal days." I still find this hard to believe, but many people don't go anywhere for their holidays. Some use their time off staying at home, puttering around and doing little odds and ends. Chores, in my opinion, that should have been done during free time around the work schedule. It is ludicrous to take a holiday to plant a garden or paint a room.

Essentially, all people do is take a break from the rat race.

For me, this methodology was insane.

It wasn't a holiday.

It was refuge.

And what was really terrifying was that the velvet rut had these people so devoted, they did not venture far from the work zone. Many would spend the precious time edgy and restless. Not knowing what to do with their "free" time, they ended up feeling anxious to get back into the fast pace of their 50-hour work week. These were rat race junkies craving the hectic tempo.

It was ludicrous.

Thankfully, this mentality had not reached the distant southern shores of Africa.

"Hey, bru. We love having you here, but you need to take a break." Scott's words caught me by surprise. What astonished me was that I was told to take a break when, in essence, I was already on one, long extended holiday from Canada. It would be a holiday within a holiday. However, his next few words, considering they were coming from my employer, were beyond surprising. They were unique, rare and had never before been heard by my ears.

"Find somebody to run your bar and go somewhere in Africa. When you come back, your job will be waiting for you. Take a couple of months for your holiday."

Take a couple of months …

I've mentioned it before, and I'll say it again, the family I worked for were incredible. Not only did they treat me as a part of their extended family, but they were also excellent employers. They were approachable, calm, open-minded, fun, liberal, intelligent and generous. And like most South Africans, the Crosbys were proud of not only their country but the entirety of the continent as well. If I insisted on staying longer in Chintsa, which I did, then they believed that I needed to explore and experience more of Africa. They felt that in order to properly do so, I would need a couple of months.

They were correct. I did need to see more of Africa. My Cape Town to Cairo journey had been suspended once I had found the beauty and serenity of Chintsa. Even though I had been able to escape to *The Kraal* on countless weekends, I hadn't taken any more than three days at one time to enjoy more of the countryside. I didn't know what the future had in store for my travels, but I knew that if I didn't see more of Southern Africa, then I would leave with regret and disappointment.

Thankfully, with a two-month holiday, I could visit practically anywhere in Southern Africa that I wanted.

I had the time to explore and play.

I had options galore.

One of the many perks of my job was that I was in a position to talk with hundreds of people who had already travelled the African continent. Where they went, where they stayed and how they got there were just a few of the essential pieces of information I was able to acquire through backpacking conversations while working behind the bar. Guidebooks weren't necessary. Besides, as a general principle, I would much rather take the recommendation of a traveller whom I've connected with than base decisions on random blurbs written by unknowns.

Amid the hundreds of backpacking gems throughout Southern Africa, a certain enticing guest house situated in Nkhata Bay, Malawi had come up in conversation quite a bit.

I had been told that *Lowani Village* was very chilled and very beautiful. It was the perfect location to unwind. The hostel was a series of guest houses that were nestled on a hillside overlooking the massive Lake Malawi, which was a body of water that stretched almost the entire length of the country.

From all accounts, Malawi was a dirt cheap destination, even by backpacking standards, and the Malawians were extremely friendly and welcoming. As an added bonus, I had been enlightened to the particulars of some of the local vegetation. Specifically, Malawian marijuana was world-renowned and implausibly inexpensive.

Basking in the sun next to a freshwater lake, smoking quality weed and being surrounded by a sociable, out of the ordinary culture seemed like the idyllic environment for my holiday.

The only hurdle was the distance. Malawi was a few thousand kilometres away from my beach in South Africa. It was a lengthy trek but even more so when I took into consideration that those few thousand kilometres were "African" kilometres. I wouldn't have the luxury of First World, four-lane tarmac highways. Instead, I would be dealing with potholed dirt roads while utilizing a variety of vehicles, none of which would pass North American safety standards. The journey would be difficult and time consuming.

Regardless, *Lowani Village* emerged as the top candidate.

I decided to make an adventure of the journey, and I put together a plan.

I decided to sacrifice some of my valued freedom and join an overland safari from Cape Town to Victoria Falls, Zimbabwe. The three-week trip would take me through Namibia and Botswana and end in Vic Falls. Although I was a little hesitant about the thought of travelling with 20 strangers on a set itinerary, it was the most efficient way for a solo traveller to cover the vast amount of space in both Namibia and Botswana without missing the bulk of breathtaking highlights.

Once in Victoria Falls, I would switch gears and use local transportation to mission through Zambia and into Malawi. I honestly had no idea how many days this leg of the journey would take. Using the local means of getting from A to B would be a new adventure. Considering the anomalies I had already encountered while in "modern" South Africa, it would be impossible to determine how long this expedition would take.

I would go one step at a time.

They would be quick steps though.

I made the decision to travel directly to Nkhata Bay from Victoria Falls without exploring Zambia. I did so because I feared that if I didn't establish a goal and final destination, the probability of getting stuck in Zambia and abandoning the Malawian experience altogether was enormous. I'd heard too many fantastic things about Nkhata Bay to miss it.

It was a good plan.

However, it wasn't perfect. I did have one, tiny hurdle to negotiate.

My South African holiday visa had expired. Technically, I was in the country illegally.

This one was my fault. Truthfully, I had neglected to keep tabs on the date. I'm not talking about the date stamped in my visa but the actual date of the year. If I'm honest, I think I had forgotten which month it was. This was one of the peculiar "problems" associated with living in Chintsa. Time had the amazing ability of vanishing.

I stopped wearing a watch ages ago, which made the actual time of day completely irrelevant. The next to go was the date of the month. This was quickly followed by the day of the week. I'd reached the point where I needed to remember if I had celebrated a specific holiday to help pinpoint the correct month of the year.

While living in Chintsa, days, weeks and months could slip away without being noticed. They obviously had. Combined with my blissful lifestyle, it was easy to understand how I let the expiration date in my passport come and go without notice or concern.

Frankly, I didn't anticipate a problem. Who was going to care if a Canadian tourist was only 14 days over his visa? The powers that be would unquestionably want foreign currency travelling around and getting spent in their relatively new and undiscovered nation. I assumed that since I was from the "western world" with "western money" to spend in their tourist-thirsty country, they would bend over backwards to extend my visa.

I thought that a polite explanation and possibly the payment of a fine would resolve the problem.

And if that approach failed, I still had another card to play.

If I couldn't sweet talk my way out of the dilemma, then I could always use bribery.

Although South Africa was progressing in the right direction, the country and the government were in their developmental stages. As a result, there existed a certain amount of lawlessness and inefficiency within branches of the South African bureaucracy. One obvious and blatant feature of this was bribery.

I had been first introduced to the world of bribery in Cape Town after I had been bumped from the flight to Windhoek. Half a pack of cigarettes was all it required to bribe the immigration officer into overlooking the two-week maximum visa and granting me a three-month extension.

Since then, I had witnessed bribery first-hand on the South African highways. More often than not, the simple statement that I am Canadian would get me waved through the speed trap. But if this didn't work, the next option would be to ask if it was possible to pay a "spot" fine.

Having become a seasoned traveller of the South African roads, I was wary of the numerous speed traps and would organize my wallet accordingly. In expectation of a pending bribe, I would have a 50 rand note ($10 Canadian) on display with the rest of my cash hidden elsewhere. A "pinkie," would be more than sufficient to bribe my way out of a larger fine and to quickly continue on the road.

Some cops would casually grab the exposed pinkie from my wallet, while others used a more clandestine approach to the illegal transaction. Either way, the bribe was finalized, and I was back on my way.

I was a bit surprised that there was such blatant and open lawlessness within the South African government departments and law enforcement agencies. However, as time went on, I appreciated that this was one of the many hurdles that a country in transition must deal with, particularly when that developing country is in Africa. It's not that North American government officials aren't subject to bribery because they most certainly are. The difference is in the clandestine nature and the amounts of the kickbacks. I would be hard pressed to bribe my way out of a Canadian traffic ticket with a 10-dollar bill. However, that same officer might be tempted by a significantly larger sum.

These Transkei traffic cops, living in the countryside on a poor wage, had nothing to lose and everything to gain.

Consequently, I made the brash assumption that either my Canadian charm or a quick slip of cash would result in a three-month extension. In spite of my suppositions, I decided that it would be prudent to deal with my immigration issue while still in the country as opposed to at a remote border crossing. The likelihood that complications could arise at a rural office was considerable. If the inefficiencies of the Home Affairs Offices in Cape Town were any indicator, then the crap in the remote border crossing would be unbearable. I was worried that if problems with my visa arose at a dingy shack of an immigration office, I could get detained in no man's land and possibly deported.

On the other hand, if all went pear shaped in King William's Town, where the nearest immigration office was located, I would still be in South Africa. I could toy with the idea of disappearing into the Transkei bush.

Nonetheless, as I drove to King William's Town, I was confident that all would go smoothly. In case I was asked, I fabricated a story about being ill in the Transkei and not being physically able to travel. I thought it was a feasible tale. By the time I entered the Department of Home Affairs, I was positive that I would leave with a three-month extension.

Similar to the Department of Home Affairs in Cape Town, this office was a zoo. Thankfully, there was a room designated to handle holiday visas. I was shown past the massive queue of frustrated South Africans and into an adjoining workspace. Crammed in this cubbyhole of a room were five women sitting around three desks. They simultaneously looked at me when I entered.

One of the ladies asked for my passport. She took a quick look at the photo. Once she had confirmed it was me, she passed it to the next lady who pulled out a sheet of paper. This lady then passed both the paper and passport to the third. This tedious process dragged on, and it wasn't until the passport, paper, pen and rubber stamp had reached the fifth and final woman that the expiration of my visa had been noticed. She made a "ssheesh" sound and shook her head in disapproval. She returned my passport and said, "I cannot give you a visa."

I looked all five women in disbelief. I was about to plead my "being sick" story when the women added, "And when you leave, you'll receive a five-year ban from returning."

The situation wasn't unfolding as I had anticipated.

I asked if there was anything that I could do.

The five women shook their heads in silence.

With my levels of frustration growing, I asked if there was anybody else, perhaps their superior, who I could talk with.

The lady sitting next to the phone let out a sigh, picked it up and dialed.

An agonizing and awkward minute later, she hung up, sighed, got up from her corner of the desk, squeezed past the others and indicated that I should follow her. She took me back past the congestion of people and upstairs to what I would describe as an official-looking office. It was only official in the sense that it was larger and less crammed than the previous. There were only three people, and they each had their own desk.

The woman ushered me to one of the desks, and my passport was handed to the immigration officer sitting there. The two spoke in Xhosa for a couple of minutes, leaving me once again uncertain about my South African fate.

After the woman had sighed and left the room, the immigration office looked at me and said, "Why are you over your visa?"

I launched into my spiel about being deathly ill in the Transkei. I made my account more dramatic by adding that upon my recovery, I discovered that my car was stuck in mud, and this further hindered my departure.

He listened to the lie and when I was finished, he sat for a moment in silence. When he let out a "sheesh" and started to shake his head, I knew that his answer wouldn't be what I wanted to hear. He said, "No. I'm afraid there's nothing that I can do."

A shot of panic raced through my body. The notion of having to leave South Africa without being able to return was one that made me sick to my stomach.

I began to initiate plan B.

I apologetically explained how much I loved South Africa and that I was normally a very reliable traveller. I explained how I had been to South Africa a couple of times and that the magic of his country had entranced me. I was laying it on thick as molasses.

However, I wasn't getting a reaction.

I threw him the bait. I explained that as a western traveller, I had lots of money that I wanted to spend in his country. I asked if there wasn't anything that he could do to help, while insinuating that I was willing to make a bribe.

"Well ..." began the immigration officer.

I recognized his tone and took that as my cue. As I reached for my wallet, I wondered what the amount of the bribe was going to be. If a bribe for a speeding ticket cost 50 rand, then the kickback for a visa extension must cost a minimum of a few hundred. I waited for him to name his price.

"We could make you a prohibited person."

A prohibited what?

That wasn't a proposal I was expecting or understood.

As it turned out, the immigration officer wasn't asking for a bribe. Instead, he was offering me an alternative. He explained that the Department of Home Affairs could classify me as a prohibited person, which in turn would provide me with an additional three weeks to leave the country. He said that they would take my photograph and record all my details such as where I was staying and when I was planning on travelling. If I departed South Africa within the specified three-week period, then I would be more than welcome to return.

However, if I failed to leave within the allocated time, immigration alarms and whistles would sound. Because they had my exact location and were, in essence, tracking me, they would swoop in, arrest and deport me. I'd be issued the notorious black stamp and told not to come back.

I really didn't have a choice.

This was my option.

I agreed to become a prohibited person.

The immigration officer began some paperwork and another officer took me to a room where my mug shot was taken. Five minutes later, I was back at the first immigration officer's desk. He produced a document and asked me to sign it

Obviously, like any intelligent individual, I read over the official-looking paper.

There were a few aspects of the application that drew my attention.

The first were the spelling and grammatical errors. However, these gaffes weren't surprising. After all, the immigration officer's mother tongue was Xhosa, not English. It was easy to overlook a few spelling mistakes, for I would have certainly made more than my share if I had to translate English into Xhosa.

The item that really caught my eye had nothing to do with the spelling lapses and everything to do with the basis for my extension. It wasn't something that I could easily overlook. It was the "official reason" the immigration officer had provided for the prohibition of my person.

"The holder of the permit may reside temporarily in (a) the Republic, (b) the Magisterial District or (c) Municipal Area of R.S.A. for the purpose of political asylum."

Political Asylum?

I reread the reason for my extension. I understood the document to say, in essence, I was granted political asylum in the Republic of South Africa.

The officer had it backwards. Other nations came to Canada for political asylum. A Canadian seeking political asylum didn't make any sense. Despite my mistrust of the Canadian government, I couldn't think of any hellish oppression that it imposed upon its citizens. Two-week vacations, the rat race or being subjected to arctic temperatures were not justifiable grounds for seeking political asylum. Even if there were valid reasons, I strongly doubt that a Canadian would ask for refuge in the Republic of South Africa.

I pointed to the line in question, explaining that I didn't think that Canadians could claim political asylum.

"Ah yes. Well, I believe you about your illness," he began to explain, although I detected a hint of recognition that he knew I was lying my ass off. "And I would like to give you an extension. However, I need a more official reason for doing so."

I gave it some thought. Despite the obvious puzzlement over my pending refugee status, the situation made a strange sense. South African immigration laws weren't designed to protect South Africa from Canadians. It's more plausible that the immigration laws were conceived with immigrants and refugees from Angola, Mozambique and Zimbabwe in mind. Canadians were probably the least of their concerns.

I put myself in the immigration officer's shoes. I couldn't imagine too many Canadians pleading their sob stories to him. On the other hand, I guessed that many Africans had. Political asylum had probably been a common request. It's plausible that the officer used the excuse he had both heard most often and was most familiar with.

I believed that he was trying to help me.

I really didn't have any alternatives.

I did the only thing I could, and I signed the paper.

Technically, I had been granted political asylum in the Republic of South Africa. This claim had to be a Canadian first. I couldn't think of any situation in Canada's short history that a citizen had been granted asylum anywhere. Not even the most disgruntled, angry, cold, Celine Dion-hating Canadian would have a legitimate claim for political asylum.

I strongly doubted that my Canadian citizenship would be affected. However, if there were any repercussions, it would be a bridge that I would cross later if and when I ever returned to Canada.

Who could have ever imagined this situation? I became a refugee to obtain a visa extension. I wouldn't have imagined it in my wildest dreams.

This made me give up making plans.

In fact, I decided to stop calling any thoughts about my future *plans*. Instead, I would call them *scenarios*. In this way, I would create a mental flexibility with regard to my future travels. And I would always bear in mind that none may happen. They were, after all, just *scenarios*.

Having said that, it was probably wise that half the distance to Malawi had been decidedly planned, organized and scheduled through the overland company, otherwise there was the strong possibility that I wouldn't get anywhere close to Nkhata Bay. I'd already made Canadian history in the unlikeliest of fashions, and I hadn't even begun the multi-country journey.

Of the thousands of scenarios that could lead me to Nkhata Bay, I just hoped one would get me there.

Anything could happen along the way …

This was Africa after all.

T.R.P
LQFTBZL
BI-89

REPUBLIC OF SOUTH AFRICA

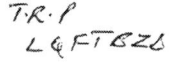

TEMPORARY PERMIT TO PROHIBITED PERSON
[Section 41 (1) of Act No. 96 of 1991: Regulation 22 (1)]

Serial No. 134167

... granted to the following person as holder of this permit to enter or remain in the RSA or part thereof as determined in part C hereof:

A. PERSONAL PARTICULARS OF HOLDER

Surname: HAMILTON   First name(s): MATTHEW CHARLES GORDON
Residential address: ▇▇▇▇▇▇▇▇▇▇
TRANSKEI
Date of birth: 74-01-28   Age: ___   Sex: M
Nationality: CANADIAN   Country of origin: CANADA
Passport or travel document No. ▇▇▇   Place of issue: PRETORIA   Expiry date: 7-02-20__

B. PARTICULARS OF DEPOSIT/GUARANTEE

File number: B6/1/20-4   An amount of (in words): waived

(in figures): R _____ Receipt No. _____ Name of depositor _____
as set in terms of section 41 (2) (a) of the Act as surety which must be deposited by or on behalf of the permit holder as guarantee that the holder will comply with the conditions subject to which the permit was issued.

Take Note
The amount deposited will be refunded when the holder leaves the Republic, and when satisfactory evidence that the conditions and requirements have been complied with, is furnished.

C. CONDITIONS

1. The holder of the permit may reside temporarily in (a) the Republic, (b) the Magisterial District or (c) Municipal Area of R.S.A for the purpose of POLITICAL ASYLUM

2. Employer's particulars (where applicable): Name _____
   Street address _____   Date of engagement _____
   _____   Period of contract _____
   Postal code _____   Date of discharge _____

3. This permit holder shall, without expenses to the State leave the Republic on or before 2022-04-26 or such later date as a duly authorised immigration officer may have endorsed on this permit for the purposes of extending the period of its validity.

4. The holder shall report to HOME AFFAIRS at intervals of 26 days/months and shall keep that officer duly advised of his place of residence. He shall give at least twenty-four hours prior notice (Sundays and public holidays excluded) of his intended departure.

5. If the holder does not leave the Republic on or before the date mentioned herein, the amount deposited under section 41 (2) (c) of the Act, shall be forfeited to the State, and the holder renders himself liable to prosecution in terms of the Act.

6. This permit is invalid, and the amount referred to therein is forfeited to the State, if the permit holder or the depositor or any other person concerned, named herein, made a false declaration or false representation when the permit was applied for or when it was obtained.

7. Other conditions: MAY LEAVE THE COUNTRY ON HER OWN EXPENSES
   Matthew Charles Gordon Hamilton

8. I/We _____ and _____ agree to the above conditions, and understand that a breach thereof may result in the forfeiture of the amount deposited, and will subject me/us to further steps stipulated in the Act.

X _[signature]_
Permit Holder   Depositor   Witness

Place: _____   Date: 2022-01-06

CERTIFICATE OF TRANSLATOR

I (full name) ▇▇▇▇▇▇▇▇▇▇
certify that I translated the content of this permit to the person/persons concerned in the language ENGLISH
and that he/she/they understand(s) the contents.

OFFICIAL STAMP

Just in case you didn't believe me: the insignificant piece of Canadian history and my favourite souvenir. Have you ever heard of anything as ridiculous as a Canadian receiving political asylum in the Republic of South Africa?

20

TRUST

JULY

I needed some weed.

Correction … I needed some *good* weed.

It had been three weeks since I last smoked anything remotely close to decent, and my nerves were frayed. This particular ganja drought was my longest spell without smoking since I had first toked way back in university. Okay, it hadn't been a total drought on this trip. I did smoke a tiny bit of ganja in Namibia and another joint deep in the Okavango Delta. But not surprisingly, weed from the desert and the middle of the swamp wasn't the highest quality. I was impressed that marijuana could even be found in the desert, but even so, it didn't stand a chance next to the potency of buds grown in the Transkei.

I needed some good weed so that I wouldn't end up killing somebody on the overland trip. I had been enduring the group for far too long. Three weeks with the same collection of people and the same fixed itinerary was beginning to do my head in. It wasn't even that I was stuck with a bad group. In actuality, I was very fortunate in the people that I was travelling with. But after three weeks in close confinements, my companions' annoying habits, even the tiniest of traits, were beginning to scratch at my brain.

I needed some good weed to help me get my head around what I was witnessing in Victoria Falls, Zimbabwe.

Not that long ago, words such as stunning, vibrant and friendly were used to describe this famous corner of Zimbabwe. Regrettably, that is no longer the case. The city was, in a word, desperate. I wish I could find another descriptor, but unfortunately there isn't a more accurate word to describe this touristy town. Even the majestic Victoria Falls, one of the world's Seven Wonders, couldn't distract me from the harsh reality that was afflicting everyone living in the area.

Desperation hung in the air.

Old and recent history, politics and the media were major contributors to this dire situation in Zimbabwe.

In November 1998, Robert Mugabe's government decided that it would seize 1503 white-owned farms and only compensate for the improvements made during ownership. They would not compensate for the land itself. Understandably, this policy didn't go over well with the white farmers who were decidedly against giving up their homes and livelihoods. Mugabe's next political move was to publish his own constitutional clause that allowed the seizure of farms. Many locals viewed this statement as approval to invade and reclaim white-owned property, which many tried and some accomplished.

Sadly, in a few isolated instances, violent and fatal encounters between armed assailants and armed farmers arose. In most cases, the victims were the farm workers who were unhappy with the seizures, knowing that their survival depended on the farmer.

Not surprisingly, the insane national politics of Mugabe and the ensuing bloodbaths had drawn the attention of the sharks. The media's "nothing but negative," grim and narrow coverage had scared the living pants off any potential travellers to Zimbabwe. The news networks, the sons of bitches that they are, had painted a picture that would have the western world thinking that every black Zimbabwean was ready and willing to bury a machete into the head of any white person.

One of the many results of Mugabe's media-hyped antics was a massive blow to the tourism industry in most of Southern Africa. Victoria Falls, a city that relied on tourism as its primary lifeline, suffered the most.

The tourist drought was unmistakable on the empty streets of Victoria Falls. Not that long ago, these were streets packed with travellers spending their foreign currency.

Nevertheless, the real consequence of this sad demise of an African nation was illustrated on the faces of the local people.

They wore desperate, pleading faces.

Walking down the street in Vic Falls was like going through a gauntlet of merchants. They frantically tried to sell me anything for whatever price they could get. It was possible that I would be one of the few potential customers to pass their way that day, and they weren't going to let the opportunity to make a sale pass them by.

One would shout, "Ten dollars," shoving a wooden elephant in my face.

"Five dollars," he would plead, not waiting for my answer to his first price.

"Two dollars! Please my friend, just one dollar! Please! Please!" The sense of urgency in the voice was evident. There was almost a trace of panic.

Sadly, it was the same state of affairs wherever I went. It was impossible to avoid it. There were hundreds of these local merchants selling anything from wooden giraffes to beadwork to elaborate mask carvings. The desperation was everywhere from the locals on the streets to the five-star hotels. There wasn't any way of escaping it.

The energy in Vic Falls was miserable and draining.

I needed to bury my head in the sand for a bit.

When I first arrived in Victoria Falls, I found a kid selling weed in the market. I tried to convince him that I would pay more money for better quality weed and that I would, if it was decent, come back for more. My reasoning with the lad didn't work. The weed he sold me was full of stems and seeds and tasted like shit. In the end, the ganja was more work than pleasure.

Nonetheless, I too was getting desperate. I returned to the market where I had scored the weed the first night. I walked around for about half an hour searching for the kid, but he was nowhere to be found. I didn't feel like going through the massive headache of trying to buy from some other kid waiting to sell me crap.

Fuck it.

I'd have a beer instead.

I was about to walk back to the hostel when I heard my name being called. I turned around to see two girls from the overland truck, Melissa and Jane, waddling towards me. Their arms and backpacks were loaded with knick-knacks ranging from necklaces to five-foot tall wooden giraffes. Judging from their mass of souvenirs, I guessed that these two had taken advantage of the locals' desperate economic situation and pillaged them of their goods for a fraction of the already low price.

I was correct in my assumption, for the girls immediately began telling me about the amazing bargains and their wonderful, newly discovered haggling skills. They bragged about how they were able to get all the beautiful carvings, artwork, necklaces and other assortments of crafts for a few dollars, an old T-shirt and some pens.

It was sickening.

There was no sense in arguing with them about how they just screwed some poor guy out of his art for a pen and how his family wouldn't be able to eat a shirt. It would be pointless. They were just 18 and naïve to the realities that surrounded them. They didn't get it, and I wasn't sure if they ever would.

I wanted to get the hell out of there.

The girls suggested that we take a taxi back to the hostel, since it was a 20-minute walk, and they had too much stuff to carry. It was hot as hell, and the walk in the heat wasn't something I was looking forward to. I'd be a monkey's uncle before I'd be seen helping the girls carry their stolen goods, so I conceded to sharing a taxi. At the very least, I would be back at the hostel and drinking my beer much sooner.

We walked a couple of blocks to the taxi rank and hopped into a cab. The girls and their hoard took up the back seat, so I sat in the front. Before we could pull away from the curb, a kid thrust his head through my open window and asked if I wanted to buy any weed. It wasn't the same kid from the night before, so I knew that I'd be starting the bargaining hassle from scratch. I didn't have the energy, nerves or patience to deal with this kid, so I politely declined his offer.

As the taxi drove away, a deep voice said, "Don't buy weed from them. They sell shit."

The voice belonged to the taxi driver, and from its raspiness, I got the impression that he was a long-term smoker. He had the type of rough, gravelly voice that suggested an automatic voice box was only a few smokes away from being added to his wardrobe.

The weed I had smoked yesterday had been crap, yet it was still the best that I had seen. As a result, I was a tad sceptical that there was any decent ganja in Vic Falls. I asked the driver if he knew what good weed looked like.

"Yep," the driver answered. He pulled open the ashtray, and it was packed with marijuana. He removed a plump, juicy bud of ganja and handed it to me.

"This," he continued without taking his eyes off the road. "This is good weed."

I had to admit, the ganja looked great. It smelled even better. In fact, it was the best-looking gear that I'd seen in three weeks. It looked as though it could have been harvested from the Transkei. Without a doubt, it looked better than the crap that I had smoked the previous night, which up until this moment was pathetically the best weed that I'd seen outside of South Africa.

I wanted to get some of the driver's ganja.

I was trying to figure out a casual way to ask the driver if he had any to sell when he leaned over and said, "Do you want to smoke some?"

I enthusiastically replied that I did.

We dropped off the girls and their booty at the backpackers and drove a couple blocks away to a quiet street where the driver parked the car. There was little chit-chat as the driver, whose name was Fred, swiftly and skilfully rolled an enormous joint. When he had finished, he looked at me with his brown, smoky eyes, smiled and stated, "My friend, you are going to get high."

He lit the joint and then passed it to me.

Fred was very accurate with his prediction.

It may have been because I hadn't smoked anything for three weeks, but Fred's joint smacked me. It was also possible that his weed was ridiculously strong, but regardless of the reason, I got goofed. I mean I got super goofed, super quick. I felt the first toke creep into the backs of my eyeballs almost immediately.

My body tingled.

My head floated.

My mind relaxed.

After three weeks of depravation and annoyances, I was finally high. And what a high it was. Sometimes weed made me stoned. Being stoned was ideal when I was chilling out on the sofa, listening to Pink Floyd and not saying a word to anyone. Other times, weed made me high. Being high was the complete opposite sensation of being stoned. When I was high, I was talkative and full of laughter.

Fred and I were both very, very high.

What developed over the course of another joint was a classic stoner's conversation. We talked about how long we'd been smoking weed and what our views were about the extensive values of ganja. We talked about the drug laws in our respective countries. We talked about the shit weed that we'd smoked, and we talked about the premium weed that we'd smoked. We talked about the different ways to consume marijuana. (Fred's favourite method was the bong.) We philosophized and talked about "the big picture." We had several one-sided discussions that would usually end with the speaker saying, "… what was I talking about?"

Then there would be laughter. Lots and lots of laughter.

As I said, it was a classic stoner conversation.

We smoked another joint and began driving back to the hostel. I decided that Fred's weed was by far the best gear I had come across since leaving South Africa and could very possibly be the best ganja that I'd find until Malawi.

I asked him if he had any weed that he could sell me.

"No," he replied. "But I can get you some if you want. It's about a half hour drive from here. I could pick it up for you, my friend."

By this time, we had pulled into the driveway of the backpackers. I was properly baked and didn't feel like sitting in a car for an hour. What I really wanted to do was lie on my back, chill and stare at the sky. The third joint brought me from the realm of being high to being stoned.

Therefore, I put forth an offer to Fred. I said that I would give him the money for the weed, and if he didn't mind, I would wait here for him to come back.

"No problem," answered Fred. "How much do you want?"

I gave him 1000 Zim dollars (about $20 Canadian) and asked him to buy me whatever that amount could get. I told him that I trusted him.

It may sound odd, but even though I had just met the guy, I did trust Fred. I certainly trusted him enough to score some ganja for me. In our time together, I didn't detect any negative vibes coming from Fred. He never said or did anything to indicate that he might have ulterior motives other than getting high with me. We'd had a great laugh together. He had been very open about his past and present life. The whole time that I had spent with Fred, I felt nothing but relaxed and safe. All my instincts said that Fred was sound as a pound.

I had no doubt that my new friend would get me the weed.

I gave Fred the cash, hopped out of the taxi and watched him drive away. I waved and smiled. I was happy for a couple of reasons. The first and most obvious was that, after three long weeks, I was finally good and high. More importantly though, I was stoked because I had just had an amazing experience with a native Zimbabwean that wasn't paid for or designed as a tour. "Smoke joint with random taxi driver" wasn't on any overland itinerary that I knew of. I didn't feel as though I had visited the zoo or imposed on somebody's rights and privacy.

I'd had a genuine, random and educational encounter.

I went to find Charlie and Jon, who were the only two people on the truck who didn't drive me insane. I knew that they would be ecstatic about my score. They were almost as desperate for weed as I was. I found them chilling in the backyard of the hostel. I lay down on the grass between them, gazed at the clouds and told them the wicked news.

Their eyes widened with excitement, and their mouths salivated in anticipation when I told them that I had just scored some primo gear. However, in spite of the fantastic news, their faces took on strange and worried expressions when I had finished the story.

"You gave him the money?"

Charlie's question was casual, and so to was my response.

"And … you think he is going to come back?"

Up until that point, I did think Fred was going to come back. Up until that point, the clouds that I had been hazily staring at resembled fluffy bunnies. However, once Charlie insinuated that I had been ripped off, my mind took a negative turn, and the clouds quickly morphed into dark, menacing evil hares from hell.

My certainty of Fred's return diminished significantly.

Shit. Had I just been scammed?

Damn. If it was a scam, what a great con it was. Pick up some stupid tourist and get him stupid stoned. Shoot the shit with him for awhile. Get him nice and relaxed. Get him so relaxed that the stupid tourist asks where he can get some of the good stuff. Tell the stupid tourist that you have to go and pick it up. Get the stupid tourist to give you the money, drive off and never be seen by that stupid tourist again.

What's the stupid tourist going to do about it? Find the driver? Not a chance. Go to the police and issue a complaint? Yeah, right. What would one say? "Excuse me, officer, but one of your taxi drivers took off with my money to buy me some weed, and he never came back." I don't think so.

It was virtually a foolproof scam.

Shit. The scam was certainly proof that I was a fool.

I wasn't upset about losing the money. It was only a few bucks. I lose more money in the cushions of my couch. What bothered me was that I had been drastically wrong in my assessment of Fred's character and motivation. This was upsetting, first, because I had been wrong, which was something that I hated to admit. But more crucially, it was a major blow to my belief that I could quickly gauge people and calculate their intentions.

This was a skill that I believed was a vital necessity while travelling alone.

Charlie and Jon began to laugh at my rookie mistake.

I knew that I was going to have to swallow my pride and admit that I had been wrong in my judgement.

As I waited for a break in the laughter to concede my blunder, something inside me told me not to. Something about the situation wasn't sitting right. I just couldn't believe that I had been duped that easily.

So with all the courage and arrogance that I possessed, I told Charlie and Jon that I thought Fred would still deliver the weed.

They laughed even harder.

I stood my ground. I told them that they hadn't been in the taxi with us and, therefore, hadn't heard the conversation. I brashly told them that there hadn't been a single trace of deception in Fred's voice or manner. He was as relaxed as me, if not more so. I confidently stated that there was no way that he had ripped me off.

Jon was able to control his laughter for a moment and said, "You wanna bet?"

I didn't have a choice. I'd been cocky enough to state that there would be weed arriving. Even though my money was sitting in some taxi with some strange man, I still believed there was a chance Fred would deliver. I'd be weak in my convictions if I didn't bet. I asked how much he wanted to wager.

"How about six beers?" asked Jon through uncontrollable laughter.

I took the bet. Fred said that it was a half an hour drive to get the weed. Therefore, with a half an hour there, maybe ten minutes or so to buy the weed, then another half an hour back, I was looking at no more than 80 minutes before I'd find out whether I was right or wrong in my belief about Fred's character.

Two hours later, there was still no sign of Fred.

I angrily conceded to myself that I had been scammed.

I was pissed off.

I wasn't mad at losing the money, and believe it or not, I wasn't even pissed at Fred. I took into consideration where he was living and the desperate situation that he was trying to survive. The money may have been jack shit to me, but that kind of dough was a shitload to him. Christ, he didn't even ask me for the money, I fucking gave it to him! I'm an honest guy, but there was a distinct possibility that I'd drive off into the sunset if some Japanese tourist handed over a thousand Canadian bucks to buy him a Big Mac.

Ultimately, I was pissed off with myself.

I was pissed off for letting my guard down.

I felt like a fucking idiot.

I had felt this way once before on my travels. While in Tenerife, I moronically lost 20 bucks in the "obvious to everybody but me" three-card monty scam. It was a feeling of absolute stupidity that made me sick to my stomach, question my intelligence and mistrust my basic common sense. The only consolation was that the Tenerife blunder had been early in my travels, and I chalked that screw-up to being wet behind the ears. I considered the mistake a lesson learned.[1]

I clearly hadn't learned my lesson. Making a similar blunder at this point in my travels and in this part of the world was what truly steamed my beans. I was in a part of Africa where a wrong move could cost me more than money.

An agonizing two and a half hours after I had handed over my money, Charlie, Jon and I headed down the hostel's driveway for a night out in Victoria Falls. My wallet and pride were paying for the first six beers. However, before we got to the gate of the property, a taxicab pulled into the driveway.

Fred was behind the wheel.

---

1. For anyone unaware, the person who seems to be continuously winning is in on the scam. When you finally put down your money, the dealer will palm the card in question and, ultimately, screw you out of your 20 bucks.

I'm not sure what I said to Jon and Charlie as I ran over to Fred's cab, but I'm positive that the comments were dripping with a victorious arrogance.

Fred had his window rolled down by the time I got there.

"I'm sorry that I took so long. My friend who I usually buy from didn't have any more, so I had to drive even further," Fred said apologetically.

He pulled a massive bag of weed from under his seat and, with a wicked smile that only a smoker could truly understand, he said, "This stuff is even better."

Honestly, it didn't matter.

It didn't matter that it took Fred longer than he had expected. Shit. What's time in Africa? I'd been on the continent long enough to know that we were on the African clock. One shouldn't expect things to happen in a specified time.

The size of the bag of weed didn't matter. The sack could have been 10 times smaller, which still would have dwarfed the pitiful bag I bought from the kid on the street the day before.

It didn't matter that the weed was a better quality. It could have been shit for all I cared.

What mattered was that Fred came back.

It mattered because it restored my faith in my capability to determine one's intentions. Once again, I believed I could establish whether someone would help me or screw me. More importantly, though, was that Fred's return radically improved my faith in my fellow man.

Fred didn't know me. As far as he knew, I was one of those rich, demeaning, ignorant tourists who came through Vic Falls waving money and haggling his people into accepting a pencil for their beautiful crafts. I hate to say it, but from the stories and from what I have seen with my own eyes, the large majority of tourists who travelled through this city were exactly that type.

Why wouldn't Fred think of me in the same negative light? Why wouldn't he take my money and disappear?

Maybe because Fred was a decent man, and he knew stealing was wrong.

Maybe because he was a good judge of character, and he saw I wasn't the typical, greedy tourist.

Maybe because Fred, like me, believed that although we lived in a world full of despair and greed, there were still some good people worth being good to.

Maybe because we knew that there were people worth trusting.

The African Elephant. Etosha National Park, Namibia

21

A TO B

JULY

It was time to hit the road again. Although it had been an interesting experience travelling across a small chunk of Southern Africa, and I was fortunate to see some truly beautiful places, the three-week overlander was only a segment of my lengthy journey. I still had another thousand kilometres of countryside to negotiate before I could begin the increasingly necessary chilling out portion of my holiday in Malawi's Nkhata Bay.

However, in order to reach this piece of what I was hoping was paradise, I had to venture into the unknown world of local African transportation.

Although I'd been travelling for almost two years, I didn't have much experience in what I would describe as "real African" travelling. My previous African travelling had been in the back of rental cars or on the comparatively luxurious South African coach lines. I was now about to dabble in true, local, public transportation, and from what I had been told, this would be a completely different experience than anything else I'd attempted so far.

Making the journey even more intimidating was my lack of a guidebook, which meant I didn't have the slightest idea how I was actually going to get to Nkhata Bay. Everything from the bus schedules to the accommodation was a mystery to me. Any information regarding the hows and wheres of this voyage I took from the mouths and experiences of other backpackers. However, despite the concerns and uncertainties, I started to get used to this style of clueless travel.

Up to now, my trip around the planet had been a series of unexpected events, usually triggered in some way by my general ignorance about the ways of the world. Quite possibly due to dumb luck, my predicaments so far had inevitably proved enlightening and beneficial to my overall, global education. If diving in headfirst had guided me safely to this point and provided me with the knowledge that it had, there was no sense in changing my modus operandi now.

Nonetheless, I decided to make this journey with Charlie and Jon. They too wanted to get to Malawi as quickly as possible, for they also loved the idea of chilling lakeside with quality ganja. Other than getting on with both Charlie and Jon, I thought that travelling with two guys across unknown African territory, even though they were as clueless as I, might be a wise decision. There was nothing wrong with having two extra sets of eyes watching my inexperienced back.

Since we would be using local land transportation, travelling from Victoria Falls to Malawi in one or even two days would be impossible. By my rough, uneducated estimation, if all things went relatively smoothly, I hoped we would arrive in Nkhata Bay in three to four days.

Honestly, I was basing our estimated date of arrival on nothing.

I had no idea.

Our scenario for the first day was to travel from Livingston, Zambia, a prospering town just a few kilometres from the Zimbabwean border, to Lusaka, the country's capital. We had crossed over to Livingston from Victoria Falls the previous day to save some time. We needed to wake at the crack of dawn in order to catch the early morning bus to Lusaka. It was a 500-kilometre journey, and it would take the entire day.

It would prove a day of learning.

My first lesson was that departure times were mere suggestions. The bus departed when, and only when, it was full. Our 7:00 AM bus didn't leave until almost 9:00 AM despite the vehicle being full, in my comprehension of the word, by a quarter past seven. My understanding of the term "maximum capacity" drastically differed from that of the average Zambian bus driver.

To my bewilderment, the driver and porters found every nook and cranny in, on top of and around the bus to stuff another family along with all of their possessions. These items included luggage, food and, in some cases, livestock. There were so many of us packed into the metal tube on wheels that I wasn't sure if the bus was destined for Lusaka or some clown act at the circus.

Finally, after what felt like a hot, sweaty and smelly eternity, the bus rumbled out of the terminal. Once we were on the road, the other realities of African transportation became glaringly apparent.

The second lesson was actually more of an African rule of the road. Pedestrians *do not* have the right of way.

I had assumed that because the majority of people using the roadways were people on foot they might have some sort of privilege or right of way, as pedestrians most certainly do back in Canada.[1]

This was a wrong assumption.

Never in my life had I seen so many narrow misses or as many people dive out of the way of a speeding bus than I did on this journey to Lusaka. It could have been my petrified mind, but it appeared that the bus driver accelerated when he saw a congestion of people approaching. It was as though he was playing some sort of terrifyingly realistic, road racing video game.

I concluded that looking out the front windscreen was a bad idea. In fact, I realized that, if at all possible, I should avoid sitting next to or looking out any windows. If I stared out my side window, I could see how narrowly we missed another oncoming, speeding bus. I had a disheartening feeling that I could only say, "Damn, that was close" so many times.

I soon realized that sitting near the front on the bus was the absolute worst place to be. Sitting in the shotgun position meant I had an unobstructed view out of the scariest window, the front windscreen. This also meant I could see the speedometer, assuming that it was working, and therefore I knew exactly how fast we were going to slam into one of the many obstacles, man, animal or metal, that littered the highway. Equally frightening was that I could also determine what the driver of the out of control piece of metal was doing. I could see whether he was drinking spirits or beer and how many he had consumed. I could see how long he kept his eyes off the road while he was talking to the person behind him. By sitting in the front, I discovered that I could establish whether the driver was attempting to avoid the mass of people cluttered on the roadside or whether he was gunning for them and trying to make them dive for the bushes. Sitting in the front left no doubt in my traumatized mind about the driver's terrifying agenda.

Following a quick stop, I "Huckleberry Finned" Charlie into swapping my front seat for his middle seat by convincing him that the front was the exciting place to be.

My logic behind wanting to sit in the middle of the bus was that I would be distracted by people and objects of all ages, shapes, sizes and smells. Therefore, I wouldn't have the time or interest to look out the window and see how close I came to dying horrifically in a fiery mass of crumpled metal and flesh. These distractions ranged from annoying to entertaining to "I can't believe I just saw that!" What provided further interest was that local African buses not only transported

---

1. In Canada, we always assume that cars will stop. Canadians will blindly step off a curb and into the middle of a street, knowing that between the polite disposition and the fear of lawsuits, oncoming drivers will stop. Canadians obviously consider it irrelevant that moving metal hurts when it slams into you. Canadians would be grease stains on the highway if they incorporated that approach here in Africa and probably almost anywhere else in the world.

people, but they also transported their goods for the village or for sale at the market. On this particular journey, the objects ranged from live chickens to a basket of fish (you can imagine the smell of dead fish on a hot, overcrowded bus) to a washing machine. Unfortunately, conversation with my fellow passengers was limited and difficult, for not many of the locals spoke English, and I didn't speak a lick of the local dialect other than "hello." Nonetheless, smiling attempts at communication provided many valuable distractions from the near-death experiences. I would much rather make stupid faces at the kids inside the bus than see the terrified faces of those outside.

Time and speed were difficult to judge, and as a result, our estimated time of arrival would be, at best, a stab in the dark. One of the difficulties was that the vehicle rarely stayed at a continuous speed for any significant amount of time. Livestock on the road could vary the speed of the bus. For example, if there was a herd of cattle on the road, then the driver might be inclined to stop, or at least slow down. But if there were only a couple of cows on the road, then the driver might possibly speed up, assuming that the cows would either move or the velocity of the bus would vaporize the beef on contact.

If there was a hill, it would be faster to get out of the bus, walk ahead, make a cup of tea and take a nap than wait for the bus to eventually struggle to the top. On the other hand, if the bus happened to be travelling downhill, then the out of control death trap appeared to reach Formula 1 speeds. Depending on how steep the hill was, the insanity of the driver and how poorly the brakes worked (brakes never worked *well*, there were just different degrees of *poor*), your speeds could vary greatly.

Ultimately, you needed a PhD in chaos theory to calculate an estimated time of arrival.

With all the obstacles and dangers throughout this journey, I honestly didn't care what time we arrived in Lusaka as long as we arrived. All that truly concerned me was that we reached Lusaka in one piece.

In the end, this was all that really could concern me. There wasn't anything that I could do about any of the other travelling hazards. I credit this recognition to the calm demeanour of my fellow African passengers. These men, women and children of all ages were dressed in their Sunday's finest, eating packed lunches and gabbing away in an incomprehensible language. They helped me accept that the sketchy conditions associated with Third World transportation were an unavoidable part of the package. For an African, it was quite a novelty and expense to travel by bus. The locals considered the actual journey as much a part of the adventure and story as their final destination.

They were correct.

This packed, shitty bus and others like it would be the only options available to my budget and me. I decided to make the most of the exceptional circumstances.

But this was a difficult task to accomplish.

After countless near misses, some apparent divine intervention and a stop at the foulest cesspool of feces, urine and vomit otherwise known as a bathroom, we arrived safely in Lusaka and were dropped in the heart of the Zambian capital.

The moment we stepped off the bus, a barrage of aggressive and determined drivers pounced on us. They all tried to entice us to get into their respective taxis. All I wanted was a smoke, but before I could light up, our bags and bodies were herded into a cab. Thankfully, my frayed nerves were somewhat mended when we arrived at the guest house. The place turned out to have quite a friendly and welcoming atmosphere. After a quick dinner and a couple of spliffs, we hit the sack. The days' travelling had exhausted us. The next day was going to be another early start, and it would be, without question, long and uncomfortable.

The morning began exactly as the previous one, with a lot of sitting around and doing nothing other than waiting for the porters to cram the bus. Frustratingly yet not surprisingly, we waited until mid morning for the pre-dawn bus to finally make its exit from Lusaka. Our day's goal was to reach the Malawian capital, Lilongwe. If everything went without incident, I thought we would arrive before the sun had set.

At least I hoped we would.

The distance we had to travel was less than the previous day's journey. However, we did have a couple of new obstacles to overcome. The first hurdle was that the bus we were travelling on wasn't an international bus and could only transport us to the Malawian border. This meant we would have to negotiate our way across the border and find another ride once in Malawi. Also, there wouldn't be a chance to exchange our money for the Malawian currency, the Kwatcha, other than through the locals on a semi-legal black market.

For reasons unknown to me, the bus dropped us off about five kilometres from the Malawian border. My only guess was that this was done to promote the local taxi industry, for when we get off the bus, more faces immediately surrounded us. And they were even more determined than the bunch that hounded us in Lusaka. Some were guiding us towards their taxis, while others wanted to exchange money. We managed to arrange both, although I'm positive that we got swindled on both counts with a lousy exchange rate and an offensive fare to travel the few remaining kilometres.

At least we were getting somewhere.

Unfortunately, that somewhere was just inside the Malawian border at a dingy taxi rank. This time the mission was to find a driver who was heading for Lilongwe. The task took much longer than I had anticipated. Mini taxis were possibly scarier than the buses because, although much smaller than the bus, they shared the same theory of overcrowding. The seats were uncomfortable without cushions, and no matter where I sat, I could scrutinize the driver's non-existent knowledge of the rules of the road. I could also detect the odour of booze on his breath, and empty beer cans rattling in the front were further evidence that our driver had been drinking.

Our particular mini taxi was so crammed that the driver had removed his steering wheel and replaced the rather essential component with a basic pipe wrench. By affixing the tool to the exposed steering bolt, the driver could slide his seat as far forward as possible, creating space for at least one more passenger.

It was on the jam-packed mini taxi that I learned to block out everything around me and mentally escape to a "happy place." This was a tough feat to accomplish considering everything picking, probing and in some case stabbing at my concentration. I had to contort my body like an Indian yoga guru, for we were once again packed like sardines. It was impossible to shuffle around my seat without displacing the entire row of people. As a miserable result, I was stuck in one uncomfortable position for the five-hour journey. The possibilities of a mental breakdown were worth betting on. Mental escape was a vital necessity in preserving my sanity.

I began to shut down.

I attempted to physically shut down so that I wouldn't cramp up. The cramping I'm talking about was not the numbness in my ass, which set in the moment I sat down. Instead, it was the spasms of muscles that I never dreamed existed.

Mentally, I had to become like an upright coma patient. I would sit dead still, blandly staring at one place in an attempt to think about a happier, more spacious and luxurious location.

Unfortunately, my mental barrier was penetrated by the fact that the daylight was quickly fading. I didn't want to arrive in Lilongwe after dark. I'd heard one too many horror stories of backpackers being mugged by thieves brandishing machetes in broad daylight to contemplate the potential dangers of arriving at night. Thankfully, we knew where we were staying. All we had to do was arrive before sunset.

Nevertheless, as the sun sank lower and lower on the horizon, so did my confidence.

Fortunately, we arrived in Lilongwe just as the sun disappeared. The mini taxi dropped us off in the heart of the city in the midst of a bustling market. The driver told us that the hostel was just down the road a few hundred metres. We thanked him. It was not so much for the ride but more for not killing us in the process. We threw on our packs and made our way down the road to the hostel.

As we walked through the market, I could feel dozens of eyes on us, or should I say, *the valuables on* us. Thank Christ we knew where we were staying, for I knew that three white backpackers aimlessly wandering around the streets would be more than a flashing light to any lurking thieves. I didn't want to be out in the open any longer than I had to. I had a nasty feeling that if we didn't get behind lock and key soon, it wouldn't be a question of *if* we got mugged but *when*.

We took a deep, collective sigh of relief when we saw the broken neon sign of our hostel.

However, I almost choked on that sigh when the man at reception informed us that all the rooms were full and that there wasn't a single bed available on the premises.

We asked if he knew where else could we stay.

He shook his head and said he didn't know.

Obviously, neither did we. Hesitantly, we left the relative safety of the hostel and began to walk down the road. Then we realized that the direction we were heading was taking us away from the city centre and, more importantly, away from the protection of the lights. We quickly turned and started back towards town. This was a critical mistake, for it indicated to any potential assailant who might be watching that we didn't have the foggiest idea where we were going. I knew that the uncertainty of our actions and our loaded backpacks in this poverty-stricken community were drawing the attention of many sets of nefarious eyes.

One set of eyes came hurrying up to us. The eyes were set into the head of a tiny, squat, middle-aged African woman who looked just as confused as we were.

"Do you know where you are going?" she asked in a perplexed tone.

The three of us shook our heads.

"Do you have any idea where you are?" she continued.

Again, the three of us ignorantly shook our heads.

The woman glanced around cautiously. "Listen, I'm a policewoman. This is an extremely dangerous part of town. There are many dangerous people around. Come with me immediately."

Adhering to her own warning, the woman turned and set off at a hurried pace. She didn't wait to find out whether or not we were following. Did the woman have a premonition about something that we idiotic white boys were unaware of? I wasn't willing to gamble my life that she didn't.

We followed her.

Besides, what other choice did we have? Charlie, Jon and I didn't have a clue where we were or, more importantly, how to get somewhere safe. I knew that it would be just a matter of time before we were mugged. We were three white tourists, weighed down with full packs and wandering around in the unknown streets of the city centre. The word "if" never entered the realm of possibility.

I gave us about two minutes before we saw the sharp end of a machete.

A soupçon of doubt passed through my head that maybe the woman we were blindly following was part of a scam. Maybe she was leading us unsuspecting lambs to the slaughter. However, the way the woman clung to her handbag along with the brisk pace of her walk led me to believe that she was as shit-scared as we were. Besides, we were screwed if we didn't follow. Truth be told, I'd much rather be mugged by this middle-aged lady than some of the nasty characters that were eyeing us.

We walked for no more than two minutes before we arrived at a large compound. With the high cement wall that surrounded the entire complex, the place looked like a prison. As we entered what appeared to be the only gate in the wall, two girls strolled up to us and began speaking to the policewoman in Chichewa.

After a minute, the woman (who, in my eyes, now ranked among the greatest heroines of all time) turned to us and said that there were rooms available and that two girls would show us to the reception. She said as long as we stayed within the complex, we would be safe.

We began to thank the woman and offer her our first-borns as gratitude for saving our lives, but she was gone. She didn't want to hear it. I don't think she cared. She had priorities, and the main one was her own life. That meant she must stop listening to the naive, asking-for-it white boys and get to safety.

No sooner had our guardian angel disappeared around the corner when one of the young girls left with the responsibility of showing us safely to reception turned to me and casually asked, "You want woman?"

I looked at the other girl for some sort of confirmation that what I had heard and what was being insinuated were one and the same. Her hand was on her slightly thrust hip, and the other hand was stroking her front. "You like?" she asked.

This was more than enough to conclude that the policewoman had put our well-being in the hands of a couple of hookers.

We politely declined their offer, not wanting to offend the ladies of the night. After all, we were still out in the open and by no means safe from the dangers of the dark. The girls, although annoyed with our refusal, led us to the reception. This place, however, would more accurately be described as a lounge, parlour or whorehouse, for there were a dozen or so scantily dressed ladies with a couple of rather nasty looking lads who I'm assuming were either their pimps or drug dealers.

Once again, I could feel all eyes in the room checking us out.

The man at reception gave us a key to the room, which we found with relative ease, for it was just around the corner from the gang of pimps and hookers. The grimy shack of a room didn't appear to be any safer. The first thing that caught my eye in our scuzzy accommodation was the used condom lying on the floor. I then noticed that there were more bars on the window than Alcatraz. A human hand and machete wouldn't have been able to reach in, but there was enough space between the bars for hoards of malaria-carrying mosquitoes to swarm through, which made our room an infested potential death trap.

We doused ourselves in bug spray and decided to go immediately to sleep. We thought along the same lines as a kid waiting for Christmas morning. The sooner we went to bed, the sooner morning would arrive, and the sooner we could get out of this hellhole.

None of us slept very well, if we slept at all, during the night. We were terrified that, at any moment, the gang of thieving pimps would kick in our door. We weren't as concerned about them taking our stuff as we were about them not wanting to leave living witnesses.

The following morning, although still in one piece, it was brutally clear that the three of us were stressed from the previous day's near-death adventure. I could see in Charlie and Jon's eyes that they were fed up with the pace of the voyage. They really needed to get lakeside and chill out for a couple of days. I have to admit that I too was getting pissed off and frustrated. After last night's close encounter, I was even more desperate to begin chilling lakeside with some Malawian cob.

We did have an option. We could spend another full day of hard travelling in an attempt to get to Nkhata Bay, or we could travel an easy couple of hours to Senga Bay, which was a little lakeside village that I had heard good things about.

It was an easy choice. We decided to go to Senga Bay.

The mission was simple. All that it involved was a quick hour and a half ride in the back of a pickup truck. Although we were once again packed like sardines in the back of the sketchy vehicle, we did have the luxury of open air and a continuous breeze to keep us cool and eliminate any sense of claustrophobia. The smiles on our faces grew as we spotted the deep blue of the lake in the distance. Our goal of getting away from moving vehicles and planting our butts down on sand was getting closer.

Initially, Senga Bay appeared perfect. We scored some weed from the guys at the guest house, which was a tiny campsite consisting of a handful of rustic huts and a tiny restaurant. We dropped our packs, quickly made our way to the beach and swam in the beautiful aqua blue water of Lake Malawi. Following a couple of spliffs on the sand, the three of us began to unwind. We laughed about our previous day's adventures and viewed them as amazing experiences as opposed to torturous hardships designed by the gods to satisfy their sick senses of humour. As we basked in the sun, we discussed the possibility of staying in Senga Bay for a couple of days rather than missioning on to Nkhata Bay the following morning and having to deal with another full day of African travelling. I considered the suggestion.

That was until we got back to camp.

The first sign that something wasn't kosher was that there were a few locals hanging around our room. The moment we opened the door, they followed us in and began eyeing our belongings. They started asking for our possessions and even went so far as to flat out demand cash. They said that they were poor, and we, as rich travellers in their country, should naturally give them a chunk of our bucks. Sensing that there was something to be had, more and more locals came into our room with the same aggressive and demanding attitude. I knew from the flimsy lock on the door that our room and belongings were by no means safe. Sadly, I knew that if we ventured too far away from our gear, it would disappear in a matter of moments and never be seen again.

The chilled atmosphere of Senga Bay was vanishing very quickly.

Later that evening, there was a confrontation between a local and another backpacker staying at the camp. Apparently there was an argument about whether or not one of the camp's employees had broken into the room of a female traveller and physically harassed her. The local in question completely lost the plot and accused the poor girl of ignorance and racism. The girl tried to calm the situation, but the frenzied local would have none of it. He was pissed off and aggressive. The relaxation and serenity of the village was being sucked out before my eyes. A quick look from Charlie to Jon confirmed what I had been feeling as well. We wouldn't be staying in Senga Bay any longer than we had to. We would move on first thing the next morning.

The next day's journey began with some disturbing news. We met a couple of Irish doctors while waiting in the village for the mini taxi to arrive. We talked about bilharzia, which was a water-borne parasite that plagued many parts of Africa including Lake Malawi. This nasty little parasite would enter the body through the skin, navigate about until it could wrap itself around the bladder or kidneys and begin the process of irreversible internal organ damage. Which areas of the lake were affected was often subject to debate depending on whom you talked to and where on the water they owned their campsite. We asked the doctors which part of the lake was infected. They told us that anywhere south of Dwangwa would be infected with bilharzia. My Malawian geography wasn't up to par, and I wasn't sure where Dwangwa was situated. I told them we had been swimming in Senga Bay and asked if it was safe.

It was clear that I was dealing with student doctors, for they obviously hadn't yet been taught the art of bedside manners. If they had, they probably wouldn't have answered my inquiry with a statement as damning as, "You're fucked."

"You're fucked" was never good to hear, regardless of who was saying it. However, the statement carried an extra layer of severity when issued by a doctor, student or not.

"Oh don't worry about it," Dr. Death laughed, obviously detecting my concern by my bulging eyes and gaping mouth. "You're fucked as in you've most likely picked up bilharzia. However, the disease won't fuck you. There are pills that you take after your last contact with the water that will kill the parasite. You guys have nothing at all to worry about."

I remembered all the kids who were swimming in Senga Bay. I thought about the women washing clothes in the lake and the men who were out fishing. I wondered if they all had bilharzia. I asked the doctors.

"They've picked it up for sure. However, it's not high on their list of worries," the one doctor continued. "Bilharzia doesn't normally affect the host until he is at least in his 40s. With famine, malaria and AIDS as prevalent as they are in this country, the locals don't live long enough to suffer from the effects of bilharzia."

In my opinion, *that* is fucked.

The next bit of news was by no means worse, but nonetheless, our situation didn't improve from it. When the mini taxi arrived, the driver informed us that he could only take us about 150 kilometres down the highway and not the entire distance to Nkhata Bay.

We were a bit confused why he wasn't driving the entire distance. None of us had really slept well for three days, and the travelling was starting to take its toll on our bodies and mental stability. We didn't want to travel a small section of the distance then have to search and renegotiate with another cab. So we asked if there were other taxis heading further in that direction.

When the driver said that there wouldn't be and that his cab was the only vehicle even heading that direction, I became even more puzzled. It seemed as if there were mini taxis everywhere in this country. In fact, it seemed as if every Malawian and his brother were mini taxi drivers. It wasn't conceivable that of all the thousands of taxis in Malawi, not a single one was heading to Nkhata Bay.

The driver must have realized he was dealing with clueless backpackers who had zero understanding that they were in the middle of dirt poor Africa and that sometimes shit happens. He explained that the river was too high and had flooded a large section of the highway. Passage to Nkhata Bay might be possible with large trucks but certainly not the mini taxis. Nonetheless, sensing that there was some money to be made off our desperation, he did offer to take us as far as the road would allow. He indicated that there was a minute possibility that a vehicle would come that could cross the river.

We had no desire to stay in Senga Bay, which meant that Charlie, Jon and I had two options if we wanted to get to Nkhata Bay. The first option would be to take a chance, grab the ride to the end of the road and maybe or maybe not get across the river. The other option would be to backtrack. This would result in another day and a half of African travelling as well as spending another night in frightening Lilongwe.

We opted for the ride to the end of the road.

A couple of hours later, our taxi reached the river, and exactly as the driver had forewarned, the waterway was impassable. On the side of the road, there were a couple of ladies selling bananas, but that was it. There weren't any other villagers, market stalls or commuters. And disappointingly, there weren't any other vehicles. It was just us. We paid the taxi driver, and in a cloud of dust, he was gone. Yet again, the three of us were on our own without a clue what to do next.

We sat down on the side of the road and did the only thing we could do. We waited.

I decided to light a cigarette.

For those who aren't aware, there is an interesting phenomenon associated with smoking a cigarette and waiting. It doesn't matter if you are waiting for a bus to arrive, your dinner to be cooked or that phone call to come through. The moment you light a cigarette, the bus comes around the corner, the fillet is done and Mom rings.

I don't understand nicotine's capability to speed up time. I just accept it.

This particular cigarette must have been a magical smoke because not only did a vehicle arrive within moments after lighting up, but the vehicle in question was a massive lorry, which was the exact type of monstrosity that could negotiate the raging river.

We waved the truck down. It came to a stop, and the driver looked down at us from his cab. We asked him if he was going to attempt to cross the river. To our relief, he nodded that he was. With hopeful faces, we asked (borderline begged) the driver if we could hitch a ride with him to our final destination. For two bucks each, he said that we could. It was an offer we happily accepted.

By this point in the journey, I think I would have paid anything.

We awkwardly pulled ourselves up and over the back of the flatbed, not knowing what cargo may be waiting. After three treacherous days of travel, I had given up all hope of comfort. I could only pray that whatever mass occupied the space would leave enough room for the three of us. And if it was livestock, I just hoped it wouldn't shit on or eat my backpack.

None of us were prepared for what we discovered.

After three days of travelling and hassles, we were finally rewarded for our misery. The sun must have been shining on someone's ass because the lorry's cargo was nothing other than couches and E-Z chairs. There weren't any other people or any livestock. It was just the three of us, a ton of space and a multitude and variety of comfort.

The driver grinded the vehicle into gear and began trudging towards the water. Amazingly, the lorry handled the raging river as if it were going through a puddle. With water smashing off the truck's side and splashing up and over the rail of the flatbed, the bad boy lorry quickly and easily crossed to the other side of the river. We were soon steaming our way towards our final destination, Nkhata Bay.

We dropped our packs, selected three different, extremely comfortable seats and skinned up a few spliffs, which were the only good things to come out of Senga Bay. We settled back underneath the hot Malawian sun and relaxed as blissfully as Greek gods. After three and a half long, trying days of African travel, it was an enormous relief to know we would be in Nkhata Bay in a couple of hours.

I stretched out on one of the couches and smoked my joint. Between the heat of the sun and my overall weariness from the previous three days, I fell into a deep, peaceful, overdue sleep within 10 minutes of putting my head back on the comfy cushion.

I dreamed of a clear, blue, bilharzia-free lake.

Some time later, Jon gently nudged me from my slumber.

Even through sleepy eyes, I could tell that Jon was excited. He was almost schoolgirl giddy. He thrust a burning joint at me and laughed through his big, goofy grin. "Wake up, mate. We're here."

22

FINDING MALAWI

AUGUST

It was becoming a game.

It was a twisted game, but it was a game nonetheless. It was a contest in which the objectives were simple and the hazards were severe and, frankly, rather disgusting. The few of us who weren't suffering from motion sickness on the overcrowded fishing boat had decided to pass the time in mild competition by guessing who would be the next unfortunate passenger to heave his guts into Lake Malawi.

At least we hoped they heaved their guts into Lake Malawi.

Despite the reassuring fact that I wasn't feeling nauseous, I had already been puked on twice. The first time was courtesy of the woman sitting across from me. She was unable to lean over the side of the boat before her spew splattered across my arm. That particular incident wasn't as revolting as some of the other vomit casualties I had already witnessed on the craft, for all I had to do to remove the mess was lean over the edge and wash my hand in the lake.

Unfortunately, the second splattering was much worse.

I knew the woman sitting next to me was going to puke. I knew the heaving was inevitable by the way her eyes rolled back in her discoloured face. Her moans and head wobbles were also strong indicators that her lunch was about to be fed to the fish. I caught the attention of my fellow competitors and motioned that I had found the next victim. Positioning was key to this game. It was easy to detect the signs of nausea when the person was sitting in close proximity. Deep breathing, for example, was a dead giveaway that a person was about to launch his guts.

The downside to this excellent positioning was that it put the competitor in direct line of the digestive exodus. When the woman could no longer hold her guts, she attempted to scuttle across the tangle of legs, including my own, that were impeding her from reaching the edge of the boat.

She didn't make it.

She puked all over my legs, lap and arm before she hung her head over the side. By that point, there wasn't much left to add to the lake.

As I sat in shock, disbelief and vomit, daunting thoughts crossed my mind. In the space of only 40 minutes, I had already been on the receiving end of these bilious emissions twice. How many more times would I get hurled on throughout what was going to be a choppy and rough, five-hour excursion?

As I splashed water across my lap in an attempt to wash off the chunks of undigested breakfast, I seriously reconsidered my decision to leave Nkhata Bay.

Life in this piece of paradise had surpassed my expectations. Within moments of arriving at *Lowani Village*, I knew that I had made the correct decision to visit Nkhata Bay. All the hard travelling, hassles, mini buses, smells, hookers, pimps and bilharzia seemed worthwhile when I sat back on the deck of *Lowani Village* with a cold beer and took in the scenic view of Lake Malawi.

The place was exquisite. The guest house was a small collection of A-frame bungalows scattered along a steep hillside that led into the amazingly blue water of Lake Malawi. Although the cottages were extremely basic, consisting of a bed and a side table, they were equally as inexpensive. Furthermore, the people at *Lowani Village* were friendly, and the Malawian cob was hands down the best and cheapest weed that I had ever smoked anywhere at anytime.[1] The chilled ambiance of this Malawian environment had an immediate and positive effect on me. *Lowani Village* was as relaxed as it was beautiful.

My mind and body had slipped into proper holiday mode. My days were simple and filled with bliss. I'd wake up in the morning, have a coffee, smoke a joint, swim in the blue, fresh waters of Lake Malawi set a mere 10 metres from my bungalow and then dry in the hot sun with another smoke. This relaxed cycle would continue throughout the day. It was interrupted only by meals and mindless chit-chat with the other travellers. Then I fell into a peaceful, stoned sleep. There was

---

1. Not only was the Malawian cob the best and cheapest weed I had ever come across, but it also came with the best presentation and packaging. Conventional paraphernalia such as Ziploc bags, bank bags, aluminum foil, newspaper and match boxes were all common and efficient methods of keeping and handling your gear. But they were never going to win any style contests. Conversely, the Malawian cob was a thing of beauty. About 30 grams of high-grade marijuana would be compressed into the shape and size of a cob of corn. The ganja cob would then be wrapped with banana leaves and tied with a string. When I wanted to smoke, I unwrapped the leaves, broke off a small section of weed and then rewrapped and tied the cob, keeping the gear fresh and dry. It was a work of art.

no doubt that *Lowani Village* was a lazy trap and the perfect environment to replenish my energies.

There was something about this particular body of freshwater that was extremely appealing. The Indian Ocean was unquestionably more powerful, but there was a unique, soothing quality about Lake Malawi that the sea couldn't provide. Perhaps it was because there weren't any sharks looming in the depths of the lake, and the chances of getting munched while basking were slim and none. Upon serious reflection, I realized that it was much more. Lake Malawi, with its deep, aqua blue waters and serene environment, created a tranquillity that was equally as influential as the ocean's power. Yet it applied its therapy in a calming manner.

Even though I needed time doing absolutely nothing to recuperate from the countless late bar nights in Chintsa, I didn't expect to travel to this part of the world and not see more of it. Despite appearances, I wasn't planning on wasting the time and potential experiences by sitting and smoking in one place the entirety of the vacation. I knew there was more to see in this struggling country than the bustling village of Nkhata Bay.

Maybe I should say I knew there was *less* to see.

My short time in Lilongwe had exposed me to some of the tragic consequences of extreme poverty such as high crime levels and violence. Then again, such troubles affect practically every major city on the planet, especially when a large segment of the population was unemployed and broke. This was certainly the case in the Malawian capital.

However, I hoped that in contrast to this violent urban atmosphere, there would be a rural setting in which poverty hadn't corrupted the lifestyle. Although Nkhata Bay was serene, it was better described as a small town than a rural village. After all, it was complete with restaurants, hotels and electricity. I wanted more basic and less 21st-century. In essence, I wanted to feel as though I had gone back in time.

I had discovered a drastic distinction between the hectic pace of a place like Johannesburg and the peaceful hills of the Transkei. The poverty had ensured that the rural lifestyle of the Transkei remained authentic and traditional. I desperately wanted to experience the peacefulness and simplicity of the Malawian villages that I had so loved in South Africa. Despite my ignorance of the country, I believed that such places existed within Malawi. It was just a question of getting off my ass and finding one.

There was a scattering of us who had been based in *Lowani Village* for an extended period of time. One of the long-stayers, a French guy named Alex, was getting itchy feet. He suggested that we travel up the lake to a tiny village he had visited in the past. He couldn't remember the name of the village, but he said he remembered exactly how to get there. The Frenchman said that the region was so incredibly beautiful and unique that the actual name was irrelevant. As far as he was concerned, all that mattered was that it was the perfect spot to disappear for a few days. A small group decided to join Alex on his return to the remote, rural community. It was an adventure that would include the five-hour water taxi ride to Ussisia followed by a 10-kilometre hike across the Malawian countryside.

Hearing Alex's charming description of the nameless village, there wasn't any question that I would join the adventure.

I was intrigued by the isolation. By the sounds of it, the village had the potential to possess the peaceful, simple atmosphere that I hoped to find. It was also a chance to get off the beaten down traveller's path. This was an always welcome endeavour that had proved eye-opening and rewarding.

Mind you, being repeatedly puked on took some of the jam out of this particular adventure, and it was putting my quest for serenity into serious debate.

As the digestive exodus continued and more passengers succumbed to their nausea, I also began to question whether we would survive the five-hour journey in this poor excuse for a boat.

Water taxis were similar to the mini taxis on the road. Both vehicles were generally unsafe for travel, overcrowded with people and goods and operated by somebody with limited knowledge of what he was doing. Our tiny fishing boat, which was powered by a sputtering, 20 horsepower motor, was packed with about two dozen people and a barrage of goods. It fought its way through the swell of Lake Malawi. One of the main disparities between a mini taxi and a water taxi was that the water taxi did have toilet facilities; people would stand up and piss off the side of the boat. Again, positioning and wind direction were key. Sometimes we got sprayed, and sometimes we didn't. When somebody stood up to relieve himself, the only thing to do was close your eyes and mouth and hope for the best.

The other glaring difference between the two modes of transportation was the terrain. Although there weren't as many impending obstacles on the water as there were on the highway, we did have one, unrelenting, unsympathetic barrier to contend with—Lake Malawi itself. Don't let the fact that we were on a freshwater lake fool you into thinking we were on a calm, glasslike body of water. Lake Malawi is huge. It stretches almost the entire length of the country and represents a fifth of Malawi's total area. It's closer to a small sea than a lake, and much like a sea, it surges and swells. On this particular day, there was some serious swell. As our boat struggled up and over a rolling wave, all I could see above the bow would be blue sky, for the craft was angled upwards as if it was a rocket ship sitting on the launching pad. When the boat would break the crest of the wave and plummet down into the valley of water, I could still see the colour blue. This time, however, it was an aqua blue wall of lake rolling towards us, which seemed destined to engulf the tiny craft.

The boat felt as though it had as much control as a bottle lost at sea.

Incredibly, the boat didn't flip, sink or get smashed.

Astonishingly, the boat didn't get lost.

It turned out that the skipper had better control of his vessel than most of the passengers had of their stomachs, for he was able to safely land on the beach in the Ussisia village. By the time we arrived at the tiny lakeside community, half the passengers had been "lake sick" and were looking considerably worse for wear. Then again, the healthier half was also looking rough and ragged; despite having retained the contents of their guts, those with sea legs had been on the receiving end at least once.

Having another person's partially digested food projected on you tends to have a damping effect on an individual's mood and appearance.

Even so, I found solace in being more than halfway to the nameless village. Plus, the remainder of the journey was on foot. This meant we wouldn't have to subject ourselves to the mercy of Lake Malawi again.

The next morning, we were up bright and early. Following a quick breakfast of bananas, we loaded up with fresh water, a few cobs of weed and our packs. We began the 10-kilometre hike across the countryside towards our Utopian destination. We began by trudging up the steep hills, which provided us with spectacular views of the lake. These views were a great excuse to stop and catch our breath. We continued back down into the lush, green valleys where the heat and humidity was as thick as the bush. Inevitably, the trail would lead lakeside where we would drop our packs and jump into the water for a quick swim to cool our sweaty bodies. Following a quick spliff, we'd throw on our gear and be on our way. It was usually up another hillside.

So the trek continued.

The hike led us through several secluded villages, and each time, the experience made me smile in awe and astonishment. Although quite surreal, it wasn't so much the serenity, simplicity or isolation of the communities that I found captivating. Instead, it was the reaction of the villagers that blew me away.

Our arrival at a village always created the same fervour.

The kids would be the first to see us coming. From the wide-eyed expressions of some of the smaller kids, I knew this was quite possibly the first time in their young lives that they had ever seen a white face. They would turn and sprint back into the collection of huts screaming, "Mazungu! Mazungu!" (This was the local way to say, "White people! White People!")

The kids were obviously alerting the welcoming committee of our arrival, for a reception fit for royalty was received when we walked into every community. Entire families would pour from their huts, stand at the entrance and wave as we walked past. They always had radiant, genuine smiles beaming across their faces.

To put this greeting into perspective, I tried to imagine my reaction if I was sitting at home in Canada watching a ball game on TV and my little brother came into the living room screaming, "Japanese tourists! Japanese tourists!" Then I tried to gauge my reaction if my father had said, "All right everybody, outside in a line. Let's welcome these Japanese strangers into our neighbourhood."

First of all, that scenario would never take place. Second, if it somehow did unfold, I know that I would ignore the old man's request and keep my ass firmly planted on the couch. And third, if for some bizarre reason I did get up and go outside to wave, I can guarantee that I wouldn't be all that happy about it.

However, here in these remote Malawian villages, overwhelming hospitality and kindness was exactly how the people greeted strangers.

We'd always spend a few minutes relaxing in the villages. It was a chance to have a look at the local lifestyle and, more importantly, to allow the locals a proper look at us. We were a novelty. The kids viewed us as new toys, and the elders viewed us as a new topic of conversation. I would have loved to know what they were saying, for their smiles and laughter originated, no doubt, at our expense. I didn't mind. I only wished that I could have participated in the discussion.

Nevertheless, the main reason we stopped in the villages was to catch our breath. The walk, although picturesque, was becoming long. Ten kilometres across, up and down rugged terrain with a 15-kilogram pack was starting to take its toll on my body. We were also fairly baked from both the sun and the copious amounts of ganja we had smoked along the way, and this made the final push rather strenuous. The thatched hut villages became sights of welcome relief. We knew that it would be a chance to find a comfortable piece of shade, drop our packs, eat some bananas and rest our fatigued legs and shoulders.

Mercifully, just when I hit a point where my muscles were screaming in agony, we came around a corner, and Alex began to laugh. He didn't need to say anything to confirm that this piece of paradise was our final destination.

I knew we had arrived.

Even if we hadn't arrived, I wasn't walking another step.

There was no need.

The place was another mind-boggling world.

If I looked up "paradise" in the dictionary, there could very well be a picture of the beach that lay before my eyes.

It had been proved again. The more difficult it is to reach a destination, the more rewarding that destination becomes. Following the unpleasantness of the water taxi, the continuous vomiting and the difficult hike, arriving in this speck of heaven felt as though I'd just hit the backpacker's jackpot. The empty, white sandy beach was no more than 50 metres long and 15 metres deep, but it was ample space for six travellers. The beach was completely enclosed by the subtropical jungle with the exception of a waterfall that poured out of the bush, cut across the edge of the sand and out into the crystal blue lake. The water in this section of the lake was the most exceptional and distinctive colour I'd ever seen. The only way to properly define this shade of blue would be to call it "Malawi blue." Although the water in Nkhata Bay was beautiful, it was still situated next to a sizable village, and I didn't doubt that a portion of the lake was the unfortunate recipient of the village's pollution. Compared to the water here, the shade of blue in Nkhata Bay could be considered brown.

We took a quick swim, rolled a couple of celebratory joints and began to make our camp. As we were doing so, I spotted an old man paddling towards the beach in a dug out wooden canoe, which was called a mokoro. He beached his mokoro, walked up to us, smiled and said in surprisingly good English, "My name is Chief Chimombo. You are welcome to stay on my beach for as long as you want."

A little dumbfounded by the gracious welcome, we thanked him for his hospitality and commented on how beautiful his village was. He continued to smile and went on to ask, "Is there anything that you need? Food? Firewood?"

We nodded that we did. The chief's smile broadened. "I'll send people."

And with a kind and sincere handshake to us all, the old man returned to his mokoro and slowly paddled away.

Within an hour, firewood and food arrived.

Chief Chimombo was a smart man. Each morning, he sent women to our campsite who carried bundles of firewood on their heads to last the day and evening. These were bundles, I might add, that I had a hard time lifting, let alone balancing on my head. This was a feature of African life that always blew me away. It didn't matter if it was in a city or in the deep rural hills, African woman would often carry whatever item they had on their heads, leaving their arms free to dangle. I've seen everything from a handbag to a sack of potatoes to a case of beer to full buckets of water. And, as was the case here in Malawi, they even carried massive bundles of wood. In the afternoons, the chief sent a man with some vegetables, bananas and a couple of chickens for dinner. It should be noted that the chickens we received were still alive. I knew that chickens didn't come from the grocery store, and I knew they spent a good portion of their time unpackaged and undivided. Nonetheless, I had never slaughtered my dinner with my own hands. The first night, I used a serrated knife to get dinner going. With the chicken wedged between my feet, I held the knife in one hand and the soon to be liberated head in the other. I gave the neck two quick slices and let go. The headless chicken ran its ghastly, final sprint and eventually collapsed to the ground. This left the city dwellers in the group, myself included, in a state of bewilderment. The following night, it was someone else's turn to play Grim Reaper, and they used a dulled machete instead of the knife. It was a choice that proved painfully slow and difficult to watch. However, despite the gory preparation, nobody turned down a piece of the open fire cooked bird when it came time to eat.

I don't mind saying that dinner was finger licking good.

That being said, the third evening, we paid the man who brought the chickens to do the fatal deed. It was money I considered extremely well-spent.

One morning, Chief Chimombo arrived at the beach with two teenagers. He said to us, "These boys are here to sell you ganja." This incredible chief, knowing that the lot of us were marijuana smokers, brought two kids over to sell us some local product. It was an attempt to put some money in their desperate and empty pockets.

Chimombo was an excellent chief. He was genuinely looking after the best interests of his village and villagers. Without being intrusive, he involved everybody in his poverty-stricken community that could earn an income from us. Other than the necessities, we were left alone. We weren't bombarded with people trying to sell us trinkets or souvenirs, as was the case in many places throughout Southern Africa. If I wanted a necklace or bracelet, I could go to the village to buy one. In the eyes of the chief, jewellery wasn't a necessity.

The weed that we bought off the local teenagers was the strongest and cheapest gear that any of us had come across in Malawi. Considering this was a safe and peaceful environment, not buying an excessive amount of top quality gear would have been borderline foolish. As a result of our cannabis gluttony, we had cobs and cobs of weed. In reality, we had an overabundance of marijuana. We were constantly smoking. We smoked throughout the morning, afternoon and evening. We had so much weed that we realized it would be physically impossible to smoke it all. In an attempt to diminish our supply, we decided to start cooking with the plant at any opportunity. When we made a pot of tea, we would always put a handful of ganja in with it.

We even went so far as stuffing our chickens with weed.

Once the decapitating, plucking and gutting was done, we'd pack the ganja between the skin and meat. The chicken would then be slowly roasted over an open fire, which allowed all the oils and fats of the skin to soak through the weed and into the meat. When the bird was cooked to perfection, we would remove the ganja and carve into the tender, juicy flesh. "Space chicken" became a staple diet. It was a delicious and mellowing dinner, and we washed it down with a warm cup of space tea. Then we would lie on the beach underneath our mosquito nets, which were our only protection from the elements, and stare up into the star-studded Malawian night. We let our minds wander as far as we would allow.

While lounging on the isolated beach, I felt a million miles (and possibly a million years) from where I had grown up. The simplicity of life in this village made it possible to believe that I could have been on a different planet. It was hard to imagine that in today's day and age, a place this basic and authentic still existed on Earth. Despite appearing centuries apart, as the ladies came down the hill carrying bundles of wood or the man arrived with our still clucking dinner, I was reminded of a universal connection we shared.

The realization of our common humanness materialized one morning as I awoke on the beach. Beneath the brilliant purples and reds of the pre-dawn sky, I stumbled to the edge of the lake to relieve myself of the excessive amount of space tea that was in my system. Standing there in silence, soaking in the beauty and serenity, I spotted a couple of fishermen on the next cove over. The two men were also standing in silence and staring at the heavenly masterpiece of an African sunrise.

They were also taking a morning squirt.

In Africa, where very little can be sanitized, hermetically sealed and camouflaged, it was clear that regardless of what part of the world we're from, despite our beliefs, religions, upbringings, cultures and futures, everyone shared the first action of the day—a good healthy piss.

It was a simple thought and possibly a crude one, but it was an observation about humankind that reassured me that in spite of the madness and violence that plagues the world, we were still one and the same.

Every night, as I lay back on the beach, digesting another deliciously simple and intoxicating dinner, I watched the local fishermen. They were marked only by a lantern, and they bobbed hypnotically in their mokoros in the darkness of Lake Malawi. Every night, I smiled.

I had found the serenity I was hoping to discover in Malawi.

By doing so, I was beginning to find the serenity that I was hoping to discover within myself.

As I would drift off to sleep on my sandy bed, I would ask if life could be any more peaceful than this.

The answer was impossible to know, but be that as it may, each night I fell asleep with a smile on my face, sensing that I was on the right track.

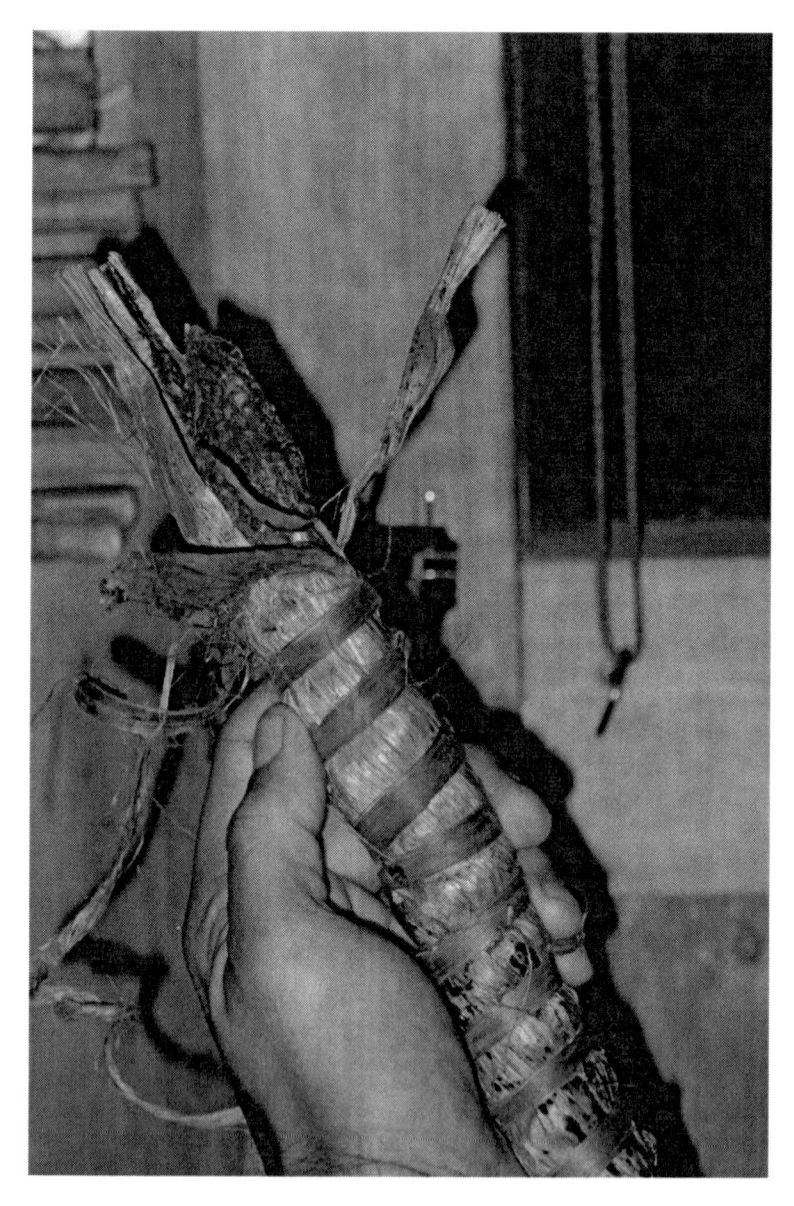

The Malawian Cob.

23
B TO C

AUGUST

Unlike any other holiday that I had ever been on, I was actually looking forward to leaving and going back to work.

Seriously.

I was completely rejuvenated from my extended time in Malawi. I felt like a million bucks, and I was excited about returning to South Africa. This enthusiasm is what happens when one is entitled to a holiday that is more than two weeks. One goes back to work refocused and not full of dread. I was the perfect example of how an extended holiday could be effective.

Not that long ago, I had been stressed and frustrated from working at *Smuggler's Cove*. I'd been in dire need of a holiday. Work at the bar had been doing my head in with endless questions about where I was from or how long I'd been travelling. I understood that they were icebreaking questions that often led to other conversation, but I no longer had the patience to wade through the repetitive small talk. The friendly inquiries were gradually filling me with an unwanted and unnecessary animosity.

However, being in Malawi with nothing to do but smoke, swim, chill out and soak in the lifestyle had completely flushed out the negative energy that had been brewing.

I was now in the proper frame of mind.

All the same, I still had one dilemma that I had to endure in order to get back to my South African home. Unfortunately, my quandary was rather daunting, for this hurdle was one that I had already experienced on my way to Nkhata Bay, and it hadn't left the best of impressions.

Ahead of me still awaited the long, tedious African journey back to Chintsa.

To make matters even more unnerving, I would be making the journey by myself. Even though Charlie and Jon were as clueless about African travel as I was, I valued having two extra sets of wide-eyes watching out for my gear and me.

Even though we would have dropped our packs the moment we saw a threatening machete, we may have discouraged would-be thieves by the simple fact that there were three of us. While travelling solo, my only deterrent would be a menacing look.

Initially, mentally preparing for the epic journey back to South Africa proved my biggest obstacle. I had become very comfortable in the setting, attitude and pace of *Lowani Village*. Even my cash runs to the town of Mzuzu, which was a mere hour away by mini taxi, required focus, preparation and determination. And more often than not, this failed due to my dread of packing into the sardine can on wheels. Chilling lakeside with a joint in my hand had much more appeal than the prospect of a fiery, crumpled death. It was a good thing that *Lowani Village* had a tab system.

With the probability of a four-day, solo journey back to South Africa looming, I needed all the focus, preparation and determination I could muster.

It wasn't going to be easy.

Therefore, to make the trip rewarding, I decided to dangle a sort of carrot at the end of the mission. I hoped it would keep me on course. I timed my departure so that my arrival in South Africa would coincide with an evening at my favourite club in the country, Durban's *330's*.

I was introduced to clubbing at the beginning of my trip when I was in London. I became immediately hooked. The pulsating music and the electric atmosphere was such a different and captivating vibe from any of the nightlife I had experienced in Canada. I couldn't help but be seduced. As my travels continued to the Canary Islands, I became even more engrossed in the club scene, for it was a predominant feature of the island's nightlife. However, it wasn't until I arrived in South Africa that I truly delved into the trance scene. South Africa was not only host to spectacular outdoor parties set in stunning, natural settings, but it was also home to some of the best clubs and DJs that I'd had the privilege of experiencing. My favourite was Durban's *330's*. I had been to Durban on several occasions, and on each visit, I made sure that I had a proper party at *330's*.

Each time was a brilliant affair.

330's was my dangling carrot.

On paper, the mission back to South Africa was relatively simple. The first leg would be an overnight bus from Mzuzu to Blantyre, which was a major city in the south of the country. Following a night in Blantyre, I would have the whopper segment of the journey—a hellacious 32-hour marathon bus excursion through Zimbabwe to Johannesburg. From there, it would be an easy eight-hour skip to Durban on the coach. I had it timed, so I would arrive in Durban on a

Friday and be rested and in prime partying condition for a Saturday night bender.

As I said, the plan looked relatively simple on paper. However, I was fully aware that with four days of rough travelling, any number of "African anomalies" could throw me off schedule. All I could do was hope for the best.

I had spent so much time talking up my departure date that when the morning arrived, I was psyched for the adventure and found it surprisingly easy to say goodbye to Nkhata Bay and my new friends. I smoked my last joint on Lake Malawi late that afternoon with Jon then made my way into the village to catch a mini taxi to Mzuzu. I arrived at the Mzuzu bus station with time to spare. I dropped my pack and sat down on the side of the road along with all the other passengers who were patiently waiting for the bus to arrive.

The Malawians were as friendly a people as I had come across anywhere on my travels. With the exception of a few thugs in Lilongwe and Senga Bay, my perception of the people was that they were calm, peaceful, hospitable and patient. These passive Malawians were the exact same type of people who were waiting with me for the bus to arrive. Everybody was sitting quietly and in an orderly line on the side of the road. Some were talking. Some were singing. Others were eating their picnic dinners. Every one was dressed in their best clothing and waiting to begin their own journeys.

It was a beautiful, tranquil scene.

However, once the bus pulled up to the stop, everything tranquil and peaceful about the setting evaporated into a cloud of hectic energy. The passive, orderly queue transformed into a mass frenzy of commuters pushing and shoving to the entrance of the bus and slowly funnelling through the cramped door. It was every man, woman and child for himself. To make the effort more of a challenge, I was hauling two heavy and bulky Malawian chairs on top of my loaded pack. This made my ability to work my way to the front next to impossible. With the number of people pushing ahead of me, I didn't think there would be any way to get on the bus. I almost conceded that I would be stuck in Mzuzu for the night.

Then a second bus for Blantyre arrived. Being at the back of the original mass, I thought I could make a quick jump over to the other vehicle before anybody else.

I was wrong.

Just as I got close to the open door, a wave of human flesh once again descended upon the one, tiny entrance. A woman, who must have been 80, elbowed me in the ribs in an attempt to gain a better position. The blow worked. The strength of the mob and my limited desire to shove and box out senior citizens forced me away from the second bus and back towards the first. I felt like a rubber duck being tossed and turned at the leisure of the ocean's currents. How I managed to work my way to the front and onto the first bus is still a mystery. One moment I was nowhere near the door. The next, a hand grabbed my shoulder and pulled me on board. I awkwardly stepped over the obstacles in the aisle and crammed my gear and myself into an extremely uncomfortable seat.

There was a family of four packed into the seats across from me: dad, mom, a daughter of about 12 and a little boy no more than three. The little guy, who was sitting on his mother's lap, was looking at me with wide, terrified eyes. I wasn't sure if he was scared because this was his first time on a bus and away from his home or if he was scared by the madness and aggressive behaviour of the other passengers. I gave him an empathetic smile and a "let's make the best of it" shrug of my shoulders.

I didn't help. The poor kid looked just as frightened.

The overcrowded bus eventually got rolling, and my vacation in Malawi had reached its conclusion. My adventure back to South Africa was just beginning.

I was becoming skilled at adapting to the conditions of African travelling. Between the four-day mission to Nkhata Bay and the few money runs I had made between Nkhata Bay and Mzuzu, I was getting the hang of adjusting, both physically and mentally, to the hardships and annoyances of Third World transportation. I had chosen a seat in the middle of the bus, systematically shut down all muscles to prevent cramping and began to mentally block out the metal seat and odd screw digging into me. I was about to escape to my happy place when I made the rookie mistake of looking out the front of the bus. Not surprisingly, I saw my life flash before my eyes.

In reality, it wasn't my life that flashed before my eyes but an oncoming truck that was trying to cut a blind corner. This was the same truck that we proceeded to slam into with a deafening bang. The sound of crunching metal is always a terrible sound, but it is much more terrifying when the metal you hear crushing is that of the vehicle you're in. I had been told that when a person was involved in an accident, time had a tendency of moving extremely slowly, as if each second was a minute. This testimony was disturbingly accurate. From the moment I saw that we were going to make impact, each second thereafter passed as though it were a slow-moving slide show allowing each horrifying detail to be etched into my brain.

The bus rocked, rattled and came to a screeching stop.

For a moment, there was deathly silence. Everybody was frozen in place. All the passengers had been holding their breath, not knowing if it would be their last.

Time regained its normal pace.

The little boy next to me began to cry, breaking the shocked silence.

The yelling began.

I had no idea what was being shouted, but it seemed clear that the verbal barrage was directed at our driver and his piss-poor driving abilities. He, in turn, was screaming in his defence. The interior of the bus had gone from church quiet to stadium loud in a nanosecond.

The luggage had been loosely attached to the roof of the bus, and the force of the impact had catapulted most of that luggage across the highway. The normally passive Malawians continued their screaming and cursing as they piled off the bus to collect their bags from the road and ditch.

The driver got off to inspect the damage to his vehicle.

My initial shock of hitting another truck was wearing off. I was able to shut my gaping mouth, pry my fingers from the seat in front of me and, of course, blink.

Holy shit, I thought, we hit a truck.

I knew that we had hit a truck. I saw the fucking thing. The driver of the other vehicle had to have been hurt. I don't care what kind of truck a person was driving; it wouldn't stand a chance against a speeding bus. A frightening memory raced through my head. I thought of all the people that normally travelled in the back of trucks.

Holy shit.

I looked around. Everybody was focused on collecting the scattered luggage from the highway, looking at the damage or giving our driver shit for the accident. To my bewilderment, not a single person went to see if anybody from the other vehicle was injured. For a country that had such a strong sense of community, I found it bizarre that nobody would be concerned with the welfare of the people from the other vehicle.

Being unhurt and in no mood to scream at the driver, I put my pack on the seat, got off the bus and walked down the highway towards the other truck. I didn't know what I would find. I also didn't know what I would or could do once I got there. But in spite of my reservations, I knew that I had to go.

Maybe it was a morbid curiosity that pulled me the 400 or so metres down the highway in the dark. Maybe it was natural instinct to help my fellow man. I don't know why I was drawn to the accident, but regardless of the reason, I wasn't prepared in the slightest for the carnage that awaited me.

The truck had flipped over on its side, and the driver was sprawled out across the road. When I approached the broken body, I could see that he had massive head injuries. The driver was unquestionably dead. I felt my stomach turn at the ghastly sight. I glanced around the highway and the overturned truck, looking for other casualties. Thankfully, there were none. The only silver lining to this tragedy was that the guy had been driving alone, and there hadn't been anybody riding in the back of the open and unprotected vehicle.

That's when I heard the cries and moans.

I froze.

The groans were coming from the darkness off the edge of the highway. I cautiously approached the side of the road, dreading what I would find.

My first fearful thought was that I had been wrong about the truck being empty and that the cries of pain were coming from the truck's passengers who had been launched into the ditch when the vehicle flipped.

Once again, I was mistaken.

The side of the highway dropped quickly and steeply into a gully about 10 metres deep, and lying at the bottom was an overturned bus with its wheels still spinning. The cries and moans were coming from within the crushed vehicle and the few passengers who were attempting to crawl out from the wreckage.

This had mutated from a bad accident into a horrific catastrophe.

I have no way of knowing what happened, but if I had to speculate, I'd guess that this bus was the second bus travelling to Blantyre which had been driving behind us. I assumed that to avoid the overturned truck, the bus swerved out of the way, lost control and went tumbling down the embankment.

What I did know was that the packed bus had many injured on board. I stood frozen in fear and shock.

I didn't know what to do or where to start.

As I was contemplating the magnitude of the accident and what needed to be done, I heard a terrifying, unmistakable sound, which to this day remains scarred on my brain.

It was the noise of a motor starting, revving and shifting into first gear.

I turned in the direction of the reverberation, and to my complete horror, I realized that it was my bus that had been making the racket. My bus was beginning to drive off into the night. That same bus was carrying everything I owned including my backpack, money, credit cards, passport, chairs and clothes.

It was carrying everything I owned in my travelling world except the most important item of all—me.

I began to run.

I didn't have time to think about why my bus might be abandoning me. I didn't have a chance to wonder why the hell these people were leaving the scene of an accident. The only thought that was going through my head was *run*!

I have never run faster in my entire life. However, despite my Olympic speed and desperate will, my legs weren't fast enough to make up the distance.

The gap between the bus and me was growing.

I continued to run with all my heart, but my legs began to give out and my lungs felt as though they were about to explode. I stumbled to a clumsy halt. I was still in disbelief that this was happening. However, the bus's red tail lights disappeared over a hill and left me in complete darkness. It was another moment forever etched in my nightmares, and the brutal reality of my predicament slapped me hard in the face.

My bus had deserted me in the middle of the night, in the middle of the highway and somewhere in the middle of Malawi with absolutely nothing to my name. I had no money, no passport and no clothing. I had absolutely zilch.

I did what any sane person would have done in this circumstance ... I completely and totally lost the plot.

I cried.

I screamed.

I cursed God.

I kicked at nothing.

I punched the air.

I punched the ground.

I was probably in this state of lunacy for a few minutes before I stopped howling. My throat was raw from screaming, and my knuckles were bleeding from punching the highway. I wiped the snot from my face, took a deep breath and attempted to get a grip on the grim situation.

I then had an extremely clear, lucid and incredibly irrelevant thought. It was a thought induced, no doubt, by the madness of the moment.

I looked down at my shoes, pants and shirt. Despite being the very last thing that should have concerned me, I deliberated whether or not my clothes were styling clubbing gear.

I realize that thought seems callous. But in actuality, it was my positive thinking working overtime. Subconsciously my brain knew that I would survive. It wasn't going to let my stranded ass die on the side of a highway. My brain knew that it was going to get back to Durban somehow. My brain knew that my friends in Durban wouldn't be able to float me the money for a new wardrobe, but they would certainly pay for my cover at the door and a few drinks in the club. What my brain didn't know was whether my clothes were of proper clubbing calibre.

As it happened, I was wearing styling clubbing clothing.

All right, maybe the thought wasn't lucid. But it was definitely positive.

And maybe it wasn't the most appropriate, but it was the best and only one that could lift me from my predicament.

The thought was positive enough to force me to deal with the problems at hand. The first was helping the injured.

I took another deep breath, turned around and started to walk back to the carnage.

I still didn't have the foggiest idea what I was going to do. Adapt, improvise and overcome were the three words that I repeated to myself as I began the terrifying walk back to the heart of the accident. But they weren't helping much.

I had zero first aid training, and even if I did, I wasn't too keen on rolling up my sleeves and diving into a Malawian bus accident. My biggest fear while travelling through African nations wasn't catching a tropical disease such as malaria. Although malaria was a dreadful, potentially fatal disease, there was an upside. The medication, which was produced overseas, came in a readily available pill form, and it had an extremely high success rate.

My number-one African anxiety was being involved in an accident such as the one in front of me. I feared being badly hurt or unconscious and being transported to a dodgy, rural hospital where who knows what would be done to me, by whom and, most importantly, with what. I was petrified about having a blood transfusion in this country. Sadly, AIDS was a disease that plagued a horrifyingly large percentage of the population. I had no doubt that the scene inside the bus would be, quite literally, a bloody mess. I also knew that with the number of passengers on board, the chance of a few of them being HIV-positive was more than likely. It was a probability.

As I stood rigidly on the highway and helplessly went over my extremely limited options, I saw headlights in the distance. They were coming from the direction of Mzuzu. As far as I was concerned, the illumination represented help. As the lights approached, I began waving my arms in an attempt to flag down whatever was coming. Thankfully, my efforts weren't in vain. I heard the vehicle downshift and slow to a grinding stop.

The vehicle was, of all things, a military truck.

Even better, it was a military truck filled with soldiers. Soldiers piled out of the back of the vehicle and began to race down the hillside. One of the soldiers came up to me, saw I was unhurt, sat me down on the side of the road and went to help the rest of his platoon with the injured. I gave little thought to the oddity and dumb luck that an army truck full of soldiers happened by this patch of highway at this time of night. Where they were coming from or where they were going didn't matter a duck's fart to me.

I was just relieved I didn't have to deal with the casualties.

Soon, the soldiers were carrying bodies up the hillside and laying them on the side of the road. Some of the victims were crying in pain from their visible injuries such as broken bones or head lacerations. Others, who weren't as badly injured, were wandering around like zombies. They were still confused, disoriented and very much in shock. Some were saying nothing. They were either unconscious or, judging from the seriousness of their injuries, dead.

As I watched this ghastly scene become more tragic by the minute, the severity of the accident started to sink in.

What really struck me in the pit of my gut was just how lucky I actually was to be alive, let alone unhurt. I had survived, scratch free, a major road accident that had taken more than a few lives and left countless injured. I was further freaked by the knowledge that the bus lying in the ditch was the one that I had attempted to board in Mzuzu. If it weren't for the 80-year-old woman's elbow and the current of people that had swept me onto the other bus, it could very well have been me lying at the bottom of the hill.

I got a cold chill up my spine.

My lost backpack and possessions became increasingly insignificant.

Then a second miraculous event happened. Another bus arrived. It came to a full stop due to the debris and bodies littered across the highway.

Although I didn't have my backpack, passport, clothing or money, I did have one item remaining in my pocket, and it was as good as gold.

I still possessed my bus ticket.

I asked the driver where he was going, and he said the bus was destined for Blantyre. I gave a sigh of relief and took a deep breath. I told the driver my story. I showed him my ticket, and to add emphasis and validity to my tale, I pointed to the wreckage and injured. The driver could see the desperation in my eyes, and he sensed the possibility that I might completely slip off the edge of sanity if he said no. He kindly and wisely let me on board.

I collapsed into a seat, and the bus slowly swerved and inched its way past the massacre splattered across the road. I stared straight ahead, for I had seen enough blood and sadness that evening to last a lifetime. There was no need to witness any more.

The bus slowly cranked into gear and drove into the night. I leaned forward and asked the driver if there was any way he could radio ahead to the other bus to inform them that they had all my possessions. He looked at me with the "silly tourist" look that I had seen once too often. I knew there wasn't any chance of this bus having a working radio, but I still had to ask. I was lucky that this one was equipped with a steering wheel.

I accepted that my backpack was gone and would never be seen again. All things considered, I came out of this accident on the lucky side. I was beginning to calm down and think a bit more rationally. I knew that once I got to Blantyre, I would be able to call Chintsa and arrange to have money wired to me. It was going to take a few days to sort out a new passport, which would be a pain in the ass. However, those tasks were a hell of a lot more appealing than dealing with a broken leg or head trauma in some rickety Third World hospital.

Then another improbability took place. We were stopped at a police checkpoint. This particular checkpoint consisted of a large stick lying across the road and a cop sitting on the side of the highway next to a fire. This was similar to the majority of police checkpoints in rural Africa.

An old, worn out policeman clambered onto the bus, gazed around and asked in a sleepy voice if there was a Canadian on board. I knew there wouldn't be another Canuck on the bus, but nonetheless, I glanced around at the other passengers. Not surprisingly, nobody raised a hand. Being the only white face on board, I assumed that the Canadian in question must have been me.

I raised my hand.

The ancient policeman saw me and said, "I have your bag."

I jumped off the bus and followed the cop to his fire. There, sitting next to his mat on the ground, were my backpack and chairs. I was speechless. I thanked him profusely as I lugged my retrieved gear onto the bus. I can only guess that the driver of my original bus, sometime after leaving the scene of the accident, realized that gear belonging to the only Mazungu on board was still on the seat. I'm further assuming that they dropped my backpack at the checkpoint, knowing that I would eventually pass through.

Although I'm often mocked for it, thank Christ I had one gigantic Canadian flag sewn onto the top on my rucksack.

This was quickly turning out to be the most peculiar roller coaster of an evening in my life.

The rest of the journey to Blantyre was uneventful. However, despite having survived an accident that claimed lives and lost and retrieved everything I owned, I was beginning to stress out. My nerves were a wreck. Even a gorgeous sunrise across the Malawian countryside couldn't chill me out. The bullet I had dodged and the bloodbath I had witnessed were replaying themselves repeatedly in my head.

I knew that I was one lucky bastard.

Nevertheless, I was stressed that I was still a long, long way from Chintsa. If a bus accident and being stranded were the first anomalies in my African journey back to Chintsa, then I was truly dreading what would be thrown my way next. Bandits? Civil war? Floods? Locusts? It could be any or all of the above, for I still had more than 30 hours of African travelling left to endure in order to reach South Africa.

The bus pulled into the Blantyre station. Words cannot express how relieved I was when I saw that my hostel, despite its grungy appearance, was located directly across the street from the terminal. The way my night had been unfolding, I figured wandering inanely through the streets and alleys of the city would undoubtedly get me mugged, and I would lose all of my gear for the second time in a matter of hours.

I walked into the gated hostel, checked into a dorm room, dropped my gear, found the bar and ordered a whiskey.

Sitting there drinking, the only thought running through my head was of the 30-hour, overnight journey from Blantyre to Johannesburg on an overcrowded, shitty bus. It was a thought that was giving me grey hairs.

It may not seem like a major problem, considering the shit that had transpired and the luck that had befallen me, but the notion of getting into another potential coffin on wheels for a 30-hour journey didn't appeal to my better senses. I was as excited about the prospect of a bus ride as the survivor of a plane crash would be about his next flight.

If I could avoid travelling by bus, I would do so at all costs.

Well ... almost at all costs.

As the barman refilled my whiskey, I asked if he knew how much flights cost to Johannesburg. His answer of 450 American dollars was extremely disheartening, for not only was the price well beyond my budget, but it was further confirmation that I would have to use the risky African bus as my means of transportation to South Africa.

I downed the second drink.

However, before I could order another whiskey to mask my worries, the barman went on to say, "You know, I've heard that the grocery store near the bank has a cargo plane that flies into Jo'burg a couple of times a week. They sometimes take backpackers on board for only 100 bucks. It might be worth checking out. The place is only five minutes from here."

Grocery store? Cargo plane? A hundred bucks?

The situation screamed that it was suspect and dodgy, but the way I viewed it, it wasn't a bus.

I had nothing to lose.

I paid for my drinks and ventured into the streets of Blantyre. In spite of the whiskey buzz, I found the grocery store with ease. I tracked down the manager, who was a middle-aged Indian guy running around and screaming at everyone in sight. Between barks, I asked him when his next cargo flight to Jo'burg was scheduled to depart and if he had space on it.

The man gave me a quick glance up and down. He said, "I've got a flight leaving in one hour. Can you be at the airport by then?"

I told him that I would do everything humanly possible to be there. I raced back to the hostel, grabbed my pack, checked out and hopped into a taxi to the airport. When I arrived, the manager was already waiting for me, pacing in front on the terminal.

He was even more hurried than when I met him in the grocery store. "We are running late. Do you have your passport?" he asked with an extended hand.

I must have been caught up in his frenzy because, without really thinking, I pulled my passport out and handed it to him.

Walking into the airport, he looked over his shoulder and said, "Wait here. I'll be right back."

I was left standing there on my own. For a brief moment, I thought my passport had just been stolen. But with all the madness I had been through the past day, that scam seemed a little too obvious and blatant. I gave my passport little thought and lit a cigarette to kill the time. Before I could finish my smoke, the manager came hurrying out of the terminal, handed me my passport and hustled me along to a truck waiting in the parking lot. Making sure he hadn't pulled the old switcheroo, I looked to see if I had the right document.

He hadn't swapped documents. It was indeed my original passport. However, there was something strange about the passport that I held in my hand. It had been stamped.

This departure stamp from Malawi was odd because I hadn't seen anyone from customs or immigration. I hadn't answered any questions. My pack hadn't been searched. I had been standing outside, leaning against the terminal having a smoke and somehow my passport had been issued a departure stamp. I wasn't sure how this was legally possible, but already being a very weird day, I decided that I wasn't about to argue.

We jumped into the manager's truck and drove to a hangar where an ancient, two-prop cargo plane awaited. It was the only plane on the tarmac, so there wasn't any uncertainty that the clump of metal with wings was my ride back to South Africa. I won't pretend to know a lot about aircrafts, but it wouldn't take an aviation historian to know that the plane I was supposed to board was very, very old. Quite possibly, it could be classified as an antique.

As I was staring at the plane and trying to determine which world war it had participated in, two pilots emerged from the hangar. Other than nobody else being in sight, I knew they were the pilots because they were wearing the blue suits, ties, hats, aviation sunglasses and even the pins with the golden wings. It was the standard pilot uniform.

I called to them to have a safe flight, but they ignored me and kept walking.

The manager looked at me and said, "They probably didn't understand you. They don't speak English. They are from Russia."

Russia?

Serious, legitimate questions were beginning to materialize in my mind. What were Russian pilots doing in Malawi flying this plane? What the fuck was I doing getting on this poor excuse for an aircraft? I had read somewhere that there was a greater chance of being in an accident on an African airline than there was being in a car accident in North America. There were a lot of car accidents in North America.

I considered my limited alternatives.

It was either risking my life for three hours on the cargo plane or risking my life for 30 hours on a bus.

When I looked at my situation that way, I didn't really have an option.

I climbed into the back of the plane.

The cargo door shut, and even though she was thousands of kilometres away, I felt my mother shiver. She certainly wouldn't approve of my decision to travel with African Cargo Airlines, and I'm sure her maternal instincts were attuned to her son about to take a gamble flying the African skies. Other than the cargo, which consisted of several crates of tomatoes and some large pieces of strange machinery, the plane was empty. Compared with the packed conditions of African transportation, the ample space inside the plane was a welcome and rare luxury.

Maybe this flight wouldn't be so bad.

However, when the door to the cockpit opened and the two pilots came out, my attitude flipped again. I initially didn't recognize them, for they weren't wearing their uniforms. Instead, they were dressed in tattered and greasy clothing. They looked as though they should be fixing the plane as opposed to flying it. Until that moment, I didn't realize the amount of confidence I placed in people simply because they dressed for the part. When a doctor wears his white lab coat and has a stethoscope hanging from the pocket, I have confidence in his diagnosis. When a pilot is dressed in his blue uniform with his golden wings, I have confidence in his ability to fly. But when these two pilots reappeared dressed like two mechanics, my faith in their capabilities diminished drastically.

But what choice did I have?

The first engine started up with a loud ch-chug, ch-chug, ch-chug followed shortly by the struggling second. The plane taxied into position on the runway and increased speed for takeoff. The aircraft rumbled and rattled as it tore down the tarmac. The plane shook so much that I think I saw a screw or two dislodge from the cabin's interior. I could only hope that they weren't important.

Just when I thought the vibrations were going to break off the wings, the plane pulled away from the ground. More importantly, it continued to climb to a cruising altitude. My uncertainties about the aircraft's potential to get and stay airborne were, for the time being, eliminated.

Although there wasn't a movie or an inflight food service, African Cargo Airlines was the most comfortable flight I had even been on. Along the sides of the fuselage were fold-down benches. I flipped one down, pulled out my sleeping bag from my backpack, put on my Discman and stretched out. This was something I'd never been able to do on a flight, and I peacefully slept through the short journey back to South Africa.

Three hours later, I was safely on the ground in Jo'burg. We hadn't landed at Jo'burg International Airport but instead a secondary small craft landing strip on the outskirts of the city. I still had an hour-long taxi ride to town, but this was beside the point; I was safely on the ground.

Standing in the small arrival terminal, I glanced up at the clock. Only 20 hours beforehand, I had been standing on a Malawian highway in the middle of the night. I had just been abandoned, I had nothing to my name, bodies were strewn around me, and I was cursing the heavens. As fate would have it, a mere 20 hours later, I was safely in Jo'burg with all my possessions, and I was days ahead of schedule. Being able to accomplish this and avoid the torturously uncomfortable bus journey was an exceptional bonus.

It was amazing how quickly one's fortunes could change in Africa.

Although I still hadn't reached my final destination, *330's*, I was positive that I would make it for the party on Saturday night. Following an uneventful journey from Jo'burg to Durban, that was exactly what happened. I was safely in Durban in plenty of time. I had plenty of rest, and I could even pick out my snazziest clubbing attire for the night out at *330's*.

I was as pumped for an evening as I ever had been.

When I arrived at *330's*, there was quite a long line of fellow clubbers waiting to gain entrance. With the obstacles I had recently overcome, a lengthy queue didn't faze me. I happily made my way to the back and waited with a smile.

I noticed that everybody seemed to be dressed in almost over-the-top clothing. I then overheard that it was *330's* 12th anniversary party, which explained the long line, extravagant attire and the fantastic energy that was coming from the crowd. I couldn't have picked a better night for a blowout bender. I became even more amped for the festivities.

As I got closer to the door, the party and what would be the end of an epic and insane journey throughout Southern Africa, I became giddy with relief and excitement.

I was going to dance my ass off.

I was going to …

"You're not coming in," a voice thundered.

It is possible that I didn't hear the bouncer, or maybe I didn't believe he could be speaking to me. I'd never had a problem getting into clubs, and I recognized this particular doorman from previous visits to *330's*. He was a monster of few words and had never received any grief from me. There was no conceivable reason why he would prevent me from entering the club.

A massive hand engulfed my chest and stopped my forward momentum.

From a butt-ugly face that looked as though it had been chiselled out of rock, a voice boomed, "I said you're not coming in. It's a costume party. No costume, no entry. Next."

No costume, no entry? Was he for real? I was dumbfounded. I wanted to grab the bouncer by the throbbing vein in his neck, shake him and scream, "Wait a second, man. Do you have any idea what kind of shit I have gone through to get here? I won't bore you with all the details, but trust me when I say it has been kind of a nightmare."

The doorman must have anticipated that I had a detailed explanation. Before I could recount my tale of woe, he pre-emptively rumbled, "I don't give a shit what your excuses are. The bosses have made it clear. No costume, no entry. Next."

I walked away from the line, baffled at what had just transpired. To be that close to the finish line and be stopped by a guy who had as many brain cells as I do fingers, just because I wasn't in costume was frustrating to say the least. However, compared to the other shit I had survived en route to *330's*, something as trivial as a costume wasn't going to prevent me from reaching my final goal.

There wasn't a fucking chance.

I hopped into a cab and went back to my hostel. It was well past midnight, and all the shops were closed, so going out and buying something to wear wasn't an option. Being a Saturday, everybody staying at the backpackers had gone out for the evening, and this meant there was nobody to ask for something to wear. My options were running out. My situation was looking dire and desperate.

Then I had an epiphany of sorts.

As I was in the toker's area and staring around the hostel's courtyard, I frantically tried to think of what to wear. Then my eyes drifted across a tree in full bloom, which resulted in a brilliant, evening-saving inspiration. I dug out my knife from my backpack and proceeded to snip away a couple dozen flowers from the tree. I then stuck the flowers through the buttonholes in my shirt, in my belt buckle and around the laces of my shoes. I even attached a few to my hat. I got another cab, raced back to the club, ignored the queue and went right up to the same doorman who had previously rejected my entrance.

He looked down at me.

I looked up at him with a pleading look in my eyes. In a tone that was somewhere between determined and desperate, I said, "I'm a flower child, man. I'm a fucking flower child."

I know doormen are bred not to, but I'm sure I saw the tiniest of smiles crack on the corner of his gargoyle-like face. "Go in," he grumbled.

I paid my entrance fee and made a direct line for the dance floor. The hard, pumping music was in full flight.

The party and people were in full flight as well.

I wound past the gyrating bodies into the heart of the dance floor. Although the floor was heaving with guys and stunning gals grooving in their own worlds to the hard trance beat, I was able to find a clear space near the middle that I claimed as my own.

I closed my eyes.

I let the beat consume my body.

I began to dance, and I smiled large.

I was at the end of my journey.

I was back in South Africa.

African Cargo Airlines' finest. This was the Russian-piloted cargo flight that transported me safely from Blantyre, Malawi to Johannesburg, South Africa.

24
HOLD THAT THOUGHT BABY ... HOW BIG?!

SEPTEMBER

Living next to the Indian Ocean, I was in the perfect environment to learn to surf.

I could see whether or not there were waves without having to leave my home. Surfers surrounded me. And, most importantly, I had loads of time to practice. After almost two years living next to the ocean, one might think that I would've become a good surfer.

Surprisingly though, I'm awful.

I did learn the basic techniques and skills of surfing when I first arrived in Chintsa. Still, I can barely stand on the board. My development depended upon my own dedication to the sport.

There is no question about it. Surfing is a cool sport. You can't help but look slick walking on the beach with a surfboard under your arm. Surfing is also a great way to get into fantastic physical shape, and then there's the added bonus that surfers have the uncanny ability to attract the most beautiful, toned and tanned girlfriends. Being a surfer definitely has upsides.

However, there are several aspects associated with the lifestyle that made me hesitant about devoting time and energy to the sport. Because of these concerns, I have never become a diehard surfer.

For one thing, I want to think and talk about subjects other than waves. Surfers seem to have one-track minds regarding surfing. I know this from the endless conversations I had with surfers in an attempt to pick up some pointers and figure out the ridiculous jargon. They talked about a wave they had caught, the wave they had missed or the wave they would catch tomorrow. Every discussion was in some way about a moving mass of water.

There were times that I got seasick listening to a surfer ramble.

Another contributing component to my reluctance was the level of depression that could and often did manifest within the surfer. If the waves were flat, then so was the surfer. Depression caused by your girlfriend dumping you for your best friend, the plummeting stock market or an overcooked steak I can understand. Thankfully, the circumstances that cause those types of miseries can usually be controlled or avoided; eat at better restaurants, keep your money under the mattress and stop dating tramps.

However, the problem with the surfing-related depression was that Mother Nature was both the illness and the remedy. She was in control of their recovery period. And at the end of the day, she can be one nasty bitch who, I imagine, was pretty pissed off with us humans for the abuse that we've been putting her through. If Mother Nature has the vengeful sense of humour that I think, then I'm guessing she screws with our psyche at any opportunity.

I don't relish the notion that an irritated Mother Nature is ultimately in control of my level of happiness.

When there aren't any waves, the dejected surfer will often sit in silence and stare for hours at the sea, desperately hoping there might be a swell building on the horizon. When the swell doesn't come, the surfer mopes away, parks his ass in front of the TV, cuddles up with his board as opposed to his girlfriend (don't laugh, many actually do this) and prays that there will be waves in the morning. This pitiful behaviour can endure for weeks if the swell doesn't pick up.

A surfer will live and die by the waves.

I don't have a problem with surfers who "live by the waves". It's the "*die* by the waves," component that I have issues with.

I have two phobias. The first is a fear of heights. Actually, it's more a fear of falling and splattering on the ground than it is of heights, but that isn't the point. I don't enjoy being anywhere that presents the possibility of a long, hard plummet. The strange thing about this phobia is that I'm not sure which event from my past triggered it.

On the other hand, I didn't need to visit a shrink to pinpoint the inception of my second terror. It wasn't my parents' fault. I certainly don't hold them accountable. I was supposed to be asleep in the back seat of the car while my parents watched the second feature at the drive-in. I wasn't supposed to glance over the headrest, but being a kid, I couldn't resist and stole a peek.

It's safe to say that what I saw scarred me permanently.

For those of you with small children, here is some free advice: being four years old is far, far too young for a kid to watch the movie *Jaws*.

I'll give Steven Spielberg some credit. He did an Oscar-worthy job at scaring the living shit out of me. And scared I was. I used to get spooked swimming in lakes, which was a completely irrational fear. There weren't any sharks prowling Canadian freshwater lakes. My phobia was so severe that I used to hear the terrorizing "daah dump" any time I swam in a pool at night. I had a panic attack and scrambled for the safety of the edge within a nanosecond of entering the dark, menacing water. I knew the only people with man-eating sharks in their pools were James Bond and the Hardy Boys. But my fear still had me thinking I was about to be munched.

The irrationality was the most annoying aspect of the phobia. I knew that my fears were entirely dumb, but even so, I remained spooked. My dread would somehow find a way to overwhelm and dominate my powers of logic and common sense. It was as though my brain knew there weren't any sharks looming at the depths of my swimming pool, but it still told the rest of my body to get the fuck out and *now*. My lump of grey matter didn't want to test the theory on the slim chance that it was wrong in its assumption.

It was stupid ... I know.

Nonetheless, the phobia was real, and all of the sudden, I was living next to a body of water that does have the monstrous reality of my fear, Jaws himself, prowling in its depths. The Indian Ocean was home to the great white shark along with a barrage of other sharks. The hammerhead, the ragged tooth, and the nastiest of them all, the bull tiger (known locally as the Zambezi, this is a shark that coincidentally *does* swim in freshwater) have all been known to devour man.

I've learned a lot about sharks since being in South Africa.

For one, *Jaws* wasn't a Hollywood exaggeration. In the famous "we're gonna need a bigger boat" scene, Cooper and Quint, after first glimpsing the beast, debate its size. They argue whether or not the monster of a shark was 25 or 30 feet long. I shudder when I think about it, but great whites do grow that enormous. Scarier still, they've been known to grow even larger. There are stories of great whites that regularly swim in the Cape Town harbour who are so massive that the local fishermen refer to them as "subs."

Another fact about sharks is that they don't enjoy the taste of human. Seal is their food of choice. To a shark, the difference between the taste of a seal and a human is comparable to the difference between a filet mignon and a burger from McDonald's. They are both edible meat, but one tastes much more delicious than the other.

The reason surfers are so often attacked is because they are mistaken for seals. To a shark, a paddling surfer has the same shape and length of a swimming seal

... a plump, slow-moving seal. Not having hands, a shark's method of trial and error involves its massive and razor-sharp teeth.

What usually happens when a shark realizes its mistake is that it lets the human go. To me, the possibility that the shark might *let go* after making a mistake was of little consolation. While the shark swam away with a bad taste in his mouth, I would be left a limb short or with my guts hanging out. My final, terrifying moments would be spent either waiting to drown or to have the shark, now attracted by the blood gushing from my stump, attack what was left of me in a vicious feeding frenzy. I can't even begin to imagine what kind of horrific final thoughts would be rushing through my mind as I sank to the depths of the sea or through a shark's digestive system.

When I surfed, I felt like bait. My position on the ocean's food chain took a lot of the fun out of surfing for me.

I knew that my fears were unfounded. I knew that very few people were killed by shark attacks. I knew more people were killed by falling coconuts or struck by lightning. But this knowledge was irrelevant. It wasn't my fear of sharks, despite my childhood nightmares, that ultimately kept me from becoming a surfer. Even with my phobia, I thought sharks were quite awesome creatures.

Truth be told, it was more a fear of the *way* I'd be dispatched to the great blue yonder that scared the living shit out of me.

Honestly, being struck by a bolt of lightning would be quite a spectacular way to leave the earth. And a coconut plunking you on the head would be a comical way to go. But being eaten was another matter altogether. Neither death was anywhere near as horrifying as the prospect of being torn to shreds by a set of razor-sharp teeth—the same teeth that belonged to the animal that would shit me out at some point in the near future.

I'm a fan of lions. Bears rock. And I think crocodiles are super cool. But the thought of being hunted, mauled or death rolled wakes me up in a cold sweat. I can't imagine being alive while some beast chews through my guts and bones ... the whole time, it's staring back into my eyes.

Fuck that.

I'll take the coconut on the head, thank you very much.

If I can avoid being made into lunch, I will do so at all costs. I don't swim in croc-infested lakes, I don't jog in game reserves, and I don't wander through woods overrun with bears with a piece of meat dangling from my neck. The reason I avoid these dangerous activities is because I don't want to put myself in a position to get devoured. Unfortunately, in order to become a surfer, I would have to disguise myself as food and flop around in an environment that possessed things that could and would eat me.

I don't think so.

For argument's sake, let's say for some suicidal reason, I decided to go for a run through a game reserve and ended up fighting for my life with a lion. Even though my chances of survival were virtually non-existent, at the very least, I'd be scrapping it out with the king of the jungle on land, which was my home turf. With sharks, the battleground would be the heaving ocean. This was an insurmountable disadvantage that I didn't want any part of.

Nonetheless, the real reason that I didn't dedicate myself to surfing had nothing to do with all the bullshit that I just mentioned. The genuine reason had everything to do with one of the baffling side effects of becoming a devoted surfer.

I knew that the day would arrive when I would be making sweet love to my beautiful, tanned, sexy girlfriend, and my well-tuned surfing ear would detect the vibrations of a surfing buddy yelling that "the waves were epic" and that "the six-foot barrels were pumping." And I, despite my love and attraction for this very, very giving surfing babe, would stop what I was in the midst of doing, put on my wetsuit and run for the ocean.

Medication could control the surfer depression, the "Jaws phobia" could be conquered, and I could even handle the thought of being digested. But I never wanted to be so addicted to something that I would stop having sex for it.

No matter how epic the mass of moving water, getting laid means more to me.

I wanted to keep it that way.

That is the real reason I don't surf.

25
LIVING IN REALITY

SEPTEMBER

On the night of the second anniversary of my escape from Canada and the start of my timeless trip around the world, I got rip-roaring smashed.

Even though the backpackers in Chintsa was quiet, and there weren't many to partake in the festivities, the few of us around did our best to consume the entire contents of the bar and party. I may have even danced on a table or two. It was another instance that proved numbers don't dictate the success of a shindig. Sometimes, the reason for the party itself can be enough to spark a bender for the ages.

As far as I was concerned, this milestone was cause to celebrate.

Despite the brilliant experiences, there had been many desperate times when I questioned my decision to leave the safety of the Canadian velvet rut. However, in the face of all the shit, all my ignorance and all the tough times that I had encountered the past 24 months, I persevered.

The bottom line was that I hadn't gone home.

Prior to my Canadian exodus, when asked how long I thought my "timeless" trip around the world would take, I usually guessed around two years. Even a few months into my travels, I still believed that in a mere 24 months, I would touch all of the continents and would have a solid grasp of what I wanted to do with my life.

This unqualified prediction was another of my numerous miscalculations.

In the two years that I'd been travelling, I'd set foot on 2 continents and 19 countries. As far as I was concerned, I'd barely scratched the surface of what the planet had to offer. In fact, the only countries I had a better comprehension of the culture and peoples was South Africa and possibly Malawi. The other countries I had visited were simply teasers and tiny glimpses. Even my four months living in the Canary Islands had been strictly spent on Tenerife, and that time had been wasted busting my hump and cleaning cutlery for gangsters. I learned more about English football than I did about Tenerife or Spain.

Notwithstanding the privilege of visiting 19 fantastic countries, I realized that simply having my passport stamped didn't justify saying I had properly experienced a place. I'd seen so many travellers fly from one city to another, take a few pictures of the view, check wherever they were off their list of "places seen" and hustle to the next. In my opinion, this rushed approach was mildly better than receiving a postcard. In order to properly absorb a place, I would need to spend time watching and listening to how the people behaved and what the people had to say.

I still had loads of places on my "must-see" list that I wanted to visit. However, I was beginning to feel that I would never be able to see them all. It was quickly becoming apparent that my list would be endless. For every one I scratched off, another three would be added. This was due to a combination of my ignorance of the planet's geography and the constant contact with other travellers. The more I travelled, the more backpackers I would meet, and ultimately, the more I discovered about this mesmerizing piece of rock that we live on.

It was a little frightening that in spite of the countless places already on my list, I knew there were still many more that I hadn't yet heard of but would in due course discover.

Frightening was the wrong word. I found it baffling that I had been so unaware of the variety and diversity of this planet and how accessible these places were if one set one's mind to it. It was this endless potential that had me skeptical that I'd ever make it around the globe and back home.

Chintsa was a perfect example of how my timeless trip could, in essence, become truly timeless. Before I began my travels, I had never heard of Chintsa, and I barely knew a thing about South Africa. The same woeful lack of knowledge still applied six months into my trip. Even when I was in Cape Town, I hadn't heard a lick about the Wild Coast and its splattering of secluded villages. Truth be told, the first I heard of Chintsa was the day I arrived 18 months earlier with Vince.

It was a magical year and a half later, and there wasn't any indication that I would be leaving the place anytime in the near future. Honestly, the thought of packing my bags, saying goodbye to Chintsa and continuing with my travels had yet to enter my mind. I knew that I would have to leave South Africa someday. I would only be able to dodge immigration for so long, but thankfully, I still had a couple of schemes up my sleeve, and that horrible date was still a long way off.

Barring any unforeseen, unpredictable circumstances, I was staying in Chintsa.

I was happy.

My tendency to fall for and get stuck in unknown, magical locations had me contemplating the eventual length of my travels. If a place that I'd never heard of had seized and captivated me for 18 months, and there remained a myriad of hidden gems on the planet, then how long was it going to take me to get home?

Frankly, I didn't care how long it took.

There was another, more significant reason for my contentment. I felt a progression in my quest to find out who I wanted to become.

Having said that, I don't think I was any closer to "finding myself" or figuring out what I wanted to do with my life, but I felt as though I was moving in the right direction. As far as I was concerned, it was equally important to figure out what I *didn't* want to do with my life. For example, I knew without question that I didn't want to work in the restaurant industry. I'm sure that my nefarious surroundings in Tenerife influenced my decision. However, regardless of the criminal element, working in the food industry was full of banalities, trivial complaints and stresses. It was not the work environment I wanted to dedicate my passion to.

Furthermore, my time travelling reconfirmed my deep-seated hatred for the cold. I always believed that surviving a cold winter was not the way to live, and thanks to my time in the heat, I'm convinced of it. I had an overwhelming feeling that wherever I settled in life, warm and sunny temperatures would be a part of the package. The prospect of the Canadian winter with the shovelling of snow and scraping of ice was as appealing as a swift kick to the nuts. Being submersed in a warm climate 12 months a year was the only way forward for this lad.[1]

As it would happen, I wasn't the only one speculating when I was coming home. My family and friends were also curious if and when I would ever return to the Canadian lifestyle. When I first left Canada, many close to me organized a pool for my potential return date. There were a few who bet on me coming home with my tail between my legs the first week. Others had me lasting a whopping

---

1. There are people who think that the cold is more appealing than the heat. It is my opinion that they have obviously never lived in a warm climate, and they are simply trying to justify the insanity of living in Arctic temperatures. They have brainwashed themselves into believing that the frozen tundra, frostbite and minus 30 degree weather surpasses the aspects of life on a beach. They've convinced themselves of this brutal falsehood to prevent winter depression from taking an even deeper hold than it already has.

six weeks until Thanksgiving. I was told the longest anybody had me staying away from Mom's cooking was three months.

However, after the first year, they started to realize I had been serious about going all the way around the world. After the second flip of the calendar, all doubters were convinced that I had been dead serious about my desire for my travels to be timeless.

"When are you going to come back to reality?"

This question was the one that I was asked most often when I called home. It was the winner by a landslide and was raised by all. Family, friends, neighbours, former teachers, ex-girlfriends and even my mom's hair stylist would ask on the phone, through emails or through the grapevine if I was ever coming back to reality. Even those who had temporarily abandoned their own realities, backpackers sitting on the other side of my bar in South Africa, would eventually question the travelling lifestyle that I was sharing with them. Inevitably, once they discovered that I'd been away from Canada for so long, they'd tell me that I was living in a dreamland and that I would have to go back to reality someday.

I'd always wonder, go back to what reality exactly?

Were they talking about the Canadian reality in which I'd begin my day by rolling over at the sound of my alarm clock, getting up, taking a shower, putting on the suit and driving my car through traffic to work? Were they talking about the same reality in which my next eight hours were spent in an office building, sitting at a desk, using the computer and sending the odd fax until it was time to drive home, once again through bumper to bumper traffic? Were they talking about the reality in which my "free time" consisted of chucking some food in the microwave for dinner, or worse, ingesting fast food, stretching out on my couch, watching some TV then falling asleep?

Not only did the thought of returning to that monotonous lifestyle make me want to tear up my passport and disappear into the African bush never to be seen again, but the more I gave it reflection, the more I realized that everything I just mentioned, whether it was the alarm clock, fax machine or rat race mentality, did not exist 100 years ago. In actuality, most of the items that I used in my Canadian, day-to-day life probably didn't exist 20 years ago.

So as far as the Canadian reality was concerned, it really hadn't been around that long.

On the other hand, when I woke up in Chintsa, I watched the sun rise over the Indian Ocean. Waves crashed against the uninhabited, 17-kilometre, white, sandy beach. The only traffic at this time of day came from the lush, subtropical dunes, which contained enough indigenous animal and vegetable life that I would often be overwhelmed with the sights and sounds. The birds and insects were in full working mode, getting a great head start on us slumberous humans. The racket these tiny creatures could produce always amazed me.[2]

Everything about my South African day that I referred to was undoubtedly a lot older than 100 years. This natural reality had been in existence for a lot longer than my Canadian reality of alarm clocks, suburbia and overcrowded expressways.

Of course, I'm not oblivious to Canada's raw, rugged, natural wilderness. It possesses more of it than practically any other country in the world. The problem, however, was that this unspoiled environment was tremendously difficult to access, and the extreme hostility of the weather made it impossible to live within year-round. This was the reason why 90 per cent of the Canadian population lives within 100 kilometres of the American border. Our wilderness is just too wild.

Clearly, my South African lifestyle does incorporate highly advanced products of the 20th century. Life there isn't about wearing a loincloth and rubbing sticks together for fire. However, the main difference between the two realities was the importance that the cultures placed upon these products. One culture understood the difference between necessities and luxuries, while the other had confused the two.

I believe that every traveller has his or her own reason for leaving the safety of home and venturing into the unknown: each person's reasons are as distinct as his or her fingerprints. One of my main motives was to get a grip on my frustrations about the Western world and to put our problems, at least what we thought were problems, into perspective.

Every country has its troubles, and sadly, South Africa isn't any different. Some of my friends and family at home, especially my mom, didn't understand

---

2. I can't ever remember watching the sunrise while living in Canada. There may have been the odd occasion when I caught the sun rising after an all-nighter, but in those rare instances, I took a quick, unappreciative glance at best. Regrettably, when it came to my normal, day-to-day, Monday to Friday swing of things, I never saw a single one. In winter, I lived in perpetual darkness, and I missed both the sunrise and the sunset while either warmly sleeping under my blankets or sitting at my office desk.

The first time I saw the sunrise in Chintsa, it took my breath away, and my ability to express myself was reduced to, "Whhhoooo…ahhhhhh…ohhhhh…" I wouldn't be surprised if the very first person to ever watch the sunrise in this part of the world, whichever millennium it may have been, uttered similar sounds.

why I desired to visit regions that most Canadians would describe as unstable. They couldn't comprehend my need to visit countries that had been affected by war, natural disasters or, as was the case in South Africa, were in the midst of rebuilding after a dark period in their history. It was hard for my family to understand, but I needed to visit countries that had issues and hazards that my Canadian society was impervious to.

There is no sense trying to sugar-coat the crime problem in South Africa. As someone who comes from a country where we rarely lock our front doors, the amount of crime and the levels of violence are quite disturbing. However, despite the high crime rate, the trouble is nowhere near as startling as the western media had me believe. The gangsters are predominately in the major cities such as Johannesburg, Durban and Cape Town, and even then, the crime and violence were territorial.

One of the biggest misconceptions about South Africa is that the majority of the black population has criminal tendencies. This couldn't be further from the truth. The large majority of the black population abhor crime, and in many parts of the rural countryside, communities sought out perpetrators and administered their own brand of harsh tribal justice. The black communities are far too aware that in this fragile time of rebuilding, the "one bad apple can spoil the bunch" philosophy remains prevalent throughout the country.

The dilemma in South Africa is that there are a small numbers of violent criminals committing a lot of crime. Essentially, the thugs are very good at what they do. In my opinion, it is this small percentage of efficient gangsters who continue to fuel the fire for the racist segment of white South Africa that still clings to apartheid.

It must be noted that another major misconception about South Africa is that the entire white population is racist. People believe that they all behaved despicably in the past and that they deserve whatever hardships come their way. Again, this couldn't be further from the truth. A significant percentage of white South Africa fought against the apartheid regime and celebrated Mandela's release. Now, they share a positive outlook about the future of their country. Unfortunately, the racist South Africans stand out more than the open-minded, and as a result, they leave a deeper impression. Regrettably, crime doesn't discriminate, and the levels of violence affect even the most liberal white South Africans.

Perhaps, this could help explain why there is so much security in the country. I got the impression that South Africans were paranoid and petrified of one another. The "he may not be a bad guy, but maybe he is" mentality had white

South Africans, both open-and closed-minded, living within homes protected like prisons.

Practically every urban residence is adorned with 10-foot high fences and electrical gates. On top of this, barbed wire, razor wire, broken bottles or any combination of the three are used to further deter any potential intruders. If a predator could somehow manoeuvre around these painful obstacles, then he would probably face a raging, bloodthirsty attack dog or some paranoid citizen who was armed to the teeth and ready and willing to pull the trigger.

To put these over-the-top security measures into perspective, there was more security around a South African church than around any Canadian military compound.

However, I don't want to dwell on South Africa's problems. Truthfully, between the division of wealth, poverty, unemployment, crime, racism, corrupt government officials, AIDS and other diseases, South Africa has more desperate issues to contend with than most countries.

Nevertheless, South Africa was attempting to deal with their own struggles rather than wasting time, energy and money on dilemmas that they couldn't solve. It was this attribute that I found so distinctive and intriguing.

South Africans worried about their own backyard.

I think the main reason South Africa was able to remain focused on South Africa was due to the fact that their media outlets weren't nearly as obtrusive as they were in North America.

With the news channels blasting away 24-7, the North American public was continuously bombarded with depressing events from around the planet. The news showed events that were totally irrelevant to the typical Canadian's day-to-day life. The purpose of these meaningless accounts was to further hammer home the belief that the velvet rut was the only way to live. To the western media, it was more important whom the president did as opposed to what he did.

There was also the glorification of undeserving media personalities, overpaid actors, athletes and entertainers. The media had transformed them into heroes and icons. Am I to accept that these people, who are paid outrageous sums of money for reading lines and hitting balls, were the ones to idolize? Was I to accept that these people were the ones we should base our moral ideals upon? I refused to do so.

Then there were the advertisements. They were absolutely everywhere. They encouraged people to eat at McDonald's and drink Coke. They would tell us to rush out and buy the newer and better products, which were just upgrades from the items already in our possession. Shrewdly, these advertisements would subdue us into believing that we needed to accept and remain within the velvet rut as our means to an end. And that end was the acquisition of Sony PlayStations, Ford Explorers and high-definition televisions.

This was all done in an attempt "to keep up with the Joneses."

My question was, who the hell were the Joneses?

Were they the people across the street or the people next door?

I hate to break it to you, but I never knew my neighbours.

I came from a social family with friendly parents, and I grew up on Withrow Avenue in a welcoming, residential neighbourhood. However, the neighbours immediately to our left had lived there for over 20 years, and I didn't know their names. The same can be said about the people who lived on the other side of the house. They had been residents for 28 years, and I'd be hard pressed to recognize them on the street.

Of course, we knew a couple of families on Withrow Avenue, but as far as having an "open door" policy or even inviting our long-time, next door neighbours in for a coffee, it just never happened.

Not every Canadian family was like this. Although I'm sure a large majority, especially urbanites, pass through existence without knowing the guy next door or the name of the girl in apartment 6A. In North America, for whatever reason, we have somehow lost our sense of community.

Again, who exactly was I trying to keep up with?

I know the life for the average black South African was tough. There certainly wasn't anything velvet about the African rut. However, I was confident that the average African not only recognized the faces of every man, woman and child in his community but knew all their names as well. In rural South Africa, keeping up with the Joneses literally meant keeping up with what and how the neighbours were doing.

I know that I am extremely lucky to have been born, raised and educated in Canada. My parents worked very hard to ensure that my brother and I were always fed, clothed and happy. Most Canadians are fortunate to enjoy a high standard of living that is tremendously rare in this world. Regrettably, the large majority of people are nowhere near as fortunate as the average Canadian. It may sound cliché, but it's true; despite the gluttonous waste of food in the western world, many inhabitants of this planet struggle to eat on a daily basis.

I felt privileged to have come from such a prosperous country, and if it weren't for my upbringing and economic environment, I wouldn't be in the position to put everything on hold, buy a plane ticket and travel the world.

I wouldn't be in a position to criticize.

Nevertheless, it wasn't the possessions or opportunities provided by Western civilization that angered me immensely. Not in the least. If it weren't for those possibilities, I wouldn't be sitting in South Africa in a position to bitch. No, what drove me insane was that we classified these possessions as necessities rather than luxuries.

We, in the western world, should be doing cartwheels every morning for the advantages, opportunities and lifestyles that we have. Education, social systems, free health care, low unemployment, low crime rates, high salaries and a stable political system are all factors that should have us laughing and skipping every day.

Yet we don't. Instead, we bitch and demand more.

And when we do get more, we aren't satisfied. We want what comes next. We want the upgrade. And we will bitch and complain until we obtain what we believe we are entitled to. If we need to neglect family and friends to work a 60 hour week to do so, then so be it. If we fall further into debt because of pre-authorized credit, then so be it. It is a never-ending, vicious cycle in which luxuries become necessities.

It wasn't until I arrived in Southern Africa that I realized how far off the path we at home had strayed. In the village, the struggles and lack of material possessions were overshadowed by the incredible sense of community that was a fundamental aspect of rural African life.

However, it was the small packages of inexhaustible energy, the African kids, who ultimately pounded home the lessons regarding priorities.

I want to make something absolutely crystal clear from the outset; these kids have nothing.

Let me say that again to emphasize my point … they have *nothing*.

These kids don't have toys. And when I say that they don't have toys, I'm not suggesting that they don't have Sony PlayStations or bicycles or action figures. I mean they don't have *any* toys.

Most of these kids don't have their own beds. The overwhelming majority don't own shoes. The lucky ones might have two sets of clothes, but even these are hand-me-downs from generations back, and the wear and tear of the decades was evident. Tragically, far too many don't have parents. They are lost to one of the many causes of early death in the harsh African reality.

However, despite these overwhelming hardships, these kids were happy. They were probably the happiest little guys and gals that I've ever seen anywhere at anytime. They were always laughing and playing. That's right. They were playing. The hindrance of not having any toys didn't stop the African kids from amusing themselves to their hearts' content, for they had tapped into something that North American kids had long forgotten.

The African children used their imaginations.

I want to point out something else about these kids. They worked hard; it wasn't always playtime for them. It was far from it actually. The kids worked in the fields. They caught mussels from the rock pools. They carried buckets of water. They babysat their younger and sometimes infant siblings. Similar to my grandpa's tall tales of childhood hardships, many of these kids did walk five miles to school. And that was if they were fortunate enough to have a school.

Yet throughout all the struggles and hardships, they remained happy.

If I took the most unspoiled Canadian kid and put him in the same environment as the African kid, the little Canuck would crack. Without TV, video games, computers or even building blocks, the North American kid would inevitably throw a temper tantrum until he cried himself to sleep in bed, which in Africa would be a blanket on the floor. He would expend all his energy and efforts sulking and would fail to grasp that he possessed the coolest supercomputer known to the planet, the imagination.

Once in the Transkei, I saw a little eight-year-old Xhosa girl sitting cross-legged on the mud floor of her family's thatched hut. Despite not having any crayons or paper, she was drawing. Instead, this little girl was amusing herself by sketching on the inside of an empty cigarette pack with a pencil stub.

The smile on her face was brilliant.

If I had transported this little girl into the heart of the biggest toy store on the planet, she could not have turned out a more radiant, genuine smile.

This little girl was happy with a nub of lead and some tattered cardboard.

The kids of Africa really got me thinking and reprioritizing.

The magic of the children's innocence and contentment with what little they possessed affected me deeply. I don't criticize my parents for the manner in which they raised me, nor do I believe that North Americans are a greedy, bad people. This isn't the case at all. I just think we have forgotten some very basic, simple and pure principles regarding our fellow human beings. And these are principles that the Africans have made paramount in their culture. I recognized that in spite of the poverty, suffering and struggles that Africans endured, there was a lot to learn in this special land from these amazing people.

There was still much for me to learn.

I believed I had found a truly enchanted location in Chintsa, and it provided me with a fountain of education and experience. I concluded that the African version of reality that I had submersed myself within was quite exceptional. Despite the madness and problems of South Africa, there was a unique energy present. It was one that was helping me open my mind and grasp what I wanted to deem important in my life.

Best of all, I had somehow figured out how to deal with the rage and anger that had been brewing in me back home. This had been a very real issue, which had been on the brink of exploding and consuming all those in my life. Through the simplicity and beauty of the Chintsa lifestyle, along with all the other features and characters that accompanied a life on the road, I'd been able to find and keep a sense of inner contentment and happiness. I honestly couldn't remember the last time I got mad at anything for any reason. Years had elapsed without my notorious temper surfacing. Even when I had been stranded in Malawi following the bus accident, I wasn't angry at my predicament or any of the people involved. Yes, I was frustrated, scared and concerned. I encountered a barrage of feelings that insane night. But anger, other than a touch directed at the Gods' twisted sense of humour, barely entered the emotional equation.

In contrast, while living in Canada, I couldn't get through a single hour without feeling the anger bubbling. This was not the way to live.

Not wanting this rage to consume me, I'd come up with an extremely basic guideline. It was one that I wanted to incorporate into all aspects of my life whether professional or personal. The straightforward blueprint was that it was good to be happy and bad to be sad. If I could apply that simplified, fundamental viewpoint to my life, I believed that I would be able to go through the ride with very few concerns.

I believed that if I was doing anything that made me unhappy, such as being stuck in the velvet rut, I had the power and ability to make a constructive change. If I was doing something that made me happy, like running a pub on a beach in South Africa, I also had the power to ensure that I remained on the same positive track.

I was very happy in South Africa.

I once heard someone say that he believed his 20s were the experimental decade. The idea was that he should experiment with as many varieties of lifestyle, environment, friendship, career, relationship and reality that he could. And through trial and error, he would be able to determine which elements were important and which were irrelevant in order to be happy in life. Then when he was 30, he would know what he wanted. He would be able to filter out the shit and create the reality that best suited him.

Much like Andy Rooney's "life is backwards" philosophy, this too made a lot of sense. Now was my time to experiment and explore. When I was in my early

20s, I had dabbled in both the academic and professional routines, and neither had appealed to me in any way. On the other hand, the ups and downs of the travelling lifestyle had inspired, educated and motivated me beyond any classroom or paycheque.

Being 26 years old, I still had a few more years to explore and experiment before I had to filter and focus.

I was planning on making the most of my time, but there was no need to rush from Africa.

I knew that there was still much more to learn.

The hands-free approach to carrying a crate of beer, a bucket of water, a bundle of wood or anything. Chintsa, South Africa

The African "baby pack." Mpande, South Africa

A Transkei "school bus." These kids were fortunate. Not only did they have a school to attend in the remote rural hills, but they had transportation as well. Mpande, South Africa

Two boys anxiously wait for their friend (top left) to make the 14-metre plunge into the rock pool below. Inspired by macho bravado, I did make this insane jump once. Common sense and my desire to live prevented any further attempts. It wasn't the height as much as the tiny landing area (more appropriate for a circus act) that quashed my daredevil instincts. Mpande, South Africa

26

THE EMAIL

NOVEMBER

"Dear Son,

Have your friends arrived yet? You must be very excited to see them after all of this time. I know that they are excited to see you in your new home. Your father and I are very happy that you have found a beautiful place in South Africa and that you are surrounded by good people who care for you.

However, on a sad note, I need to tell you that Grandma (my Mom) has been diagnosed with cancer of the uterus. Honey, she has lived a long and happy life and she has expressed no desire to 'ride off into the sunset' (in her words) going through chemotherapy, being sick and confined to a hospital bed fighting for who knows how long. She would rather die quickly and gracefully.

Having said that, this will most likely be her final Christmas. Sweetie, I know that you are very happy where you are in South Africa but you might consider coming home for the holidays. I know that your Grandmother would be ecstatic to see you. Your Father, brother and I have missed you dreadfully as well.

Please give it some thought.

I'm sorry to have to be the bearer of bad news but please don't let it spoil what will be an amazing time with your friends.

Missing you very much,

Love Mom"

I've never been a fan of emails. I didn't create an email address until I began my travels, and since obtaining the cyber residence, messages to my friends and family have grown few and far between. This is probably because I've lived so long on the beach, and I would much rather be doing something in the sunshine than sitting behind a computer indoors. There was the added consideration that I was dealing with African Internet connections, and the time it took to load pages was painstakingly slow. An hour could be devoted to sending one email with the strong possibility that the bastard would only vanish into cyberspace.

I didn't have the patience for writing emails in the best circumstances.

Granted, emails are a quick and easy way to stay in touch with a lot of different people in a lot of different places. However, the heart of the message is lost in the impersonal and effortless manner in which it is delivered. Handwritten letters require time and effort to write and post. A telephone call indicates that somebody wants to hear my voice and have a conversation. On the other hand, emails require next to no effort (unless you're in Africa). This makes it possible for horrible, life changing news to be delivered in such a bland and monotonous manner that the severity of the message can be overlooked.

In this instance, there was no question regarding the gravity of Mom's email.

My grandmother and I had always been very close. I attended university in the city where she lived, and during those four years, we had a chance to spend quality time together that strengthened our already strong relationship. I was and had always been her "sweetheart." Before I began my travels, believing I could be away for a couple of years, I made a point of spending time with and saying goodbye to all my grandparents. Two years was a long time in "grandparent years," and a lot could happen to their health in that period. I wanted them to know how I felt before I left home in case it would be the last time I saw them. All three (my mom's father had been dead for almost 25 years) told me that if anything should happen to them while I was travelling, I shouldn't come back. They said a flight home for a funeral would be economically pointless, and they understood that I loved them.

However, this situation was a little different. I wouldn't be going home for a funeral. Grandma was still very much alive, and I had a chance to spend more time with her. It was a luxury most people aren't able to enjoy with those they love. It had been over two years since I had been back to Canada, and as much as I loved Chintsa, I knew that blood family was still blood family. If I asked, any member of my family would be there for me in a heartbeat.

How could I not do the same for them?

I couldn't.

I needed to leave Chintsa.

I needed to go home.

But I wasn't finished with my travels.

I had just scratched the surface of the planet, and there was too much more to be seen and experienced. Maybe Grandma's health was the reason that I needed to motivate my Africanized ass, pack up and move on from Chintsa. However, her illness wasn't cause to call it quits on my plan to travel the planet. I wasn't ready to return to the velvet rut.

Christmas in Ottawa was going to be a short stopover. I did not intend to stay any longer in the cold than I had to. I'd heard too many horror stories of long-term travellers returning to their homes after extended time away only to find themselves overwhelmed with the drastic change to their realities. I'd heard nightmares of people sinking into depression for months on end after returning to the stagnant lives from which they had run. I'd heard tales of continuous moping, whining, not knowing what do to and constantly wishing they were back on the road. I'd heard these symptoms were common and almost to be expected.

I vowed not to let this happen to me.

Therefore, to prevent this distressing state of mind from setting in, I purchased a return flight to London, which I booked for three weeks after my return to the winter homeland. By doing so, I would be able to eliminate any feelings, thoughts or traces of post-traveller depression. Instead, I could focus on spending quality time with my friends and family. I would be able to enjoy rather than dread being at home.

In the end, it was crucial that I was able to eliminate additional stress, for I knew that saying goodbye to Chintsa was going to be difficult enough. I knew that Chintsa would always be a home away from home and that the family here would always be my second family. But leaving right before the fantastic insanity of the holiday season was going to be a colossal mental task to overcome.

Furthermore, no matter how much I pretended that it didn't concern me, I was anxious about seeing my friends after all this time. More precisely, I was anxious about seeing the changes, great or non-existent, in my friends.

Two years is a long time. Much had changed in the lives of my Canadian mates. Some had married and had children; others had established careers and bought property. My life had also changed, but a vastly different set of circumstances had been involved. Although there was an iota of doubt, I remained confident that those closest to me would be, despite their changes, still "brothers."

It was the fringe buddies whom I was concerned about.

Not only were my experiences and the places that I'd visited completely foreign to them, but I knew that my views and perspectives would differ from theirs. They had devoted two years towards the fast-paced North American lifestyle, while I'd worked for pittance and lost my shoes on a beach.

There could be a conflict of ideals.

I was also apprehensive about returning into the heart of the western world. I had mellowed out significantly during the past two years, and although living in South Africa had been a major influence upon my new-found serenity, it wasn't the only reason that I had chilled. Southern Africa had provided me with a captivating classroom. I hoped that the lessons learned would remain intact, and I hoped to apply them in whatever setting or environment that I settled in.

This was the theory, at least.

Returning to North America amid the Christmas season, which is a time when getting has become more important than giving, would put my presumption to the ultimate test.

As good luck would have it, before I had to deal with the challenges of home, I had some exciting times ahead. It seemed that some of the people that I missed from home also missed me. Instead of waiting for me to pack it in and go back to Canada, my two closest friends, Woody and Russell, had decided to come visit me in South Africa. Woody was out for a three-week vacation, and Russell, much like myself in that he was a little lost in life, had decided to dabble in the world of extended backpacking. I was thrilled to have two friends from home visit so that they could share in my African experience and possibly understand why I got stuck in such a distant land for such an extended time.

I didn't think there would be any problems or drastic, incompatible changes in our personalities, but I couldn't be 100 per cent sure until my friends physically arrived and we stood face to face. Granted, they were my best friends, but I hadn't seen them in over two years, and no matter how I looked at it, two years was a long time.

However, my concerns were unwarranted.

Any remaining doubts about reconnecting with my friends were eliminated within 10 seconds of their arrival in Chintsa. I saw Russ and Woody the moment they walked into the bar. I stopped whatever I was doing and ran from behind the counter. The three of us were hugging and laughing a nanosecond later. We immediately began insulting each other, which although bizarre to outsiders, was a classic trademark of our friendship. It was a sign that everything was going to be sweet. Scott told me to take a break, so we grabbed a handful of beer and trekked down to my cottage.

It was as though time had stood still.

There were a few minutes of awkward, feel each other out, break the ice conversation, but after that, it was old school. We were laughing at the same shit we had laughed at two years ago. We pounded a couple of beers, smoked a couple of spliffs and caught up. Woody and Russ recounted tales of what my other friends were doing with their lives.

Some things, thankfully, never change.

Hanging out with my mates in South Africa for the next three weeks was one of the highlights of my travels. My friends also served a fantastic, secondary function by helping me mentally prepare for the adjustments that I would inevitably have to make once I returned to Canada. Even though there may be a few people at home whom I will have lost touch with, there will always be those who remain close despite time, distance and change. This reassurance further fuelled my desire to continue travelling and explore the planet, for I knew that I could stay away from Canada for an extended period and not lose those who mattered most.

As far as I was concerned, losing contact with a few distant friends from high school was an easy sacrifice to make for the mind-boggling experiences of my past two years.

People come and go from our lives.

Still, there was a part of me that was gutted about leaving South Africa and saying goodbye to my new family and friends. I was able to balance any traces of sadness with feelings of excitement and anticipation about what country would be next on my world travels. There was still a lot of planet to experience. I knew that it was now or never to commence the next leg of my adventure, or it was possible that there wouldn't be a next leg. Time had this marvellous tendency of disappearing in South Africa, and I had a feeling that if I stayed in Chintsa for much longer, then I'd get stuck permanently.

Twenty months was twenty months. South Africa had plenty of time to leave its unmistakable impression on my heart and soul, and it most certainly had done so.

It was time to go.

As time passed, the less bummed I was about going home. I was actually becoming quite stoked about seeing my family and friends. Following a whirlwind three weeks of Christmas cooking, Mom's TLC and snow, I'd be out of Canada and back on the road to continue backpacking the planet.

With my escape flight safely secured, there wouldn't be any pressure to find work, and I would have a definitive answer to the inevitable barrage of questions from family and friends regarding my future. "Are you settling down?" now had a retort.

I was excited about the visit until I received Mom's email.

> Dear son,
> Both your father and I are extremely excited about your decision to come

home. We have both missed you dreadfully.

However, before you arrive, you should be aware that things will be a little different when you get here. Your father and I are no longer together. We have separated, and I have moved to Florida where I'm sharing accommodation with another man. The weather here is 80 degrees, and we are playing golf everyday.

I do hope that you can keep an open mind and not take sides on this situation until you've heard all the facts. Please try and remember to incorporate some of your new-found calmness and do not let anger dictate your emotions. The man whom I am living with is very kind and gentle. I hope that you can understand.

Your father, brother and I will be at the airport when you arrive.

Love always,

Mom

I felt as though I'd been kicked in the nuts.

I read the email again slowly. I made sure I hadn't misread a sentence or overlooked the punchline. To my shocked disbelief, the email read exactly the same. I felt physically ill. My mind was racing with thoughts of denial and embarrassment. I didn't know which was more disturbing—my Mom choosing to inform me of the family disintegration via email or her thinking I would give a rat's ass that she was playing golf in a hot and sunny Florida. The weather was 80 degrees? Had my Mom gone insane? Did she honestly think it mattered to me that she was getting a tan? The only messages that I could ascertain from Mom's email was that she and Dad had split up and, worst of all, they had lied to me in the process.

The next chunk of time was a bit disjointed. I remember turning off the computer and attempting to get the hell out of the crowded office before I broke down. I recall crying uncontrollably as I ran past Woody, down the hill and to the solitude and relative safety of my cottage. I didn't stop to talk, for I knew that my tears were just clearing a path for the anger and rage that was about to blow off the scale.

Although it had been over two years since I had cracked with anger, the acidic taste of rage is not easily forgotten, and it overwhelmed me now. It choked me with its bitter flavour.

By the time I arrived at my cottage, I was literally growling and frothing at the mouth.

Every muscle tensed.

Every vein throbbed.

I searched for something to destroy.

I picked up the wooden lounge chair from the sundeck, which weighed a hefty 35 kilograms. Its only fault in the universe was being an inanimate object in my warpath, and in a moment of rage-induced strength, I hip launched the heavy bastard deep into the bush.

I let out a primordial yell.

I stormed into the cottage where I kicked, punched, overturned, head-butted and drop-kicked every piece of non-living matter I could see.

I moved back to the patio to let fly the other, innocent chair when, through blurred eyes, I saw a face cautiously peering around the corner of the cottage.

It was Woody braving the wrath of my temper.

He had come to say goodbye. He had a flight to catch. As shitty luck would have it, Woody was returning to Canada that fateful morning. I had originally planned on going to the airport to see him off, but after I opened my emails, all plans to inflict myself on the general public had flown out the window.

It was safest that way.

Although it was visibly obvious that I was in no shape to go anywhere, I nonetheless apologized to Woody and explained that I wouldn't be able to go with him to the airport.

Woody didn't need any apologies. "I know man. I mean, I don't know, but I understand," my best friend consoled. "I'm sorry that I have to leave you like this, man. Call me in a couple of days when you feel like talking, okay."

He put his hand on my shoulder. "You gonna be alright, brother?"

I felt my heart move into my throat and tears well up in my already-swollen eyes. Woody was truly one of my best friends.

Through uncontrolled body sobs, I nodded that I would.

We hugged goodbye.

I was, once again, left alone with my anger.

Thankfully, the initial explosion of rage and the superhero feats of strength had subsided. I was wary that there might be anger aftershocks, but for the moment, I had stopped being destructive. I rolled a massive joint and smoked it. I rolled another joint and smoked that one too. I didn't stop. I slipped into a stoned, almost hypnotic state and stayed that way for the next 24 hours. I barely moved from the chair. My brain needed to block out all other thoughts and attempt to process the life changing news that had been cyber-dumped on me.

Nobody, regardless of age, wants his parents to split up, and the revelation of my family's secret really caught me off guard. It wasn't so much that they had gone their separate ways that had me upset. And as much as it made me sick to my stomach, it wasn't even that Mom was shacked up with some guy in Florida. No, those were other issues altogether and ones that I would deal with at another time. What really felt like a bullet to my heart was the manner in which they kept their separation from me and the manner in which I was told.

I couldn't believe that my parents had lied to me for as long as they had. I had spoken to Mom on their anniversary in August, and she had given me some bullshit story about their romantic evening on the town. Did they feel that they were protecting me? Didn't they think that I'd find out at some point? Did they not realize that their lie could only backfire whilst hurting me tremendously in the process?

Worst of all, the lies and deception had rocked some of my core beliefs. Beliefs such as family, true love, commitment, honesty and respect were now all in question. These had been deep beliefs that had remained intact throughout my travels despite the changes in my perspectives, and they had been ones that I thought would never be challenged.

My parents' love for one another used to be my strongest argument when I defended the existence of these beliefs in today's world of infidelity, divorce and broken families. I used to say that despite the statistics, marriage could work. All one had to do was look at my parents to see the blueprint for success.

Now, everything had been shattered.

My parents' lies had unsteadied my beliefs. It was as though my core principles had been detonated into the air, and where and how they would resettle was impossible to predict. How could I believe in commitment and true love when my strongest argument in their support was now working against me? I thought that family was supposed to be open and honest with one another, especially when times were difficult. I thought that family could count unconditionally on one another.

How could they have lied to me for so long?

I spent the rest of the day and night secluded in my cottage. I believed it was safer for everybody and everything that way.

I had some serious thinking to do.

I didn't sleep a wink the entire evening.

The next morning, Russell bravely ventured into the cottage to see how I was doing. We had been friends long enough to know that when I was raging, it was best to stay away and to give me time and space to cool off. I picked up an overturned chair and asked him to sit down. I rolled us a spliff.

I explained that there were a few things that I needed to say out loud in order to get my head around the insanity and that I didn't expect him to have an answer to my rambles. I began to talk. I rolled another joint. I continued with my rant. The only time I stopped talking was to wipe the tears from my eyes or to light another joint. Russell, another very close friend, sat there and absorbed every piece of rage and confusion that consumed me.

When I was finished airing my anger and frustrations, all Russ could utter was, "Jesus, man. I don't know what to say."

He stared at the floor in silence for a minute. "Besides," he continued, letting his notorious, devilish grin consume his face, "I think I'm too stoned to say anything."

Laughter can be an amazing remedy even for the bleakest situations.

It felt good to smile.

It was vital for me to talk, even though I never expected my friend to have any answers. If I hadn't got a few things off my chest, I'm sure I would have exploded.

I had survived the initial shock and rage of being lied to by the people closest and dearest to me. I now had to decide what to do about it.

My first thought was to write my brother and tell him to inform my parents that they could both go fuck themselves. If their lies were any indication of how much they respected me, then I was going to take my ticket home and smoke it. They could explain to Grandma why I wasn't going to see her again before she died.

However, I thought better of this point of no return course of action. If I didn't go home to spite my parents, I would hurt two innocent people whom I loved. I would hurt my dying grandmother and my brother. And I was sure my brother was having an even harder time than I because he was living among that madness and dealing with the shit on his own. I knew that I needed to go home for no other reason than to support him.

I had to go home because, ultimately, this was my family.

Family was one aspect of my life that I promised myself I would never run from. My family was never part of the reason why I had to leave Canada. They were intelligent and supporting, and they had always provided me with unconditional love. If anything, they were the ones who kept me clinging to my sanity during the years I was trapped in the rat race. When I made my decision to go travelling, I knew that my family was a rock-solid unit and that they would survive without me.

In spite of this solidarity, I made a promise that if any problems should arise with my family while I was travelling, whether it was an illness or crisis, I would return home.

This was a crisis.

My parents had angered and hurt me beyond explanation, and they had shaken many of my core foundations and beliefs. But despite my confusion and uncertainties, the one belief that I clung to was the power, strength and importance of family. There were devastating cracks in this belief, but it hadn't been entirely destroyed. If there was a chance, I still felt that it was well worth repairing.

I spent some time thinking about what I wanted to say to my mom and dad. Although I had stopped throwing objects into the jungle, I was still mightily pissed off. I sat down at the computer, and despite its impersonal nature, I wrote Mom and Dad an email that unmistakably portrayed my emotions and thoughts. I didn't think there would be any way to avoid anger seeping into my letter, but to be sure that I hadn't gone too far, I reflected upon my words before I sent the message.

When I awoke the following morning, I felt exactly the same way and didn't change a syllable.

I realized that it is possible to convey the most heartfelt emotions via email and that there are times when a communication without conversation is actually a good thing.

> Mom and Dad,
>
> It's safe to say that I'm not handling the news of your past letter well. In fact, I'm having an impossible time.
>
> I can't remember the last time I cried as hard as I did the other day after Mom's email came through. I have never felt so hurt in all my life. How could you drop a bomb like that then casually talk about the weather? Are you mad? The emotions I experienced that day reached all-time maximums. I was devastated, hurt, embarrassed and angry. Anger doesn't even begin to describe the emotion I experienced. Why was I so mad? Because you lied to me! You haven't been honest with me for God knows how long. Half-truths and flat out lies! And because of your lies, you have made me a liar. I have talked about how wonderful and in love my parents were and how lucky I was to have such a great family to way too many people. It was all bullshit.
>
> Most importantly, your actions have destroyed so much that I believed in. My beliefs in honesty, commitment, love and strength of family have all been rocked. Lines and points of no return have been crossed. None of it was

my fault.

It was quite coy of you to keep your separation a secret from me until I had purchased my ticket home. If it weren't for Grandma and Mike, I'd tell you to shove my ticket up your asses. I'm leaving a place that I don't want to leave, which is a place filled with love, and I am instead returning to a place of … what? Home? Hardly. More like complete uncertainty and anything but love. Thanks very much for making this a shitty Christmas.

Since the two of you have kept me out of your lives for so long, don't expect to hear from me until I get back to Ottawa. All I know about you Mom is that you are somewhere in the state of Florida. Thanks for a phone number. You asked me not to take a side, so that is the way it is. And don't, I repeat, don't pick me up at the airport! I've travelled the world for over two years. I'm sure I can handle Ottawa International back to Withrow Avenue. I don't want to see you after all this time and bullshit at a fucking airport. Stay away. I'll be home when I'm home.

Your pissed off son.

P.S. If you have never believed anything I've said, then you had better believe this. If I ever meet this motherfucking "gentle" cocksucker you are "sharing your accommodation with," I will kill him.

27

CULTURE SHOCK

DECEMBER

The first of what would prove to be many culture shocks had occurred a mere 20 minutes into my travels. The thickness of the Glaswegian brogue caught me unprepared. So much so that it had almost scared me back to Canada with my clueless tail tucked between my legs and before the ink in my passport had dried. Thankfully, I persevered through my fear of not being able to communicate; from then on, the culture shocks were welcome and enlightening occurrences.

For example, the open and truly liberal mentality of the Netherlands, and particularly Amsterdam, had blown me away in a stoned haze. Working for gangsters in Tenerife had been a revelation into the motives of the criminal element and it had helped shed some of my naïveté. And practically every day in Southern Africa, I experienced at least one thing that made me shake my head in disbelief. Yet it always helped me appreciate some of the pure and basic principles, morals and ideals that I wanted to govern my life.

However, in the two years, two months and 26 days that I'd been exploring the planet, it was safe to say that the culture shock I was in the midst of experiencing was the biggest one to date. Despite all the eye-opening experiences and lessons in all the amazing countries, this change of scenery was staggering.

I wasn't enjoying it.

I wasn't happy about it.

It was freaking me out.

It was freaking me out because it shouldn't have been freaking me out. There shouldn't have been any wide-eyed surprise or apprehension about what I was transfixed upon. This wasn't uncharted territory. This wasn't a place that I was ignorant about. In fact, for the first 24 years of my life, I had known nothing else.

In spite of the familiarity, I was being slapped in the face with a noteworthy culture shock.

As the 767 started its decent towards Ottawa International, my eyes were glued to the cabin window. They were fixated on the white, frozen landscape below. It had been a very long time since I'd seen snow, and now there was a ton of it waiting below.

Maybe it wasn't culture shock that I was experiencing but rather, and probably more accurately, "environmental shock."

Concerns about my pending family crisis and my potential anger were temporarily supplanted by the horrors of the cold.

The last time I had to tolerate anything remotely resembling cold weather had been over two years prior when I departed Vienna for Spain in search of work. Once I settled in the Canary Islands, I never again subjected myself to negative temperatures and had lived an endless summer ever since.

There had been a brief moment while staring out the window that I had been captivated by the splendor and beauty of the Canadian countryside. I had forgotten how stunning an endless, snowy landscape is. Perhaps there was a miniscule part of me that was mesmerized by the serenity of the pristine, white blanket. Perhaps I was hypnotized by its purity. However, my misguided sentiments of nostalgia were avalanched by the recollection of the intensity and brutality of the cold.

I wasn't ready for the Canadian winter's bite and sting. My bones were chilled just thinking about the arctic temperatures I would be subjected to. The viciousness of the cold would be compounded by my acclimatization to warm weather. I spent my first winter in Chintsa running around in shorts and a T-shirt, and I had never been cold. Conversely, by the time my second South African winter rolled through, my blood had thinned, and I found myself shivering beneath the covers on more than one evening. I spent a large part of that season dressed in long pants and a jumper, which was a drastic contrast to my beach wardrobe the previous year.

If a South African winter now gave me the chills, I was concerned that I would freeze to death in the Canadian cold.

I wasn't physically prepared.

My mental status wasn't much better. Saying goodbye to Chintsa and my friends had been much more difficult than I ever dreamed.[1] The first stream of spontaneous tears arrived about five days before my departure date. The only

---

1. Sabrina had been bang on with her prediction. Africa did get into my heart, and I had an overwhelming urge to stay. From the moment I boarded the plane to leave, I felt an overwhelming urge to return. Any readers considering a trip to Africa…you're forewarned.

consolation was that these breakdowns would happen at night in the seclusion of my cottage. It often occurred as I was going through the emotional process of packing up my belongings. Regrettably, for the last couple of days, if the thought of leaving even flickered through my head, I would burst into tears regardless of company or situation.

I was struggling because I knew that I was leaving a special home and special people. On my last night in Chintsa, the Crosby family threw me a heart-melting going-away party. It brought a lump to my throat the size of a grapefruit and reduced my ability to speak to sobs. The next morning, when I drove away from *Smuggler's Cove* and my wonderful view of the Indian Ocean disappeared from sight, I became an uncontrollable blubbering mess.

I'm aware that real men do cry, but this outburst was absurd.

I spent the large majority of the 12-hour flight to the UK staring out the window into the darkness and contemplating some of the decisions that I would have to make once I was home. They were difficult questions with unpredictable answers.

Once in London, I caught up with Charlie and Jon, who both happened to be living there. The three of us hit the nightlife and a proper bender with my mates helped numb the hurt and take my mind off my impending anxieties. Charlie, who was an Australian and still in a travelling mindset, was not suffering from any of the settling down blues that afflicted me. On the other hand, Jon, who was a Londoner at heart, understood my concerns about returning home, for he was currently experiencing the stresses of being back in the old lifestyle after spending ages away. He helped suppress my worries by smoking a ton of dope with me, including a massive cannon of a joint moments before I went to Heathrow to catch my flight home.

However, in spite of the copious amounts of ganja, as the plane was making its final descent into Ottawa International, I realized that there was no way to prepare for the trials and tribulations that awaited me. The mixture of emotions and thoughts racing through my mind made it difficult to focus. Having said that, one particular sentiment was able to overshadow the others.

I was pissed off.

I was pissed off because my parents had split up.

I was pissed off because they had lied to me.

I was pissed off because I had to leave South Africa.

I was pissed off because I was going to freeze my ass off.

I was pissed off because I was pissed off.

Damn, had the last two years been a waste? Had the rage that had consumed me prior to my travels been lying dormant for the past 24 months? Had my anger been slowly brewing and building and waiting for the perfect opportunity to explode?

I hoped not.

I didn't want to be pissed off.

I didn't want to be angry.

I prayed that some of my new-found calm and serenity had been absorbed and still lingered inside. I reminded myself to keep everything in perspective. I needed to remember what the real problems of the world were. I told myself that my parents' separation was quite irrelevant compared to the hardships and struggles that 90 per cent of the world endures every day. In the big picture, my family's hurdle was a miniscule, insignificant bump.

For too many people, as I had seen on my travels, the only goal for the day was to survive.

Trying to figure out why my parents were unhappy was a trivial task in comparison to basic survival.

Nonetheless, the family obstacles that awaited me were real, and they were mine. They needed to be resolved. I thought I might have an opportunity on the flight to quietly think and prepare for what I wanted to say once I was home with my folks. I'd gone over how I wanted to approach my parents countless times the last couple of weeks in South Africa. However, nothing that I came up with completely tackled all of my issues.

As my luck would have it, I wouldn't have a moment to focus on the flight.

In part, it was my fault. I was late getting to the airport due to a combination of delays on the London subway, the Christmas season pandemonium at Heathrow and, in all likelihood, the joint I had smoked with Jon just prior to leaving his flat in London. I had to literally run to my departure gate and was the last passenger to board, drawing the annoyed looks of those already seated and impatiently waiting. Upon discovering that the individual sitting next to me was as wide as he was tall and that his flab devoured a substantial portion of my seat, it pushed what little patience I had remaining to its limit. I found it difficult to concentrate when my entire body was being crushed against the fuselage by a wall of human flesh.

With the continuous fear of being squashed, I wasn't able to sleep or mentally prepare for the confrontation with my parents. I had to pay strict attention to the "man house" next to me in case he decided to shift. Hours later, when I caught sight of the Canadian snow, I was snapped back into reality. When the plane touched down on the frozen runway and the captain announced the outside temperatures of negative 24 degrees, I became borderline frantic.

Both the cold and my parents were close.

My fears about surviving the wintry weather were heightened the moment I stepped from the plane's bulkhead onto the terminal's ramp. The cold that had crept through the cracks pricked at my skin, made my eyes water and literally took my breath away.

The Canadian cold was going to be miserable.

Nevertheless, it was still going to be awhile before I felt the bitter iciness against my flesh. With entire families travelling for the Christmas season, the customs terminal was complete bedlam. I conceded the lost time and fell to the back of one of the passport lines. As we slowly advanced, I began to wonder what kind of questions immigration might ask me.

Although I was mildly intrigued whether the Canadian government would have any record of one of their citizens being granted political asylum, my main concern was with the Canadian Revenue Agency. I was worried that the government would notice that I hadn't paid any form of taxes in over two years. I was worried my name would attract warning signals the moment it was typed into the computer. I was concerned that the government would find a way to charge me even though I hadn't taken a cent from the system in all that time. Based on my experience with the Canadian bureaucracy, I didn't fancy my chances. If I had to guess, I'd say that they would find a way to charge the living hell out of me in back taxes.

The bastards would probably have some way of fining me for having been granted political asylum.

As my luck would have it, I never got the chance to find out.

While standing in the queue of impatient, weary travellers, I noticed a customs officer making his way up the line with a very active terrier, who was sniffing away at the passengers. When the duo reached where I was standing, the dog froze, sniffed around my feet, flipped onto its back and began to roll and frolic. Others in the line, upon seeing the dog's playful display, made comments such as, "Ohhh, look at the little pup" and "Isn't that cute."

I wanted to slap them all.

I knew exactly what the dog's little trick was indicating, and there was nothing cute about it. Having another man's fingers shoved up my ass in a fishing expedition didn't fall under any definition of the word "cute" that I was aware of. By the way that Lassie was rolling around, I knew that unpleasant experience was in my not so distant future. There was no question in my mind that this particular little pup had been trained to smell marijuana.

An anxiety attack took up a strategic position and prepared its assault upon my central nervous system.

"Excuse me, sir. Would you please come with me?"

It was an order and not a question.

The customs officer took possession of my day pack and ushered me towards the interrogation room. As we walked away, I could feel the eyes of my fellow passengers glaring at me in disgust and whispering to one another, "You see … he did look like trouble."

Although I kept a cool exterior, my insides shat their pants. Thankfully, that first jolt of panic was eliminated when I took a quick, mental inventory of my pack and body.

I was 100 per cent positive that I had nothing illegal with me.

Despite my love for the harmless plant, I would never cross an international border with marijuana on me. That was my golden rule on the road, and it was one that I would never consider bending or breaking. As far as I was concerned, there was no need to risk being busted at the border with ganja, for it existed everywhere on the planet. I'd been able to find and smoke weed in every country that I'd been to on my travels, including the swamp and the desert. It was impossible to put a financial value on my freedom.

The risk was not worth the reward.

The officer escorted me into a small, windowless room. He closed the door and began searching my day pack. I looked around for where he kept the latex gloves.

"Do you know why I've pulled you from the line?" he began the interrogation. His head was down as he rummaged through my pack in search of illegal substances.

I had a feeling that any attitude could result in an extra finger being used in the examination of my rectum. Therefore, I answered the officer's question as honestly and politely as I could. I told him that I assumed his dog had smelled marijuana on me.

Without looking up from his search, he continued. "That's correct, sir. Are you travelling with any marijuana?"

Again I answered truthfully. I told him that I was not.

Unzipping the front pouch of my pack, he asked me a very direct question. "Do you smoke marijuana?"

I'd been honest to this point, and I figured that there was no sense in lying now. I conceded that there was no way to avoid a strip search, and since I had absolutely zero to hide, I answered with a confident and bold, "Yes."

The officer stopped his search, and for the first time, he looked directly at me. "Do you smoke often?" he asked.

I assumed that there were only so many fingers one could insert into another's anus, and it was this theory that ultimately influenced my truthful answer of, "Every single day."

"When was the last time that you smoked?" he asked, now with a clearly exasperated tone.

I looked at the clock on the wall and figured out the time zone difference between Ottawa and London. By my rough calculations, it had been about 12 hours since I smoked a joint with Jon. I told the customs officer my approximate guess.

The customs officer shook his head. He said, "Our dogs can smell marijuana on people five days after their last contact with the drug. If you smoked only a few hours ago, then this is most likely what our dog detected. I'm wasting your time and mine. I do, however, still have to search your bags."

By his unperturbed tone and demeanour, any trepidation about having my butt penetrated by another man's finger had vanished. This was as welcome a relief as I could have hoped for. My entire body, including my rectum, relaxed.

Honesty proved not only a virtue but, in this potentially piercing predicament, a wonderful tool. I'm certain that if I had lied to the customs officer and answered, "No, I don't smoke marijuana," he would have known that I was talking shit. His dog had obviously smelled weed on me, and if I had lied, any credibility would have been lost. My deceit could provide the customs officer with just cause to search my ass. I wasn't smuggling any weed, so what did it matter if I told the officer that I was a smoker? It was his job to prevent illegal substances from *entering* the country. He shouldn't give a rat's ass what I smoked in other countries just as long as I didn't try to smuggle some home.

After the officer had searched my day pack, he said that, as a formality, he also had to examine my backpack. We went to the baggage area and waited for my gear. We waited along with the other travellers. I could once again feel the disdainful glares of my fellow passengers, who were obviously assuming that they had been travelling with a criminal. When my pack came down the conveyor belt, the officer took possession of it, and we returned to the interrogation room. Walking away, I could hear the whispers and comments. They were no longer subtle or discreet, and they were all littered with condescending judgment.

When the officer finished his half-assed search of my backpack, he told me that I was free to go. I began to head down the hallway to where the other passengers had been waiting when the officer said, "You don't have to go that way. You've cleared customs. You don't have to go back into that mess again. You can go through this door and out into the arrival terminal. Have a merry Christmas."

I returned the wishes, exited the second doorway and headed down the corridor to the arrival foyer. I passed a connecting hallway at the end of which I saw, to my overwhelming delight, my fellow passengers still waiting to clear customs. All the snobs who had looked down their noses at me were now attempting to clear Canadian customs four days before Christmas. From the barrage of open suitcases, I guessed it was going to be a slow and tedious process. I wanted to shout, "Yeah right they have nothing to declare. Search them all!" but I knew that a good percentage would be subjected to the unpacking and repacking of their many pieces of designer luggage without my verbal influence. They would be searched for no other reason than it was Christmas, and everybody was travelling with presents.

That is, everybody except the ganja-stinking backpacker.

I smiled and waved at the condescending bastards.

I stood there for a minute, relishing the satisfaction of seeing their luggage unpacked and smuggled items lying across the tables. I let the moment linger a little longer than I probably should have. I did so because I knew that once I left the airport, a world of uncertainty would be waiting.

However, I knew that I was just delaying the inevitable. I couldn't avoid going back to the family home.

It had to be done.

I took a deep breath and walked towards the exit. The doors to the arrival hall swung open.

Since I forbade my parents from coming to the airport, I had asked Woody to pick me up. I hoped we would hit the local pub for a few pints so that I could gather some liquid courage before entering the madness that awaited me at home.

I spotted Woody almost immediately. But I was more than surprised to see the faces of so many people whom I loved and missed. Standing in a smiling and waving group were a pile of my closest and oldest friends, my brother Mike and, despite my warning, my mom and dad.

Upon sight of me, Mom, who was an Olympic calibre sprinter in her youth, began a charge in my direction that produced overturned luggage and jostled passengers. One of the casualties was a frail, old woman. Her only mistake had been getting between a mother and her cub, and she was sent sprawling as a result of a forearm shove to the back.

Emotions were barreling through me as quickly as Mom was approaching. The main reason I had instructed my parents not to be at the airport was because I didn't know how I would react once I saw them. There was the potential for an emotional explosion, and I was afraid it would be dominated by anger and rage. I didn't want to deal with my temper in the middle of the airport and in front of countless strangers. As much as I wanted to be cool, calm and collected, I didn't know if I could or would be. I didn't want to have it all come apart at Ottawa International.

When Mom was a few metres away, I could see that her face was streaming with tears. Unquestionably, they were maternal tears of joy for having her baby home safely after having been away for so long. However, they said much more. They were tears of pain and sorrow. They were tears that were pleading for understanding and forgiveness.

Mom hugged me for dear life and sobbed uncontrollably on my shoulder, releasing all the emotions that had consumed her. If I had let go, she would have collapsed into a puddle on the floor.

I didn't want to let go.

Despite the anger and rage that had been roaring through my veins, and despite everything that I wanted to say or even scream, I knew that there were only a few words that I could express.

There were only a few words that I trusted to be true.

There were only a few words that made sense among all this insanity.

As I hugged Mom for the first time in over two years, the only words that came from my heart were, "I love you Mom ... it's going to be all right."

It *was* going to be all right.

... TO BE CONTINUED

REFERENCE

www.madmattysworld.com

ABOUT THE AUTHOR

Matt Hamilton, almost 10 years after his initial venture of travelling with just a pack on his back, is calmly clinging to his youth and still very much trying to find himself. Although born and raised in Canada, he considers the warmer parts of the planet his home, ideally in environments where shoes are optional.

978-0-595-45677-2
0-595-45677-4